MARY BERRY
& LUCY YOUNG
COOK UP A
FEAST

MARY BERRY
& LUCY YOUNG
COOK UP A
FEAST

DK

LONDON, NEW YORK, MELBOURNE, MUNICH, AND DELHI

Project Editor
Michael Fullalove

Designers
Carolyn Hewitson, John Round

Photography
William Reavell

DK LONDON

Project Editor
Andrew Roff

US Editors
Rebecca Warren, Shannon Beatty

Project Art Editor
Kathryn Wilding

Senior Jacket Creative
Nicola Powling

Senior Presentations Creative
Caroline de Souza

Managing Editors
Dawn Henderson, Angela Wilkes

Managing Art Editors
Christine Keilty, Marianne Markham

Production Editor
Ben Marcus

Production Controller
Alice Sykes

Creative Technical Support
Sonia Charbonnier

DK INDIA

Head of Publishing
Aparna Sharma

Managing Art Editor
Romi Chakraborty

Senior Editor
Saloni Talwar

DTP Designer
Tarun Sharma

First American Edition, 2010

Published in the United States by DK Publishing
375 Hudson Street
New York, New York 10014

10 11 12 10 9 8 7 6 5 4 3 2 1

177770—August 2010

Published in Great Britain by Dorling Kindersley Limited.

A catalog record for this book is available from the Library of Congress.

978-0-7566-6206-6

DK books are available at special discounts when purchased in bulk for sales
promotions, premiums, fund-raising, or educational use. For details, contact:
DK Publishing Special Markets, 375 Hudson Street, New York, New York 10014
or SpecialSales@dk.com.

Color reproduction by MDP, Bath
Printed and bound in Singapore by Star Standard

Discover more at
www.dk.com

Contents

In the 20 years we've worked together we've written cookbooks on a vast range of subjects. One of the many joys of publishing them is the feedback we get from you, our readers. We take your comments extremely seriously. And if there's one request that's kept on coming, it's for a book to serve numbers—a party book, with recipes for anything from a family get-together in the kitchen to a full-on feast. It's an area we feel well qualified to write on—in our personal lives as well as in our professional lives, there's nothing we like so much as cooking for family, friends, and neighbors—no matter the number.

At the same time, we're well aware of the worries that many of you have about cooking for more than six—you tell us about them at our cookery demonstrations and in your letters and emails. "What can I make for so many people?" "How can I keep the food hot and will there be enough?" These are the sorts of question we're asked and these are the sorts of question we bore in mind as we wrote this book.

In *Cook up a Feast*, we give you all the advice you need to make cooking for a crowd easy and stress free. There are recipes for summer and winter, for formal occasions and informal occasions, inside the home and out. We give timings for conventional ovens, together with prepare-ahead and freezing information. And at the back of the book there's a choice of menus for lots of different kinds of event.

We kick off with **the basics**—how to plan your feast and how to guarantee there's enough for everyone to eat. We tell you ways to get the most from your kitchen (the center of the action at any special occasion) and let you in on a few cheats and shortcuts to make life easier. We also give you ideas on setting the scene and on how to keep your cool on the day itself. Then it's on to the recipes.

To get your feast off to a flying start, we begin with a chapter on **Party bites**—the mouthwatering mouthfuls you serve with drinks. Following hot on its heels there's a selection of **Starters**, then a chapter on **Special main courses**. We've long been fans of the kind of casual gathering where various people bring along a dish. It's a style of entertaining that's now so popular it's got its own name—the **Potluck party**—and in that chapter we give you a collection of all-in-one dishes that are ideal for preparing ahead and transporting to your chosen venue. **Buffets** are another classic way of entertaining and we've teamed our buffet recipes with those for **Bowl parties**, a new kind of get-together, where guests can tuck into hearty food served in individual bowls. **Italian food** is such a perennial crowd-pleaser, it seemed only fitting to devote an entire chapter to it, while in **Summer in the Backyard** you'll find our favorite dishes for picnics, barbecues, and other al fresco meals. The finale to any feast is the dessert, so toward the back of the book there's a selection of **Desserts** with that all-important wow factor. Which leaves just one meal uncatered for—snack time. There are so many occasions when a cup of tea or coffee and a choice of sweet and savory treats hit exactly the right note. The recipes in **Snacks for a Crowd** are just the ticket.

To take the effort out of estimating quantities, for the vast majority of recipes we give a list of ingredients to serve six and a list of ingredients to serve 12, with notes on any special equipment you'll need. And because celebrations are often larger than that, throughout the book we flag up dishes that are particularly suitable for cooking for a dozen people upward.

So here it is—the much-requested long-awaited book to answer all your party needs and put your mind at rest when cooking for a crowd. We hope each and every one of you enjoys it and finds the inspiration and confidence you're looking for as you plan your special day.

Remember—no feast is worth stressing over. Whatever happens, fun will be had by everyone—including you!

Mary Berry   Lucy Young

The mere thought of cooking up a feast is enough to send many people into a spin. So what better place to start than with answers to seven of the questions most commonly put to us.

Preparing a feast Q&A

Q *"I'm only used to cooking for four or six and am a bit daunted by the idea of feeding lots of people. What's the best way of going about it?"*
A "The recipes in this book are all designed with entertaining in mind, so that's already a great starting point. Begin with some forward planning and get yourself organized—decide what kind of occasion you'd like it to be, where you'll have it, and when. Then it's time to draw up some lists—write down the names of your guests and what you'll give them to eat. Plan your shopping list and work out the cooking times, so that you know when the dishes need to go into the oven or on to the burner. There's more information on planning on pages 10–11."

Q *"I'm worried there won't be enough for everyone to eat. How can I be sure I'll get it right?"*
A "If you follow our recipes to the T, everything will be fine—we have worked out all the quantities for you. Serve plenty of bread or potatoes with your main course, and offer a second dessert. If you know your guests have really huge appetites, make extra quantities of the main-course recipe, but make sure you choose a dish that can be frozen after the party in case there's some left. To double-check you're on the right lines, turn to pages 12–13."

Q *"My kitchen's tiny. Will I have enough space to prepare food for lots of people?"*
A "Don't let the size of your kitchen put you off—you can turn out delicious food even from the galley kitchen of a boat. As long as you have a standard-sized stove, a fridge, freezer, and a surface to work on, you'll be fine. Keep the menu simple and prepare ahead. Store food you've made in advance in your fridge or freezer. If you're short on space, ask a neighbor if you can make use of their fridge for a few hours. For more advice from us on getting the most from your kitchen, turn to pages 14–15."

Q *"I don't have the right equipment to cook large quantities of food. Will I have to go out and buy lots of new stuff?"*

A "In a word, 'no'. You can entertain on a large scale—and without spending lots of money—with just the minimum of equipment. Inexpensive throwaway dishes are one option (not very green, we know, but then you probably don't have parties all that often). Alternatively, you could borrow from friends or you could improvize—we do that all the time. On pages 16–17 you'll find our guide to the equipment you need for a party."

Q *"I'd like to give my party a theme, but I'm a bit stuck for ideas. Do you have any suggestions?"*

A "Themed parties are such fun and they can be as formal or as informal as you like. Forget about the theme to begin with and plan your party as you would any other. What's the reason for it, who's coming, and where's the venue? Think of a few of your favorite things to do and eat and see if they are an inspiration. What's happening in the world at large? Is there a TV show you love? Pick a country, then choose recipes that come from there. You'll find some of our ideas on page 19. Once you've chosen your theme, make sure you spell it out when you're sending out the invitations. Then get down to the planning, so that you carry your theme through to the decorations, music, and food."

"To stop last-minute panics, prepare well ahead. That way, you'll be able to relax, knowing that everything is organized."

Q *"I love having people over for a meal, but it always seems like so much hard work. How can I make life easier for myself?"*

A "Keeping your menu simple is the best way of cutting down on the amount of work. Serve one course—an all-in-one dish, say—plus a dessert. Another way is to organize a potluck meal, where the cooking is shared among the guests—you ask people to bring a salad or dessert, for example, which means you only need to provide a main course. Potluck parties share the cost, too. The other option is to do a bit of cheating. You'll find some of our crafty shortcuts on pages 20–21."

Q *"I just know I'll lose my nerve the minute our guests arrive and end up ruining the food. How can I avoid a last-minute panic?"*

A "Simple. Prepare the food well ahead, so that all you need to do is take it out of the fridge or reheat it. Plenty of the recipes in this book fit that bill. With your menu taken care of, you'll be free to spend the day of your party making all the final preparations. For a guide to the things you need to think about then, turn to pages 22–23."

Whatever the occasion, when we're having a party the first thing we always do is sit and plan it. Careful planning and meticulous organization are key to success. These are our seven golden rules.

Planning the occasion

Cook with the seasons

A visit to the supermarket can be just the inspiration you need when you're planning your menu. The bright pink shoots of young rhubarb, for instance, are irresistible in spring, and perfect for the creamy, lemony dessert on page 254. Soft fruits such as strawberries and raspberries follow close behind in midsummer. Leeks, chicory, and parsnips are at their best in winter, while tomatoes are wishy washy and anaemic. Steer well clear is our advice.

For an early summer menu, you can't beat asparagus.

1 Choose what kind of feast

Decide between formal and informal. Will it be supper in the kitchen or on the patio, a bowl party or a buffet? Is your feast in honor of a special event such as a birthday or anniversary? If it isn't, invent one—we often do! Do you have enough space to entertain the number of people you would like to invite? Do you have the room for all your guests to sit down or would you rather they mingled and munched? Do you have a contingency plan if you're hoping to eat outdoors and the weather turns bad?

2 Be realistic

There's always the temptation to pull out all the stops to give your guests the best time you can. But, from experience, we'd say you are probably making more work for yourself than you need to.

Instead of pushing yourself to the very limit (and exhausting yourself in the process), it's far better to stay inside your comfort zone. Be realistic rather than ambitious. Remember, simple well-cooked dishes will always outshine more complicated recipes that might not go according to plan. And your guests would much rather find you relaxed and ready to chat than stressed out—and flat out—in the kitchen.

3 Look at your guest list

Keep firmly in mind who your guests are and devise a menu to suit them. Are there children coming? Or vegetarians? Theirs might not be the only dietary considerations—certain ingredients, such as raw eggs, are best avoided by pregnant women, the elderly, and the young alike. Nuts are a problem for some allergy-sufferers, as is shellfish. This is such a perennial favorite, however, that

rather than taking it completely off the menu, we tend to provide an alternative dish for those guests with the allergy.

The number of guests you've invited is also likely to determine what you cook. If you're inviting lots of people, for instance, a buffet, bowl party, or cocktail party would fit the bill. If people will be standing up as they eat, it makes sense to prepare something that's easy for them to eat with a fork.

To give you a helping hand, at the back of the book, you'll find menus we've put together for all sorts of occasions. Take a look through them—at least one is bound to suit yours!

4 Bear in mind the timing

Having guests for brunch or lunch is likely to be a much less elaborate affair than a smart dinner party. People will expect less to eat, too.

The time of year is another consideration—guests are generally starving on Thanksgiving, but rather more well fed by the day after. In general terms, warming dishes will hit the spot in winter, while a selection of cold foods is good in summer.

5 Calculate the work load

With your proposed menu to hand, jot down what you can prepare ahead and what you can freeze in readiness for your big day. Will you be comfortable putting the finishing touches to dishes while your guests are there? Or would you rather it was just a simple matter of putting them in the oven?

Dishes you can reheat and serve are ideal if you want to spend as much time as you can with your guests or if you think you might get flustered. Even better are cold dishes that will be sitting there ready for you to bring out and serve.

For a fuss-free relaxed way of entertaining, have a bowl party. Your guests enjoy their main course in a bowl—standing up or sitting down.

"Your guests would much rather find you relaxed and ready to chat than stressed out—and flat out—in the kitchen."

6 Fine-tune your menu

When you've taken these factors into consideration, fine-tune your menu and plan the cooking times with military precision. Then write it down—not on the back of an old envelope, but on a proper piece of paper that you can keep somewhere safe for reference. And cross things off as you go along—it will inspire you with confidence.

Remember to make a note if a dish can't be served straight away—roasted meats, for instance, need 15–20 minutes to rest before you carve them, and some tarts are tricky to cut when hot. Check, too, that you'll have enough room in your oven or on your stove top and that you won't be trying to finish off too many dishes at once.

7 Head for the supermarket

If you have lots of shopping to do, tackle it in two hits. Make a list of those things you can buy well in advance—pantry ingredients, for instance—and compile a second list of all the produce such as fruit and vegetables that you need to get at the last minute so they are as fresh as possible. Run through the big day in your head, trying to think of items such as ice cubes, matches, and napkins that you might otherwise forget until it's too late.

Consider having a potluck party

If reading all of this is making you realize you don't really have enough time to organize a feast on your own, think about throwing a potluck party, where you ask friends, family, neighbors, or colleagues to share the load by bringing along a dish. These potluck parties are all the rage right now—and for good reason. They are an excellent way of cutting down on the amount of work and expense involved for everyone. For more information, turn to page 132.

All-in-one dishes like our shepherd's pie (page 141) are ideal for transporting to a potluck party.

From experience, we know it's better to serve too much food than not enough. That said, you don't want so much left over that you do not know what to do with it. Here's how to get the quantities right.

Serving the right amount

Almost every recipe in this book is designed to serve six or 12. These quantities depend to some extent, of course, on who your guests are—if you have invited a group of your girlfriends over for lunch, for instance, they are unlikely to eat as much as a gang of growing teenagers or the guys from the local baseball team.

In general, though, we tend to err on the generous side. And to make doubly sure that there will be enough food, we always provide a plentiful supply of bread or potatoes, so that guests with a healthy appetite can tuck in and help themselves.

Time of day
How much food we serve depends on the time of day. Lunch, for instance, is generally a lighter meal than dinner. Here's what we serve when.

Brunch One course with salad or bread.

Informal lunch A light main course plus a fruit salad or simple dessert.

Sit-down lunch A main course and a dessert, with a first course for very special occasions.

Informal dinner A main course and a dessert, with a first course for very special occasions.

Formal dinner Party bites, first course, main course, and dessert. In other words, the works!

Main courses
Unless you're serving a buffet, you are only making extra work for yourself by offering a choice of main courses. The one exception is curries—a selection of two or three always goes down well. When serving 12 people, never be tempted to make two different dishes for six—the servings can look rather small. Prepare two dishes for 12—you can bank on most people wanting to sample both.

Desserts
Even if it's only one sumptuous dessert plus a fruit salad, we always serve a choice of dessert at any gathering of eight people or more. That way, anyone with a corner to fill can do just that. Most people have a sweet tooth, in any case. And if you're still worried about guests leaving with an empty tummy, place a cheese board on the table.

Cooking for more than a dozen people
If you're planning on entertaining more than a dozen guests, look out for our "Great for a crowd" stamp throughout the book. These are our favorite recipes for larger gatherings. To make life easier for ourselves, they are often dishes we can prepare in advance and freeze. For some of them, you'll need to invest in a big 2½ gallon (11 liter) pan. Buy a long-handled spatula, too, and remember that food in a large pan needs stirring more frequently, as it is much more likely to catch on the bottom. The large plastic storage boxes you find in DIY stores are perfect for storing cooked food in—but check that they are food safe and will fit into your fridge or freezer.

SERVING QUANTITIES FOR LARGE NUMBERS

To help you serve side dishes, garnishes, and accompaniments in the right amounts to large numbers of people, here are our suggested serving quantities.

FIRST COURSES

Soup
10fl oz (300ml) per serving, although the exact amount depends on the vessels you are serving it in. Soup bowls usually hold 10fl oz; mugs a little less. For 12, you will need 3 quarts (3.5 liters) soup; for 20–25, 5 quarts (6 liters) soup

Arugula (as a garnish)
7oz (200g) for 12; 14oz (400g) for 20–25

MAIN-COURSE SIDE DISHES

Baby new potatoes
3lb 3oz (1.5kg) for 12; 5½lb (2.5kg) for 20–25

Baked potatoes
1 medium potato per person

Mashed potatoes
8oz (225g) (unpeeled weight of potatoes) per serving. So 6lb (2.7kg) for 12; 10lb (4.5kg) for 20–25

Roast potatoes
Three small potatoes per serving

Green salad/mixed leaf salad
11oz (300g) for 12; 1lb 2oz (500g) for 20–25

Tomato salad
1 small or ½ large tomato per serving

Rice/bulghur wheat/couscous
1lb 5oz (600g) for 12; 2¾lb (1.25kg) for 20–25

Noodles
4oz per person

Bread
1 large baguette cuts into 10–12 slices

Green vegetables
About 2½oz (75g) per serving. So 2lb (900g) for 12; 3lb 3oz (1.5kg) for 20–25

Gravy
1 quart (1.2 liters) for 12; 1½ quarts (1.4–1.7 liters) for 20. If your guests are helping themselves from the gravy boat, make a little more, as they may serve themselves rather generously

FOR A BUFFET

Poached salmon
6–6½lb (2.7–3kg) salmon (head on, gutted) for 12; 13lb (6kg) salmon for 20–25

Ham
2 slices per serving (if accompanied by another meat or fish); 3 slices per serving (if served on its own)

Roast filet of beef
5–6oz (140–175g) per serving when hot; 3½oz (100g) per serving when cold (cold beef is easier to carve thinly)

FOR DESSERT

Heavy cream
1¼ pints (600ml) for 12; 2½ pints (1.2 liters) for 20–25

Crème fraîche/yogurt
14oz for 12; 28oz for 20–25

Custard
1 quart (1.2 liters) for 12; 2 quarts (2.4 liters) for 20–25

Ice cream
1 scoop per person as an accompaniment; 2 scoops per person served on its own

FOR A CHEESE BOARD

Serve 3–5 cheeses, about 1lb 10oz (750g) in total for 12; 2¼lb (1kg) for 20–25. The most popular is Cheddar. Accompany with your favorite savory crackers, a good chutney, and some fresh figs or grapes

Never is the kitchen more the heart of the home than when you're entertaining. Everything needs to run like clockwork, especially if it is also the setting for your feast. So time for some kitchen knowhow.

Kitchen knowhow

When you're cooking for a crowd, you need every spare inch of your kitchen. Big pots and pans and large serving platters all require space, so start by clearing away as much clutter as you can. The more surfaces you have to work on, the better. And you may well need them later to serve or arrange the food out on.

Unless all the dishes you're serving are cold, you'll need to think about how you'll use your oven. With lots of party food to prepare, it's likely to be working overtime. What will you be cooking in your oven and what will you be cooking on the stovetop? And when will you be cooking it? Maximizing the space in your fridge and freezer calls for careful planning, too.

"When you're planning your menu, aim to spread the work load between your oven and your stovetop."

If your fridge is crammed, put bottles in buckets of ice and water. Don't submerge the labels or they might come off, making it tricky to know what's inside.

Get the most from your oven
When you're planning your menu, aim to spread the work load between your oven and your stovetop. Pick one dish you can cook on the stovetop and a couple in the oven, or vice versa.

The tasks you're likely to need to perform at the last minute include cooking, reheating, and keeping dishes hot. Make sure you have all the room you need, and adapt your menu if you foresee a problem. Not every dish is suitable for reheating, remember—lasagnas and fish pies, for instance, need to be served freshly cooked, although they can often be prepared up to a certain point in advance and then cooked to serve. This is the sort of information you'll find in the Prepare ahead box on each recipe, so check there.

A second oven or a hot plate makes life easier (even if you only use it for warming the plates) and a microwave is great for reheating dishes you have made in advance. Remember that it may be impossible to get large containers into it, and the reheating time can be quite long for big dishes.

Keeping food hot
It is essential to keep hot food hot. Use the stovetop to keep pans on a gentle simmer or put things into a low oven, but only after they have come to a boil on the burner. Turn to page 23 for our guide to reheating food.

Get the most from your fridge

Platters and serving dishes make poor use of the space in a fridge. They might even be too big to fit in. We keep food we've prepared in advance in plastic bags or containers. It helps to put sweet things and savory things on separate shelves to make them easier to find.

If you do put plates or dishes of food in the fridge, cover them carefully with plastic wrap or foil and then sit them flat on a shelf.

Insulated containers—the kind you use for picnics—are ideal for keeping food cool. Make sure you have plenty of ice blocks ready in the freezer.

If you're running out of space in your fridge, there are some items you can take out until everything is back to normal. There are also items that must definitely stay in.

• You can take any beer, wine, and soft drinks out. You can still serve these chilled by putting them into buckets of icy water. Be careful not to cover the labels because they will soak off in time. If you have lots of people coming, you could fill the bath with cold water and ice. Spread an old towel out in the bottom beforehand to prevent scratching and to stop the bottles falling over. Ground coffee, bottled sauces, and jars of pickles and chutney will also be fine out of the fridge for a few hours. The same is true of fresh fruit and vegetables.

• Cooked meats, salamis, and pâtés should be kept in the fridge until you are ready to serve them. Salads with pasta, rice, or vegetables in them also need to be kept chilled, as do ready-to-eat seafood and dips.

If you've cleared out everything you can and still don't have enough space in the fridge, make sure the dishes you're going to serve last stay in there. The rest should be okay at room temperature for up to 4 hours—unless it's a blisteringly hot day.

Get the most from your freezer

Transfer food to plastic containers or bags. Small portions freeze quickest. They take less time to defrost, too. And make sure you label them so that you know what they are when you are ready to defrost them. You don't want to reheat what you think is a chicken and leek pie only to find when you serve it that there's rhubarb inside.

Make use of your freezer as a back-up for extra bread, rolls, butter, baby peas, and ice cream, just in case the number of guests you are expecting increases at the last minute. And clear space for freezing any leftovers.

Fridge safety

The average domestic fridge isn't that big and when it's full to capacity, it has to work overtime to cope. As a result, the temperature inside can rise, even if the weather outside isn't that warm. A fridge that's full to capacity doesn't allow the cold air to circulate freely either, which can sometimes mean foods are inadequately chilled.

Check frequently that yours is working at the correct temperature—39–41°F (4–5°C)—and adjust the controls to lower the temperature, if necessary. If your fridge doesn't have a temperature display, invest in a fridge thermometer—it's an inexpensive piece of equipment that could potentially save you and your guests from food poisoning.

Defrosting food

If you've frozen food ahead of time, it's important to defrost (thaw) it completely before cooking. We always advise defrosting in the fridge because it's the safest method of doing it. Overnight should be fine for small dishes, but a large deep dish can take up to two days. If time is against you, however, you can defrost non-meat and non-fish dishes at room temperature for a maximum of six hours. Once thawed, transfer to the fridge until needed. Never defrost in a warm oven or warm cupboard—the risk of attracting bacteria is high.

Clearing up

The kitchen is also the place where you'll pile all the dirty china and cutlery. Ask someone to help you clear and wash the dishes or to put them in the dishwasher while you get on with the next course. And ask someone else to put leftover food in the fridge or freezer. This is where family comes in!

Transfer food into plastic bags or containers to keep it in the fridge or freezer—they make better use of the limited space available.

Once you've fine-tuned your menu, check you have all the pots, pans, and dishes you'll need. If you don't have absolutely everything, don't worry—there are often ways around it.

The right equipment

If you haven't cooked for a crowd before, there's a chance your kitchen might not be equipped for it. When money's no object you can simply go out and buy all the new items you need. But that may not be an option. It might not be necessary anyway. Help is at hand—in various guises.

The majority of recipes for 12 in this book can be cooked in two standard dishes for six rather than in a single huge one. There's even an advantage to doing this—smaller dishes are a lot less heavy

"Our preserving pan has saved the day on so many occasions—we've used it as a mixing bowl, cooked potatoes or a ham in it, even used it to stir a cake in."

Perfect timing

With so much going on in the kitchen when you're cooking for a crowd, it's worth putting your mind at rest by investing in a good digital kitchen timer. They are relatively inexpensive, extremely simple to use, and the best models can time up to four dishes at once.

to handle. If you don't have a second dish, borrow one from a friend or buy a foil dish. The cooking times for two dishes should be the same as for one large dish, but keep an eye on the food toward the end of cooking—the important thing is that it's cooked right through to the middle.

Foil dishes

You can buy a whole range of inexpensive foil dishes at your local supermarket or department store. They are available online, too. They're not as sturdy as porcelain cookware, so always sit them on a baking sheet, particularly when you're taking them in and out of the oven, and take care not to puncture them.

Because they are made of metal, cooking times are slightly less. Again, check toward the end of cooking to see if the food is done.

Improvising

Take a look around your kitchen to see if there are any pieces of equipment you can improvise with. A roasting pan, for example, can stand in as an ovenproof dish, and we find no end of uses for our preserving pan. To check the capacity of a dish, fill it with water from a measuring cup. Slightly too big is better than too small—for obvious reasons.

For serving

Presentation is so important. If you don't own any serving platters, you could use trays covered in foil, bamboo mats, or leaves—grape or banana leaves for savory dishes, currant or fig leaves for sweet dishes. A wooden chopping board or marble pastry board would would make an admirable serving platter, too. Even a pitcher can come in handy as a container for breadsticks.

If you're worried about breakages, consider using non-breakable options. It's not only bread that looks appetizing in a basket—our party bites look spectacular presented in a shallow wicker tray, as do cupcakes, muffins, and scones. Pretty plastic or melamine serving dishes are another option. You'll find lots to choose from in the stores. There are even some trendy designer versions.

Glasses

Don't have enough glasses to go round? Then check with a local caterer or party supply store to see if they rent glassware. Throwaway glasses are another option and are a particularly sensible idea if you're eating outside.

Some basic cookware and tableware

Walk into a department store or kitchen store and you'll see a bewildering array of equipment. There's a pot or pan, it seems, for every method of cooking and a utensil for each technique. In this book we've aimed to keep fancy equipment to a minimum and to use standard-sized pieces whenever possible—ovenproof dishes, for example, should have a capacity of 2 quart (2 liters) for six and 4¼ quart (4 liters) for 12. Here is some of the other equipment you'll need to cook up and serve up a feast.

Bowls

There are so many things you can put in pretty bowls at a party— dips and salads, to name but two.

Ramekins

Ramekins (5fl oz/150ml) are ideal for serving individual soufflés and crème brûlées.

Salad bowl

For tossing and serving salads, use a large glass, wooden, or china bowl—deep or shallow.

Loaf pan

You can do more than bake bread in a 1lb (450g) loaf pan. It's great for loaf cakes, terrines, and pâtés.

Muffin pan

You need a muffin pan for muffins, a cupcake pan, and a mini-muffin pan for tartlets.

Tart pan

An 11in (1½in/4cm deep) removeable bottom tart pan is essential for quiches and tarts.

Foil dishes

Platters, casserole dishes, and tart pans made of foil are a godsend, not least because they cut down on the amount of washing up.

Casserole

A 4 quart (5 liter) casserole that's heavy and deep is a versatile item that can be used over direct heat as well as in the oven.

Cake pan

A 12 x 9in (30 x 23cm) pan will yield enough cake—or sticky toffee pudding—for a dozen people. Some makes come with a storage lid.

Preserving pan

Not essential, but if you have a preserving pan you could stir a cake or boil a ham in it.

Fish steamer

Large steaming pans capable of holding whole fish can be purchased at kitchen stores.

Platters

Serving dishes come in all shapes and sizes. We particularly like thin banana-shaped dishes.

Whatever the occasion you're cooking for, you'll want to create the right atmosphere by setting the scene. Flowers, candles, and music all have their part to play. You could give the event a theme, too.

Setting the scene

Start off by deciding which area of your home you are going to entertain your guests in and, whether it's your kitchen, living room, patio, or dining room, set it up as much as you can the day before. That way, you'll have plenty of time to make any last-minute adjustments.

If you're having a stand-up party, remove any unneeded furniture and arrange what's left so that guests can move easily around the room. If there isn't enough seating to go around, clear as many surfaces as you can for people to perch on. One large rectangular or oval table placed close to a wall is best for the food. Smaller tables dotted around the walls of the room work well if you have more space, as they encourage people to move and mingle. Provide a separate table for drinks and glasses, and make space here and there for dishes for guests to dispose of their cocktail sticks and olive stones in and for them to put their glasses down.

Lighting
The right lighting will instantly establish the mood for your party. Avoid overhead lights at all costs—they're very unflattering, especially for an evening

Tealights twinkling in glasses add a touch of romance to any table and cost next to nothing.

"We kick off with some easy listening, then—as the party revs up—Mary reaches for the Rod Stewart and Lucy puts her iPod on Party shuffle."

Make the table look pretty with napkins and china in a coordinating accent color.

event when it's all about glamour. Stick to strategically placed table lamps and standard lamps. Candlelight is particularly lovely, lending sparkle and romance to any occasion. Place candles in clusters around the room. Ideal spots for them are at the back of a table (so they can't be knocked over easily), around the hearth of a fireplace, and on a mantlepiece.

Flowers

A simple arrangement of flowers makes a stunning centerpiece for the table. Even a small vase of blooms will add the finishing touch if you're short on space. We generally choose a bouquet of one kind of flower, and often decorate the table with a pot plant, such as an orchid or geranium.

Music

Music is great for creating an ambience, but never play it so loud that people have to shout, and be careful about what you choose—straight-ahead jazz or heavy metal would be too intrusive and not to everyone's taste. We like to kick off with some easy listening then—as the party gets in full swing—Mary reaches for the Rod Stewart and Lucy puts her iPod on Party shuffle.

Themed parties

We love coming up with different themes for parties. But rather than full-on costume parties, we'll often ask people to color-code their clothes to black and white or to come in a wig— something simple for people to do, but with a large element of fun. Of course, many occasions already have a theme—you could be entertaining guests after the christening of the newest member of the family, for instance, or celebrating the landmark birthday of a friend. Match the decorations—and the food—to the event. Curries would be perfect at a Bollywood bash, chili for a Mexican theme, and pasta for an Italian party.

Flower arrangements don't need to be big. This bunch of anemones, hellebores, and roses would look magical at Christmas.

It's all in the details

One of the lovely things about entertaining is sitting down after your guests have gone and looking back at the day, thinking of all the little things that went well. It could be how succulent the lamb was, how pretty the flowers looked on the table, and how happy people looked as they stood around and chatted. That's why we think that setting the scene is so important— joyful memories for you and joyful memories for them.

If you're on the last minute, you might appreciate a helping hand. Luckily, cutting the odd corner won't affect the final quality of the dish—so long as you choose the right corners to cut.

Cheats and shortcuts

There are many ways you can cheat and make cooking for a party easier. A quick visit to your local supermarket or delicatessen will provide you with all the ready-prepared ingredients you need to rustle up a speedy dish like the Express Mediterranean platter on page 83, for instance. Hummus, olives, and a selection of cold meats— what could be more delicious and trouble free to serve as your first course.

Bags of prepared salads are an excellent timesaver, too. Buy the different varieties of leaves in separate packages, then you don't end up getting enormous amounts of shredded iceberg lettuce (not our favorite), and mix them together when you are about to serve them. A bottle of good-quality vinaigrette won't go amiss, too.

You can also get ready-prepared vegetables in bags—broccoli and cauliflower trimmed and broken up into florets, carrots peeled and chopped, peas and beans podded. Serving a vegetable side dish has never been so easy. You could also team frozen vegetables with fresh vegetables—frozen peas go well with softened zucchini, for instance, and frozen baby fava beans can be mixed with any variety of fresh bean.

On the facing page, you'll find a list of the cheat ingredients we always have to hand in our fridge, freezer, and pantry. From ready-baked tartlet cases to cans of chickpeas and corn, they're all designed to take some of the pressure off the busy cook.

Think simple and in season—if you have no time to make an elaborate dessert in the summer, serve fresh strawberries or raspberries with cream or make our Magenta fruit compote with white chocolate sauce on page 264. Simplicty itself.

Equipment
Certain pieces of equipment can save you time and effort as well. Cake-pan liners take the fuss out of lining cake pans. They are also guaranteed to be a perfect fit. Throwaway foil containers, such as tart pans, casserole dishes, roasting pans, and platters are not only convenient, they don't need washing either. You might appreciate that more than you think at the end of the day.

Other than a bit of chopping and some stirring, little preparation is required to turn out a dish as spectacular as our 21st-century coronation chicken on page 187.

CHEAT INGREDIENTS

These store-bought items are perfectly acceptable to use when you're cooking up a feast and want to reduce the amount of work you have to do.

IN CANS

apricots (in natural juices)

black-eyed peas (in water)

butter beans (in water)

chickpeas (in water)

corn

flageolet beans (in water)

pears (in natural juices)

red kidney beans (in water)

white peaches (in natural juices)

IN PACKAGES/BAGS

French bread (part-baked)

ladyfingers

meringues

ready-to-eat dried apricots

pre-cooked sliced bacon

soft bread dough

stock cubes

IN JARS/BOTTLES

marinated artichokes

mayonnaise

onion marmalade

pepperdew peppers

pesto

roasted peppers

salad dressing

tapenade

tomato purée

FROM THE REFRIGERATOR

crawfish tails

custard

dinner rolls

filo pastry

pie crusts

puff pastry

quail's eggs (cooked and ready peeled)

salad leaves

soft bread dough

tartlet cases

FROM THE FREEZER

baby fava beans

baby peas

chestnuts (ready peeled)

onions (ready chopped)

soft fruits such as raspberries

And to drink…

For a delicious soft drink that's almost as good as homemade lemonade, we mix together bottles of store-bought carbonated apple juice with grapefruit or cranberry juice (two-thirds apple juice to one-third fruit juice is about right). Then we float a few lemon or orange slices on top. Hey presto! Some sliced strawberries and tiny sprigs of mint look pretty in summer.

"All it takes to rustle up a dish like the Express Mediterranean platter on page 83 is a quick trip to the supermarket."

Preparing ahead

Okay, so preparing food in advance isn't exactly cheating, but it is a simple way of making life easier for yourself on the day. Throughout this book we give you advice on preparing ahead, but there are other little shortcuts, too. When you're making the gravy for the Mini pork en croûtes on page 120, for instance, you can mix all the ingredients together, ready to add the juices from the meat at the last minute. We do this all the time.

We also keep fresh white breadcrumbs, grated Cheddar, grated Parmesan, and nuts in separate plastic containers in the freezer. They thaw in minutes, ready to cook with, and taste as fresh as the moment you put them in there.

Our top 10 speedy dishes

Smoked salmon on rye (page 46)	10–15 mins prep
Express Mediterranean platter (page 83)	10 mins prep
Chicken with pesto and Taleggio (page 104)	10 mins prep
Teriyaki steak (page 113)	5 mins prep
Seafood linguine (page 164)	5–10 mins prep
Mushroom stroganoff (page 198)	10 mins prep
Rhubarb and lemon pots (page 254)	10–15 mins prep
Heavenly lemon cheesecake (page 259)	10–15 mins prep
Mango Eton mess (page 273)	10–15 mins prep
Lemon and lime puddings (page 274)	10 mins prep

It's the day of your feast and the countdown's on. If you've prepared ahead and kept yourself well organized, the pressure shouldn't be too intense. It's now time to make the final preparations.

On the day

Take a look at your menu. What's sitting in the fridge waiting to be transferred to a dish or platter? What needs to be reheated or have the finishing touches put to it? And what has to be put together from scratch? Even if it's only the potatoes you're serving with your main course or a salad you have to dress, make sure they're on your list.

Organize the equipment

Clear a space next to your stove and lay out all the equipment you'll need—knives, utensils, oven gloves, a kitchen timer. Try to think of everything.

Well ahead of time, get out all the plates, bowls, serving platters, and cutlery you will need.

Clear a space on a counter and pile the serving platters on it. Don't forget dishes for sauces and a basket for bread.

Sort out all the plates, bowls, cutlery, napkins, and serving utensils you'll require and place them on your dining table or buffet table. If you're serving food hot, have the plates or bowls ready to put in the oven to heat through.

Set the table

If you're having a buffet, arrange a stack of plates or bowls at one end of the table, with the cutlery and napkins at the other end. The flow of traffic can go from right to left or from left to right, depending on the layout of your room. To show you how this works, we've set the table for a buffet on pages 212–213 and for a bowl party on pages 178–179.

For a large sit-down meal, it's a good idea to have a seating plan. For special occasions, you might want to have name cards. If it's a family affair and you have young children, get them to decorate the cards for you. If you're having flowers in the center of the table, arrange them in tall vases or low vases so that people can still see each other and chat.

Ask for help if you need it

If you think you'll need help at some point during the party, make sure you line up volunteers in plenty of time. You might need someone to take people's coats and bags, for instance (we usually put them on a bed), or someone to go around with a plate of canapés or a bottle of wine. If you have any last-minute cooking to do, you might well appreciate a helping hand in the kitchen, too, even if it's only asking someone to toss the salad. But beware of enlisting too much help—people could end up getting in your way.

Warm the plates and platters

Plates must be piping hot for food you're serving hot. Platters may need heating, too. The easiest way to do this is in a low oven. If your oven's already in use, you could either run them through a quick wash in the dishwasher (there's no need for any detergent) or stack them over a pan of simmering water. Swap them around every so often so they all get hot. Hot plates and hostess carts may not be high fashion any more, but they will certainly come in handy if you have one.

Taste the food

In the same way that you taste food as you're making it, it's important to taste it again before you serve it. Adjust the seasoning, if need be—that way, you can present it with confidence.

Serving cold food

If you've prepared food ahead and kept it in the fridge ready to serve cold, transfer it to platters just before serving. If you want to cover the platters with plastic wrap, make sure it's only lightly secured under the rim—when too tightly wrapped, it can be time-consuming to remove and there's always the risk of damaging the arrangement as you do so.

"Don't provide outsized serving utensils—they are practical, but the food will go in no time."

Portion control

Whether you're serving individual plates of food or letting guests help themselves, it's important to keep an eye on the size of the portions.

If you're serving guests, make sure the portions are a sensible size—you don't want to overwhelm people (particularly women) by putting too much on their plate to begin with. They can always have more.

If you're serving food on platters for guests to help themselves, don't provide outsized utensils—they may seem practical, but guests will make full use of them and the food will be gone in no time. When serving pies and lasagnas, we often lightly mark portion sizes on the surface with a knife so guests know where to cut. This works well with whole fish, too. Again, don't make the portions too large.

The drinks and glasses

At a buffet, set the drinks and glasses out on a separate table. Site it well away from the door—the first thing guests generally do at a party is pour themselves a drink and you don't want them blocking the entrance to the room. Provide the right glasses for the drinks on offer—wine glasses (both red and white), beer glasses, and glasses for water or soft drinks—and make sure there are plenty of them. Some non-breakable glasses or plastic tumblers are a good idea if there are going to be children present. You might want to supply an ice bucket and some straws, too. A corkscrew and a bottle opener are essential items, as is a container for corks and caps.

Red wine can be swirled easily in a large-bowled glass to release aromas.

White wine will keep cooler in a narrow glass with a stem to hold it by.

Beer tastes better from a chalice glass, which also maintains the head.

Soft drinks or water are best served in tall highball glasses.

Reheating food

If you're going to reheat food, it needs to be done thoroughly. There can be serious health risks if you don't. We've indicated in the recipes when you can prepare a dish ahead and reheat it. If it doesn't say you can do this, don't do it—you'll spoil a dish like our beef stir-fry, for example.

If you've kept food you've prepared ahead in the fridge, allow time for it to come to room temperature before you reheat it. This can take much longer than you think—up to a few hours for a big dish. It depends to some extent on the temperature in your kitchen.

Whenever possible, reheat food in a wide shallow pan or dish—it will heat up more quickly than in a small deep one.

On the stove top, use a large-based pan that covers the whole of the hot plate. If you are reheating a casserole, bring it up to a boil, then cover with a lid and leave it to simmer gently, stirring occasionally to prevent it burning.

Before you preheat the oven, arrange the shelves so that you know the dishes will all fit in. Preheat it well ahead of time and, halfway through cooking, switch the dishes around in case your oven has hotter parts to it.

Remember that the more dishes you're reheating in the oven at the same time, the longer they'll take. Check toward the end of cooking to see if they're done—they must be piping hot in the middle.

Party bites

Party bites is our name for the tiny dishes that delight the eye and excite the palate at the start of a special occasion. To get your feast off with a flourish, choose the right ones and present them with flair.

Party bites

Antipasti, tapas, mezze, canapés—there are so many names for party bites. Little surprise then that the recipes for this chapter come from all around the world. At their most sophisticated, party bites are exquisite tartlets topped with half a quail's egg. Somewhat humbler—but no less satisfying—are slices of baguette baked in the oven until golden and crisp, then topped with a mouthwatering mixture of slow-roasted tomatoes and herbs. Which you choose depends to some extent on the occasion—formal or informal—as well as who your guests are. But here are some general guidelines.

What to serve

● Offer a selection of meat, fish, and vegetarian canapés. That way, you can guarantee you're catering for all tastes.

● Unless you're having a cocktail party, offer just a small selection of bites. People are much more likely to remember them if you don't give too much choice.

● Offer a selection of hot and cold eats. The advantage of doing this is that you'll be able to prepare the cold canapés completely ahead of time, which will help you spread your work load and leave you free to put the finishing touches to the hot canapés. In summer, though, it's perfectly acceptable to serve just cold canapés.

● Think about the dishes that follow. If you're serving fish as your starter or main course, you might want to ring the changes and have party bites that are vegetarian or have meat in them. If you're serving curry, it might be fun to extend the theme with some Asian-style canapés, such as chicken satay or meatballs with a hot dipping sauce.

What to serve them on

● Use light platters or plates to serve the canapés on. In our experience, heavy platters can soon become a chore to hold, particularly when guests want to stand and chat.

● China, wood, melamine, thin slate, or flat wicker trays are ideal.

● Throwaway foil serving dishes are another option. You'll find them in supermarkets and department stores, as well as online. We often cover them with red currant or black currant leaves so you can't see the foil. Grapevine leaves also work well—ask for them at specialty food stores.

● Think about the color. Food always looks appetizing against white, but it can look equally stunning on black or silver. Avoid colors that will overpower the food or make it look anemic.

● Small mugs are ideal for serving soup when guests are standing up, but don't fill them to the brim or you'll take too much of the edge off their appetites.

● If you have the time, decorate the serving platters—fresh herbs tied in bundles with raffia look pretty. Sprigs of holly add a festive touch at Christmas and a small bouquet of sweet peas or roses is good in summer. Even some wedges of lemon or lime would do.

Other things you might need

● If the party bite comes with a dipping sauce, serve it in a ramekin or small bowl.

● Some party bites call for toothpicks or skewers. Use a selection of toothpicks—wooden, bamboo, glass, or plastic (but not for hot food). Even though they have to be soaked in water for a few hours before use, we prefer wooden skewers to metal ones because they're nice to handle and don't get hot.

● Place piles of small napkins—fabric or paper—in obvious places around the room for people to help themselves.

CHEAT *If you've run out of serving dishes, take a look around your kitchen to see what you can use instead. A chopping board, tray, or pastry board will do the job. If it's seen better days, give it a quick makeover with some foil, sushi mats, or grapevine leaves.*

How many party bites to serve

Whatever party bites you choose to prepare from the recipes in this chapter, these are the numbers to serve per guest.

● **8–10 per person** at an occasion such as a cocktail party where you're serving no other food. Serve up to five different types—cold and/or hot—depending on the number of people you've invited.

● **3 per person** at a meal with no first course. Serve two different types of canapé—cold and/or hot.

● **1–2 per person** at a meal with a first course. Serve just one kind of party bite, either cold or hot.

How to serve party bites

● If you've kept the canapés in the fridge, take them out about an hour before you want to serve them so they have a chance to come up to room temperature. The flavors will improve as a result.

● When serving hot canapés, work out timings carefully in advance—you don't want to keep people waiting. Nor do you want everything in the oven at once. And allow a little time for them to cool down before you take them out to serve.

● Assemble the canapés completely and then transfer them to the plate or platter. If you try to assemble them directly on the platter, it can get rather messy—and you won't have time for mishaps.

● Arrange the canapés in neat lines. For some reason, odd numbers—three, five, seven, and so on—look better than even numbers.

FOR KIDS *If you have a troop of ravenous children or teenagers on the prowl, your party bites will be wolfed down in a flash. We always steer them toward a batch of sandwiches or bigger canapés that we've prepared especially for them.*

"Start with your most stunning party bite—just like the curtain going up at the theater, this is your signal that the action is about to commence."

● Canapés always look more appetizing if they're served without a toothpick stuck in them—even if you need one to eat them. We always put the sticks in a separate container on the serving platter. A shot glass is ideal. Remember to dot little bowls here and there for people to dispose of them.

● Serve dipping sauces in a separate bowl or ramekin and let guests help themselves.

When to bring out the party bites

● Don't bring out your canapés until most of your guests have arrived. You don't want them to have been gobbled up by the time everyone gets there.

● If you need a hand to take them around, ask a good friend—anyone who's single, there without their partner, or who doesn't know many people will probably jump at the chance.

● Start with your most stunning party bite—just like the curtain going up at the theater, this is your signal that the action is about to commence.

● To begin with, serve one kind of canapé per plate or platter, so you can keep a track of which guests have had what.

● Once the party bites have started to disappear, serve mixed plates or platters rather than half-empty ones—these can look rather sad and uninviting.

● Allow 45 minutes to an hour for guests to enjoy their canapés before you serve your first course or main course. Don't rush things—you want to keep the atmosphere relaxed.

● At a cocktail party you expect to last for 2–3 hours, serve the party bites for a couple of hours and then wind down.

● As a sign that it's finishing-off time and the curtain's about to come back down, we serve something sweet—brownies or cupcakes presented in paper truffle cases.

These are smart enough to impress royalty! They're quick to assemble, too. Use vacuum-packed Parma ham, because you need evenly cut slices. Serve the rolls hot or warm.

Asparagus, goat cheese, and Parma ham filo rolls

Makes 48–60

18 asparagus spears, trimmed
12 slices Parma ham
6 tbsp soft spreadable goat cheese
6 sheets filo pastry
  (each about 7 x 10in/18 x 25cm in size)
1 stick butter, melted

1 Cook the asparagus in boiling salted water for 2–3 minutes or until just tender. Drain and refresh in cold water, then dry on paper towels.

2 Lay two slices of ham next to each other lengthwise on a board. One edge should overlap slightly. Spread 1 tablespoon of the goat cheese over the top so the ham is completely covered.

3 Arrange three asparagus spears end to end along one of the long edges of the ham. Trim them slightly if they are too long, then roll the ham up tightly.

4 Brush one sheet of filo with melted butter, sit the ham along one end, and roll tightly into a long sausage. Make five more sausages in the same way, then transfer to the fridge to firm up.

5 To serve, preheat the oven to 400°F (200°C). Slice each sausage diagonally into 8–10 slices, then arrange on a baking sheet and bake for 8–10 minutes or until golden and crisp.

PREPARE AHEAD
The rolls can be made up to the end of step 4
up to 12 hours ahead. Not suitable for freezing.

These are divine. They are also tiny, but you could make them larger if you prefer. Just remember to bake them for a few minutes longer—and keep your eye on them.

Sausage and apple filo rolls

Makes 80

1lb (450g) pork sausagemeat

1 small crisp apple, peeled, cored, and coarsely grated

1 tbsp wholegrain mustard

1 tbsp freshly chopped sage

salt and freshly ground black pepper

10 sheets filo pastry (each about 7 x 10in/18 x 25cm in size)

1 stick butter, melted

1 Put the sausagemeat, apple, mustard, and sage into a mixing bowl, season with salt and freshly ground black pepper, and mix well.

2 Divide the mixture into 10, then roll each one into a sausage about the diameter of a breakfast sausage link and as wide as a sheet of filo.

3 Brush one sheet of filo with melted butter. Arrange a sausage down one side and roll it up. Repeat with the remaining filo and sausages, then chill in the fridge for 30 minutes.

4 To serve, preheat the oven to 400°F (200°C). Slice each roll into eight diagonally and arrange on two baking sheets lined with non-stick baking parchment.

5 Bake for 8–10 minutes or until golden and crisp. Serve hot or warm.

PREPARE AHEAD AND FREEZE

The rolls can be made up to the end of step 4 up to 12 hours ahead. Alternatively, you can bake them and reheat to serve. Freeze the uncooked rolls for up to 2 months.

This recipe is an excellent choice for big gatherings. Both children and adults love this wonderful combination of savory and sweet, and they are quick and easy to prepare.

Golden dough balls with cheese and chutney

Makes 32

a little all-purpose flour to dust
13.8oz can refrigerated pizza crust
scant 1oz (25g) butter
3½oz (100g) mature Cheddar
   cheese, grated
1 tbsp milk
salt and freshly ground black pepper
1 egg yolk
2 tbsp freshly snipped chives
3 tbsp mango chutney

VARIATION

As a variation on this scrummy recipe, cut small slices of chargrilled red peppers from a jar and arrange them in a cross on the top of each dough ball when they come out of the oven.

1 Lightly dust your work surface with flour. Roll the pizza crust out to a rectangle approximately 10 x 16in (25 x 40cm). Cut into 16 strips, and roll each strip into a ball. Slice each dough ball in half horizontally.

2 Melt the butter in a saucepan, add the cheese, and stir to melt. Add the milk and stir until smooth. Leave to cool slightly, then season with salt and freshly ground black pepper and stir in the egg yolk and chives. Transfer to the fridge to firm up—when the mixture looks like soft butter, it will be easier to spread.

3 Preheat the oven to 400°F (200°C). Line a baking sheet with non-stick baking parchment or foil. Spread the cheese mixture over the cut side of each ball, and place onto the baking sheet. Spoon a small blob of the chutney on top.

4 Bake for 14–16 minutes or until golden brown and hot. Arrange on a platter and serve immediately.

PREPARE AHEAD AND FREEZE

The dough balls can be made up to the end of step 3 up to 12 hours ahead. Freeze without the chutney for up to 1 month.

These warm canapés are always a hit and they're a cinch to make. If you'd like to serve them as a starter, you'll need three to four per person. Serve them with a little ramekin of satay sauce.

Mini chicken satays

Makes 24

Special equipment 24 skewers (see below)

4 large skinless boneless chicken breasts
4 tsp white wine vinegar or rice vinegar
4 tsp superfine sugar
2 tbsp sunflower oil or sesame oil
a little olive oil, to fry
a sprig of cilantro, to garnish

For the satay sauce

1½ tbsp olive oil
1 large onion, finely chopped
1 small jalepeño, seeded
  and finely chopped
3 garlic cloves, crushed
1 tbsp medium curry powder
6 heaped tbsp crunchy peanut butter
1½ cups water
1 heaped tsp superfine sugar
juice of ½ large lime
salt and freshly ground black pepper

SKEWERS

We prefer wooden skewers to metal ones. Soak them in water for about 8 hours before use so that they don't burn during cooking.

1 Slice each chicken breast into six thin strips, then place them in a mixing bowl. Add the vinegar, sugar, and oil and toss together well. Leave to marinate in the fridge for about an hour.

2 To make the sauce, heat the oil in a frying pan over high heat, add the onion, jalepeño, and garlic and fry for 1 minute. Cover with a lid, lower the heat, and cook for 5 minutes or until the onion is starting to soften.

3 Stir in the curry powder and fry for 1 minute. Add the peanut butter, water, sugar, and lime juice and stir over high heat until the sauce is thick and shiny, then season with salt and freshly ground black pepper. Spoon into a serving bowl and leave to cool completely.

4 Thread each strip of chicken on to a skewer—it should be fairly flat so that it will fry evenly, with room at one end so it can be held comfortably.

5 Heat a little olive oil in a large frying pan and fry the chicken skewers for 1–2 minutes on each side or until golden all over and cooked through. You may need to do this in batches. Garnish the sauce with the cilantro sprig and serve with the warm chicken skewers.

PREPARE AHEAD

The sauce can be made up to 3 days ahead. The skewers can be threaded up to 2 days ahead. Not suitable for freezing.

Asian food always goes down well at a party. The consistency of the sauce is thin—as is traditional—but you can thicken it at the end with half a teaspoon of corn starch mixed with two teaspoons of water.

Pork meatballs with Asian dipping sauce

Makes about 50

1lb (450g) lean ground pork

1 red chile, halved, seeded, and finely diced (see below right)

1 tsp freshly grated ginger root

½ onion, coarsely grated

1¾oz (50g) saltines, finely crushed

1 tsp five-spice powder

1 egg yolk

small bunch of cilantro, roughly chopped

zest and juice of ½ lime

salt and freshly ground black pepper

a little sunflower, to fry

For the dipping sauce

juice of ½ lime

2 tbsp light brown sugar

½ cup plum sauce

1 tbsp soy sauce

¼ cup cold water

1 Put the first nine ingredients into a bowl and mix together with your hands. Season well with salt and freshly ground black pepper, then shape into about 50 small meatballs.

2 Heat a little oil in a large frying pan, add the meatballs, and fry slowly for 10 minutes or until lightly golden and cooked through. You might need to do this in batches. Keep warm while you make the dipping sauce.

3 Put all the ingredients for the sauce into a small saucepan and heat until the sugar dissolves. Transfer to six tiny ramekins or two larger bowls and serve them next to the meatballs on the plate.

PREPARE AHEAD AND FREEZE
The meatballs can be made and fried up to 2 days ahead. The sauce can be made up to 3 days ahead. Freeze the uncooked meatballs for up to 2 months.

SEEDING CHILES

Cut the chile in half lengthwise, then scrape out the seeds with a spoon. You might want to wear plastic gloves if you have sensitive skin.

We've been serving a version of this canapé for years and they are still one of our most popular. Our assistant, Lucinda, also has a catering company and she says these are always the first to go.

Sausages and mustard mash

Makes 20

20 cocktail sausages
3½oz (100g) mashed potatoes
a little milk (optional)
a little butter (optional)
salt and freshly ground
    black pepper

whole-grain mustard
a little freshly grated
    Parmesan cheese
paprika, to dust

1 Grill the sausages, turning them halfway through, until cooked and evenly brown. Set aside to cool completely.

2 Heat the mashed potatoes in a pan (if they are a bit stiff, stir in a little milk and butter—the mixture should be smooth and fairly loose). Season with salt and freshly ground black pepper and add mustard to taste. Transfer to a piping bag fitted with a plain narrow tip (don't worry if you don't have one—you can use a teaspoon).

3 Slice each sausage open lengthwise. Squeezing the ends of each one together gently, pipe or spoon the mashed potato into the opening.

4 Arrange on a baking tray, sprinkle with the Parmesan, and lightly dust with paprika.

5 To serve, preheat the oven to 400°F (200°C). Reheat the sausages for 10 minutes or until hot throughout. Transfer to a platter and serve. Do warn your guests they may be hot!

PREPARE AHEAD AND FREEZE
The sausages and mash can be prepared up to the end of step 3 up to 1 day ahead. Freeze at the end of step 3 for up to 1 month.

These are our take on the crispy duck pancakes you get in Chinese restaurants. And very good they are, too. We use filo pastry because it is much easier to roll than store-bought pancakes.

Duck and hoisin spring rolls

Makes 18

1 boneless duck breast, skin removed
a little olive oil
salt and freshly ground black pepper
6 sheets filo pastry
3 tbsp butter, melted
3 tbsp hoisin sauce, plus a little extra
  for dipping
¼ cucumber, sliced in half lengthwise,
  seeds removed, then cut into
  2½in (6cm) long matchsticks
3 scallions, cut into 2½in (6cm)
  long matchsticks

1 Preheat the oven to 400°F (200°C). Meanwhile, rub both sides of the duck breasts with a little olive oil, season with salt and freshly ground black pepper, then fry over high heat for 2 minutes on each side or until golden brown on the outside and still pink on the inside. Allow to cool slightly, then cut into very thin slices.

2 Lay a sheet of filo on the work surface and cut it into three 4 x 5in (10 x 12cm) strips (the dimensions of the filo will depend on the brand, but cut strips that are roughly this size). Brush the edges of each strip with melted butter.

3 Spoon a little hoisin sauce near the bottom of each strip (leaving a gap around the edges), then sit a couple of slices of duck on top, followed by a few of the cucumber and scallion matchsticks.

4 Fold the sides of each strip in, then, starting at the bottom, roll them up into neatly shaped spring rolls. Make 15 more in the same way.

5 Brush the spring rolls with a little more melted butter, arrange on a baking sheet, and bake, turning them halfway through cooking, for 10 minutes or until golden. Serve warm with extra hoisin sauce to dip into.

PREPARE AHEAD
The spring rolls can be made up to the end of step 4 up to 8 hours ahead. Not suitable for freezing.

Every can of water chestnuts we open seems to contain 21, but you may end up with one more or one less. It doesn't matter in the slightest for these, our version of the traditional devils on horseback.

Bacon and water chestnut bites with mango chutney

Makes about 21

7 strips of thin bacon
¼ cup mango chutney
5oz can water chestnuts, drained
  and dried

1 Preheat the oven to 425°F (220°C). Lay a strip of bacon on a chopping board. Hold on to one end of it with one hand and place the back of a knife on it near your hand. Pressing the knife down firmly, pull the bacon toward you so that the entire length of it runs underneath the knife, stretching as it does so. Cut across into three equal pieces. Repeat with the other strips.

2 Lay all of the bacon strips on the board. Spoon ½ teaspoon of the chutney on one end, sit a water chestnut on top, then roll the strips up and arrange them on a baking sheet.

3 Spoon a little more chutney on top of each bite, then bake, turning them halfway through, for 20 minutes or until crisp and golden. Serve hot with a toothpick.

PREPARE AHEAD
The bites can be made up to the end of step 2
up to 24 hours ahead. Not suitable for freezing.

These are utterly delicious—crispy bacon and egg mayonnaise tartlets, each topped with half a quail's egg. To make the eggs easier to peel, do it when they are just cool enough to handle.

Crispy bacon and quail's egg tartlets

Makes 24

12 large hen's eggs
12 quail's eggs
2 tbsp mayonnaise
dash of Tabasco
2 tbsp freshly snipped chives
salt and freshly ground black pepper
4 strips of bacon
24 store-bought pre-baked mini
   pastry shells
celery salt, for sprinkling

1 Put the hen's eggs in a saucepan. Cover with cold water, bring to a boil, and boil for 5 minutes. Add the quail's eggs and boil for a further 3 minutes. Drain and cover with cold water. Peel as soon as they are cool enough to handle.

2 Put the mayonnaise, Tabasco, and half the chives into a bowl with some salt and freshly ground black pepper and mix together. Quarter the large eggs, add to the mayonnaise, and mash well with a fork. Cut the quail's eggs in half and set aside.

3 Fry the bacon in a non-stick frying pan until crisp, then drain on paper towels and set aside.

4 Spoon the egg mayonnaise mixture into the pastry cases and sit half a quail's egg cut side up on top of each one. Snip the bacon into pieces and arrange a piece next to the quail's eggs.

5 Sprinkle with a pinch of celery salt, garnish with the remaining chives, and serve at once.

PREPARE AHEAD
The tartlets can be prepared up to 3 hours ahead.
Not suitable for freezing.

Made a little larger, these fritters are also great for brunch. You'll find the crispy bacon in a packet at the deli counter of the supermarket. Fry some bacon strips yourself, if you prefer.

Corn and feta fritters

Makes 30

¾ cup self-rising flour
2 eggs
3½fl oz (100ml) milk
salt and freshly ground black pepper
¼ cup freshly snipped chives
5.5oz (150g) can corn, drained
2oz feta cheese, finely crumbled
a little sunflower oil, to fry
7oz (200g) low-fat cream cheese
3½oz (100g) cooked bacon,
  broken into pieces

1 Put the flour into a mixing bowl, make a well in the center, and add the eggs. Whisk by hand, gradually adding the milk, until you have a smooth batter. Season with salt and freshly ground black pepper, then stir in half the chives along with the corn and feta.

2 Heat the oil in a non-stick frying pan, add the batter to the pan half a teaspoon at a time, then fry for 2–3 minutes on each side or until golden and cooked through. You may need to do this in batches. Set aside to cool.

3 Put the cream cheese into a bowl, add the remaining chives, and season with salt and freshly ground black pepper.

4 Using a teaspoon, spoon the cream cheese mixture on top of the fritters, then top with a piece of crispy bacon. Arrange on a platter and serve.

PREPARE AHEAD
The fritters can be made up to 1 day ahead and assembled up to 6 hours ahead. Not suitable for freezing.

Matchsticks of celery root coated in mustardy mayonnaise, remoulade is a classic starter. Here, the mixture is teamed with arugula and wrapped in wafer-thin slices of rare fillet steak.

Beef remoulade rolls

Makes 24

2 large tenderloin beef filets
1 tbsp olive oil
salt and freshly ground black pepper
1 small celery root
¼ cup good-quality mayonnaise
1 tbsp Dijon mustard
large handful of arugula

1 Rub the steaks with the oil and season with salt and freshly ground black pepper. Heat any remaining oil in a non-stick frying pan, add the steaks, and fry for 3 minutes on each side or until still rare (this will depend on the thickness). Set aside to cool completely.

2 Peel the celery root with a sharp knife, chop into pieces, then cut into thin matchsticks with the matchstick attachment of a food processor. Immerse in boiling salted water for 3 minutes or until soft. Drain and dry on paper towels.

3 Put the mayonnaise and mustard into a bowl, season with salt and freshly ground black pepper, and mix well. Stir in the celery root.

4 Slice each cold steak into 12 thin slices (you may get more depending on the size of the steak). Spoon a little remoulade on one end of each slice, put a few arugula leaves on top, then roll them up and arrange on a platter. Serve with toothpicks, if you wish.

PREPARE AHEAD
The remoulade can be made up to 3 days ahead.
The rolls can be made up to 8 hours ahead. Not suitable for freezing.

These are always a hit. As a twist on the traditional recipe, we use rye bread, pumpernickel, or pumpkin-seed bread. You'll find the cucumbers in jars near the pickles and olives at the supermarket.

Smoked salmon on rye with cucumber pickle

Makes 60

¼ cup light mayonnaise

2 tsp whole-grain mustard

1 tsp lemon juice

1 tbsp freshly chopped dill, plus extra
   to garnish

4 rectangular slices of rye bread,
   pumpernickel, or pumpkin seed bread

7oz (200g) smoked salmon slices

4 cucumber dill pickles, drained
   and very finely chopped

1 Mix the mayonnaise, mustard, lemon juice, and dill in a small bowl.

2 Lay the bread on a chopping board and spread evenly with the mixture.

3 Cover the mayonnaise with smoked salmon, then cut each piece of bread into 15 squares. Top each one with chopped pickle, arrange on a serving plate, then garnish with dill and serve.

PREPARE AHEAD
The bites can be made up to 6 hours ahead.
Not suitable for freezing.

Dips are so easy to serve at a party. Here are two of our favorites. The scorching chile one will certainly sort the men from the boys!

Dip platter

Garlicky herb dip

Serves 6–12 (depending on what you serve it with)

1 jalepeño, halved, seeded, and cut into three
3 small scallions, finely chopped
3 garlic cloves, halved

small handful of flat-leaf parsley
small bunch of chives
6oz (200ml) tub full-fat crème fraîche

1 tsp Dijon mustard
1 tbsp lemon juice
salt and freshly ground black pepper

1 Put the jalepeño, scallions, garlic, and parsley into a processor and whiz until very finely chopped. Add the remaining ingredients, season with salt and freshly ground black pepper, and whiz again until smooth.

2 Spoon the dip into a bowl or ramekin and chill. To serve, place in the center of a large plate, with your choice of dippers (see right) around the edge. The dip also goes well with potato wedges or dolloped on a baked potato.

PREPARE AHEAD
The dip can be made up to 3 days ahead. The flavors will get stronger the longer it keeps. Not suitable for freezing.

Scorching chile dip

Serves 6–12 (depending on what you serve it with)

10 pepperdew peppers, drained, rinsed, and cut in half
1 red chile, cut in half
2 tsp freshly grated ginger root

6 tbsp mayonnaise
2 tbsp mango chutney
3½oz (100g) full-fat cream cheese

a few drops of Tabasco
salt and freshly ground black pepper

1 Put all the ingredients into a processor and whiz until smooth. Season with salt and freshly ground black pepper.

2 Spoon the dip into a bowl or ramekin and place in the center of a large plate. Arrange your choice of dippers (see above right) around the edge.

PREPARE AHEAD
The dip can be made up to 4 days ahead. The flavors will get stronger the longer it keeps. Not suitable for freezing.

DIPPERS

Vegetables are the classic dippers and always popular. Our favorites are peppers, carrots, cucumber, fennel, and celery—all cut into matchsticks or thin slices. Halved baby corn and small Little Gem lettuce leaves are also ideal.

If you're serving chips, tortillas, or bread, choose plain varieties so they don't overpower the flavor of the dip. Toasted naan and pita bread are perfect for dipping.

Breadsticks are inexpensive and come plain or flavored. They are great for dipping because they hold their shape.

We like our blinis quite thin, but the thickness is entirely up to you. If you make them too thick by mistake, simply slice them in half horizontally and you'll have twice the number.

Homemade blinis with salmon and crème fraîche

Makes 30

heaping ¾ cup self-rising flour
½ tsp baking powder
2 eggs
¼ cup milk
2 tbsp freshly snipped chives
1 tbsp sunflower oil

For the topping

3½oz (100g) cream cheese
3 tbsp crème fraîche
2 tbsp freshly chopped dill, plus a few
   sprigs to garnish
1 tsp lemon juice
7oz (200g) smoked salmon

1 Put the flour, baking powder, eggs, milk, and chives into a bowl and mix to make a smooth batter. Heat the oil in a frying pan, add the batter half a teaspoon at a time, and fry for 1–2 minutes or until little bubbles form and the blinis start to curl at the edges. Turn over and lightly brown the other side, then transfer to a wire rack to cool. You may need to do this in batches.

2 For the topping, mix the cream cheese, crème fraîche, chopped dill, and lemon juice in a small bowl, then spoon a little on to each blini.

3 Top the blinis with a small swirl of smoked salmon and a tiny sprig of dill. Arrange on a platter and serve.

PREPARE AHEAD AND FREEZE
The blinis can be made up to the end of step 1 up to 2 days ahead. They can be assembled up to 6 hours ahead. Freeze at the end of step 1 for up to 3 months.

The time spent roasting the tomatoes is worth every moment—the depth of flavor they acquire is wonderful. Teamed with a herby cream cheese, they make a wonderful cold canapé.

Crostini with slow-roasted tomatoes and herbs

Makes 30

1 stick of soft bread dough or a very thin baguette
a little olive oil
15 small cherry tomatoes
salt and freshly ground black pepper
dash of superfine sugar
2 tbsp cream cheese
2 heaped tsp freshly chopped mint
2 heaped tsp freshly chopped basil

1 Preheat the oven to 275°F (140°C). Meanwhile, cut the bread into 30 thin slices and brush both sides with a little of the oil.

2 Slice the tomatoes in half and arrange cut side up on a baking sheet. Sprinkle with a little salt, some freshly ground black pepper, and a dash of sugar. Cook in the oven for 30 minutes or until just softened and beginning to shrivel.

3 Heat a little olive oil in a frying pan and fry the slices of bread over high heat until golden brown on both sides. Set aside to cool.

4 Mix the cream cheese and herbs together in a bowl and season with salt and freshly ground black pepper. Spoon on to the cold crostini and top each one with a cold tomato half.

PREPARE AHEAD AND FREEZE
The crostini can be assembled up to the end of step 4 up to 6 hours ahead. Freeze without the topping for up to 4 months.

These are so popular whenever we serve them. Boursin cheese comes in foil packs and is flavored either with pepper or garlic—we use the pepper version (Boursin Poivre) for this recipe.

Crostini with Parma ham and peppered cream cheese

Makes 30

For the onion marmalade

1 tbsp olive oil
1 red onion, thinly sliced
½ tsp balsamic vinegar
1 tsp brown sugar
salt and freshly ground black pepper

1 soft bread dough (see below) or thin
   white baguette
a little olive oil
½ x 5.2oz (150g) packet Boursin Poivre
6 slices Parma ham

CHEAT

If you are short on time, use onion marmalade from a jar. Soft bread dough is available from supermarkets. It is half cooked and very thin—perfect for making crostini. Use a thin white baguette if you can't find it.

1 Preheat the oven to 325°F (140°C). Meanwhile, make the onion marmalade. Heat the oil in a saucepan, add the onion, and fry over high heat, stirring, for 5 minutes or until lightly colored. Cover with a lid and cook slowly for 20 minutes or until soft. Add the vinegar and sugar and stir over high heat for a few minutes until combined and glossy. Season with salt and freshly ground black pepper, then set aside to cool.

2 Cut the bread into 30 slices. Brush each side with a little olive oil, then arrange on a baking sheet. Bake for 30–45 minutes or until crisp. Leave to cool.

3 To serve, spread a little Boursin on top of each of the crostini. Snip each slice of Parma ham into 5 pieces and arrange on top of the Boursin. Top with a little marmalade, arrange on a platter, and serve.

PREPARE AHEAD AND FREEZE

The marmalade and crostini can be made up to 1 week ahead. The topping can be added to the crostini up to 6 hours ahead. Freeze the crostini without the topping for up to 4 months.

The addition of Parmesan cheese and pesto makes the pastry for these tarlet cases out of this world! For more filling ideas for tartlets, see pages 54–55.

Hummus and feta tartlets

Makes 48

Special equipment 12-hole mini muffin pan; 2in (5cm) round pastry cutter

For the tartlet cases

1½ cup (6oz) all-purpose flour, plus
   a little extra to dust
2½oz (75g) freshly grated
   Parmesan cheese
5 tbsp cold butter, cubed
2 tbsp pesto
2 tbsp cold water

For the filling

7oz prepared tub hummus
4 small carrots, grated
juice of ½ lemon
salt and freshly ground black pepper
7oz (200g) feta cheese, crumbled
7oz (200g) mixed pitted olives,
   sliced in half

1 Preheat the oven to 350°F (180°C). Meanwhile, put the flour, cheese, and butter into a food processor and whiz until the mixture resembles fine breadcrumbs. Add the pesto and water and whiz until the dough just comes together. Turn out on to a floured work surface and knead lightly into a ball. Roll out very thinly and then stamp out 48 rounds with a 2in (5cm) round cutter (don't worry if you don't get exactly 48). Use 12 of these to line the muffin pan.

2 Bake for 12–15 minutes or until golden brown. Turn out on to a wire rack to cool and bake the remaining tartlet cases in the same way.

3 When the tartlet cases are completely cold, spoon a little hummus into the base of each one. Mix the carrots and lemon juice together in a bowl and season with salt and freshly ground black pepper. Pile a little carrot on top of the hummus, then arrange some feta and half an olive on top. Serve cold.

PREPARE AHEAD AND FREEZE
The tartlet cases can be made up to 10 days ahead and kept in the fridge. The tartlets can be filled up to 4 hours ahead. Freeze the empty tartlet cases for up to 2 months.

Four delicious toppings for blinis or crostini. Each is enough to top 30. Prepare the blinis according to the method on page 50 and the crostini according to the method on page 52.

Toppings for blinis and crostini

Mozzarella, pesto, and cherry tomato

heaping ½ cup pesto
5½oz (150g) mozzarella, broken
   into pieces
8 cherry tomatoes, quartered

Spoon a little pesto on to each blini or crostini, top with a piece of mozzarella and then a quartered tomato. You should have two quarters left over.

Quail's egg, hollandaise, and asparagus

15 quail's eggs
30 asparagus tips
salt and freshly ground black pepper
¾ cup store-bought hollandaise sauce

Put the quail's eggs into a pan, cover with cold water, and bring to a boil. Boil for 3 minutes, then plunge into cold water. When cool, peel and cut in half. Cook the asparagus tips in boiling salted water for 2–3 minutes or until tender. Drain and refresh in cold water. Spoon a blob of hollandaise on to each blini or crostini, sit half a quail's egg and an asparagus tip on top, then sprinkle with freshly ground black pepper. Serve cold or reheat in an oven preheated to 325°F (160°C) for 10 minutes or until warmed through.

Crab, cream cheese, and chili dipping sauce

6oz can white crabmeat, drained
3 heaped tbsp cream cheese
3 tsp chili dipping sauce
salt and freshly ground black pepper

Mix the ingredients together in a bowl, season with salt and freshly ground black pepper, then spoon on to the blinis or crostini.

Parma ham, pepperdew pepper, and cream cheese

½ cup cream cheese
10 slices Parma ham, each cut into three
6 red baby bell pepperdew peppers,
   drained and cut into five slices

Spread the cream cheese on to the blinis or crostini, then arrange a swirl of ham and a slice of pepper on top.

Four excellent fillings for tartlets. Each recipe makes enough to fill 48 cases. Prepare the tartlets according to the recipe on page 53, but leave out the pesto.

Fillings for tartlets

Rare beef, beet, and horseradish

½ tbsp olive oil
8oz (225g) filet steak
1 large cooked red beet, peeled and
   coarsely grated
scant ½ cup creamed horseradish sauce

Heat the oil in a frying pan, add the steak, and fry for 3 minutes on each side or until cooked on the outside and rare on the inside. Leave to cool, then cut into 48 thin slices and arrange in the tartlet cases. Sprinkle with grated beet and a blob of horseradish sauce.

Goat cheese and Mediterranean vegetables

2 medium zucchini, cut in half lengthwise
   and thinly sliced
2 red peppers, halved, seeded,
   and cut into tiny dice
olive oil, to roast
salt and freshly ground black pepper
3½oz (100g) firm goat cheese,
   cut into cubes

Preheat the oven to 400°F (200°C). Toss the zucchini and peppers with a little olive oil and season with salt and freshly ground black pepper. Place vegetables in a roasting pan and roast in the oven for 15 minutes or until golden and tender. Spoon into the tartlet cases and top with the goat cheese. Serve cold or reheat in an oven preheated to 325°F (160°C) for 10 minutes or until warmed through.

Shrimp cocktail with mango

12oz (350g) cooked shrimp
½ cup mayonnaise
1 tbsp tomato ketchup
2 tsp creamed horseradish sauce
1 tbsp lemon juice
salt and freshly ground black pepper
1 small mango, halved, stoned, and the
   flesh cut into 48 cubes (see page 273)

Mix the shrimp with the mayonnaise, ketchup, horseradish sauce, and lemon juice. Season with salt and freshly ground black pepper and spoon into the tartlet cases. Top each with a cube of mango.

Dolcelatte, watercress, and pear

2½oz watercress
1lb (450g) dolcelatte cheese, cut into
   48 small cubes
1 ripe pear, peeled, cored, and cut into
   48 small cubes

To serve cold, divide the watercress among the tartlets, then top with a cube of cheese and a cube of pear. To serve warm, top with the cheese and pear, then reheat in an oven preheated to 325°F (160°C) for 10 minutes or until the cheese has melted. Add the watercress before serving.

A selection of blinis, crostini, and tartlets (see overleaf) ●●●➤

Our best starters

If you haven't served nibbles with drinks, the first course is your opportunity to get off to a good start with a dish your guests can't wait to tuck into. The recipes in this chapter fit that bill perfectly.

Our best starters

When you're choosing a first course, look at your menu as a whole.

● If you're serving fish as a main course, offer a meat or vegetarian dish as your starter, and vice versa.

● A simple first course is good before a more elaborate main course—you don't want to spoil people's appetites or fill them up before the meal has barely begun. But a rich or elaborate starter is fine before a simple main course.

Hot or cold?

A cold first course makes life easy when you're serving large numbers of people and is ideal in summer. Hot soup is perfect in winter, but bear in mind that if you're working singlehandedly it can be trickier than you think to serve soup to a crowd—it has to be piping hot, as have the bowls you pour it into.

Again, look at your menu as a whole. You might feel more relaxed if you know one course is made, ready to take out of the fridge and serve.

*"If your guests are sitting down to eat,
put the starter on the table before they
come in so the scene is set."*

Serving cold starters

● Remember to put out any accompaniments, such as bread and butter, toast, or rolls.

● Dress salad garnishes at the last minute so the leaves don't go limp.

● If guests are sitting down to eat, put the starter on the table before they come into the room so the scene is set.

● At a more informal occasion, where guests are not sitting down at a table to eat, go around with the first course on a platter—this is a very sociable way to entertain.

Serving hot starters

● Before you serve the food, have everything you need to hand—oven gloves, utensils, kitchen timer, and so on.

● If you're serving your first course on individual plates, place them on a work surface and arrange any garnish on them, then all you need to do is add the hot food.

● It's quicker, easier, and less messy to pour soup from a large pitcher rather than trying to serve it with a ladle.

● Make sure soup bowls are piping hot—soup gets cold extremely quickly.

● Assemble your guests before you do any last-minute reheating or cooking.

> **FOR LUNCH** *Some of our starters, such as the tartlets on page 67 and the mousseline creams on page 71, are substantial enough to serve as a light lunch. For hungry friends, you might want to serve a couple, but one is fine for us.*

Vibrant in color and quick to make, this soup is ideal for any winter party. Serve with croûtons or crispy bread.

Sweet potato soup with cumin and ginger

Serves 6

1 tbsp olive oil

2lb (900g) sweet potatoes, peeled and cut into ½in (1cm) cubes

1lb (450g) carrots, cut into ½in (1cm) cubes

¾in (2cm) piece fresh ginger root, peeled and finely grated

1 tsp ground cumin

5 cups vegetable stock

salt and freshly ground black pepper

heavy cream, to garnish

chopped chives, to garnish

Serves 12

2 tbsp olive oil

4lb (1.8kg) sweet potatoes, peeled and cut into ½in (1cm) cubes

2lb (900g) carrots, cut into ½in (1cm) cubes

2in (5cm) piece fresh ginger root, peeled and finely grated

2 tsp ground cumin

10½ cups vegetable stock

salt and freshly ground black pepper

½ cup heavy cream, to garnish

chopped chives, to garnish

1 Heat the oil in a deep saucepan, add the sweet potatoes, carrots, ginger, and cumin and fry over high heat, stirring, for 10 minutes or until starting to brown.

2 Add the stock, bring to a boil, then season with salt and freshly ground black pepper. Cover with a lid and simmer over low heat for 20–30 minutes (35–40 minutes for 12) or until the sweet potatoes and carrots are tender.

3 Carefully scoop out half the vegetables into a bowl using a slotted spoon. Whiz the remainder in a processor or blender until smooth, then return to the pan.

4 Add the reserved vegetables, bring to a boil again, and check the seasoning.

5 To serve, garnish with a swirl of heavy cream and some chopped chives.

PREPARE AHEAD AND FREEZE
The soup can be made up to 3 days ahead.
Freeze for up to 3 months.

The onions are caramelized in sugar in this traditional recipe. We toast the croûtons to make a perfect winter starter or lunch dish.

French onion soup with mustard Gruyère croûtons

Serves 6

1½ tbsp butter
4 large onions, thinly sliced
2 tsp soft light brown sugar
6 cups chicken stock
1 tbsp corn starch
salt and freshly ground
   black pepper
1½ tbsp balsamic vinegar

For the croûtons

1 small thin baguette stick
1½ tbsp butter, at
   room temperature
2 tbsp Dijon mustard
1¾oz (50g) Gruyère,
   finely grated

Serves 12

3 tbsp butter
8 large onions, thinly sliced
2 tbsp soft light brown sugar
12 cups chicken stock
2 tbsp corn starch
salt and freshly ground
   black pepper
¼ cup balsamic vinegar

For the croûtons

1 large thin baguette
3 tbsp butter, at room
   temperature
¼ cup Dijon mustard
3½oz (100g) Gruyère,
   finely grated

1 Melt the butter in a deep saucepan, add the onions, and fry for 5 minutes, stirring. Lower the heat, cover with a lid, and cook for 20 minutes or until completely soft.

2 Remove the lid, stir in the sugar, and continue to fry the onions over high heat for 10 minutes or until lightly browned. Add the stock, bring to a boil, cover with a lid again, and simmer for 5–10 minutes.

3 Mix the corn starch in a cup with a little cold water to make a thin paste, then stir into the soup. Season with salt and freshly ground black pepper, add the vinegar, and stir well. Bring to a boil, stirring continuously, until slightly thickened.

4 To make the croûtons, preheat the broiler. Slice the bread into 18 thin slices (36 for 12), butter both sides, then toast on one side until golden. Turn the croûtons over, spread a little mustard on the untoasted side and top with the cheese. Slide back under the broiler for 3–5 minutes or until the cheese is golden and melted.

5 Serve the soup in hot bowls with three croûtons per person.

PREPARE AHEAD AND FREEZE
The soup can be made up to 3 days ahead. The croûtons can be assembled up to 6 hours ahead and broiled just prior to serving. Freeze the soup without the croûtons for up to 3 months.

This is a hearty, healthy soup full of flavor and goodness. Serve it piping hot with some crusty bread.

Puy lentil and pearl barley soup

Serves 6

1 tbsp olive oil
1 large onion, finely chopped
2 carrots, finely diced
2 garlic cloves, crushed
3½oz (100g) dried Puy lentils
3½oz (100g) pearl barley
24oz jar tomato purée

5½ cups chicken stock or
  vegetable stock
salt and freshly ground
  black pepper
2 tsp sugar
1 tbsp balsamic vinegar

Serves 12

2 tbsp olive oil
2 onions, finely chopped
2 large carrots, finely diced
4 garlic cloves, crushed
8oz (225g) dried Puy lentils
8oz (225g) pearl barley
2 x 24oz jar tomato purée

11 cups chicken stock or
  vegetable stock
salt and freshly ground
  black pepper
1 tbsp sugar
2 tbsp balsamic vinegar

1 Heat the oil in a deep frying pan, add the onion and carrots, and fry over high heat, stirring, for 10 minutes or until lightly brown.

2 Add the garlic, lentils, and barley and fry for 1 minute. Blend in the tomato purée and stock and season with salt and freshly ground black pepper.

3 Bring to a boil, cover with a lid, and simmer for 40–45 minutes (50–55 minutes for 12) or until the lentils and barley are tender.

4 Add the sugar and vinegar, check the seasoning, and serve.

PREPARE AHEAD
The soup can be made up to 3 days ahead.
Not suitable for freezing.

Our lovely friend Jane gave us the idea for this recipe. It's creamy and luxurious—ideal before a light meal. Serve with croûtons.

GREAT FOR A CROWD

Honey-glazed parsnip soup

Serves 6

1 tbsp olive oil
2lb (900g) parsnips, roughly chopped
2 large onions, roughly chopped
4 celery sticks, sliced
1 leek, roughly chopped

1½ tbsp honey
5 cups vegetable stock
salt and freshly ground black pepper
½ cup heavy cream

Serves 12

2 tbsp olive oil
3lb 3oz (1.5kg) parsnips, roughly chopped
4 large onions, roughly chopped
8 celery sticks, sliced
2 leeks, roughly chopped

3 tbsp honey
10 cups vegetable stock
salt and freshly ground black pepper
1 cup heavy cream

1 Heat the oil in a deep saucepan, add the vegetables, and fry over a high heat for a few minutes. Stir in the honey and fry for 4–5 minutes or until the vegetables are becoming golden brown and caramelized.

2 Add the stock and season with salt and freshly ground black pepper. Cover with a lid, lower the heat, and simmer for 20–30 minutes (35–40 minutes for 12) or until the parsnips are completely tender.

3 Transfer to a processor or blender and whiz until completely smooth.

4 Return to the pan to reheat, stir in the cream, and check the seasoning. Serve piping hot.

Great for a crowd... At the end of step 2, pour the contents of the pan through a sieve into a large bowl. Transfer the vegetables to a processor and whiz till smooth. Add a little of the cooking liquid and whiz again, then put the purée and the rest of the cooking liquid into a pan, stir well, and continue to step 4. The soup freezes well.

PREPARE AHEAD AND FREEZE
The soup can be made up to the end of step 3 up to 2 days ahead. Freeze at the end of step 3 for up to 1 month.

SERVING SUGGESTION
If you really want to impress your guests, serve a few mouthfuls of this soup in little coffee cups between your first and main courses, as they do in posh restaurants.

These are perfect as a first course, but you could equally serve them as a light lunch. Serve warm with dressed salad leaves.

Fennel and smoked salmon tartlets

Makes 8

Special equipment
8 x 4in (10cm) tart pans

For the pastry
1½ cup (6oz) all-purpose flour, plus a little extra to dust
6 tbsp butter
1 egg
1 tbsp water

a pat of butter
1 large fennel bulb, roughly chopped
1 small red chile, seeded and chopped
5½oz (150g) smoked salmon, chopped
large handful of freshly chopped parsley
¾ cup heavy cream
2 eggs
salt and freshly ground black pepper
1¾oz (50g) mature Cheddar cheese, grated

Makes 12

Special equipment
12 x 4in (10cm) tart pans

For the pastry
3 cups (12oz) all-purpose flour, plus a little extra to dust
175g (6oz) butter
1 egg
1–2 tbsp water

a pat of butter
2 medium fennel bulbs, roughly chopped
1 large red chile, seeded and chopped
7oz (200g) smoked salmon, chopped
large handful of freshly chopped parsley
1¼ cup heavy cream
3 eggs
salt and freshly ground black pepper
2½oz (75g) mature Cheddar cheese, grated

1 To make the pastry, put the flour and butter into a processor and whiz until the mixture resembles breadcrumbs. Add the egg and water and whiz until it forms a ball. Roll the pastry out thinly on a lightly floured work surface, then cut circles with a 5in (12cm) cutter or the bottom of a saucer. Place in the pans and chill for 20 minutes.

2 Heat the pat of butter in a frying pan, add the fennel and chile, and fry for 1 minute. Cover with a lid and cook over low heat for 15 minutes or until soft. Set aside to cool.

3 Preheat the oven to 400°F (200°C) and put a baking sheet in to get hot (two sheets for 12). Meanwhile, divide the cooled fennel mixture among the pastry cases, then sprinkle over the smoked salmon and parsley. Whisk the cream and eggs together in a measuring glass, season with salt and freshly ground black pepper, and stir in half the cheese. Pour into the cases, then sprinkle over the remaining cheese.

4 Bake for 20 minutes (25 minutes for 12) or until golden brown and the pastry is crisp.

CHEAT
If you don't have time to make the pastry yourself, you can use store bought—use 8oz (225g) pie crust pastry for eight tartlets and 12oz (350g) for 12 tartlets.

PREPARE AHEAD AND FREEZE
You can make the tartlets up to 2 days ahead.
Freeze for up to 2 months.

Mary was given this recipe by a friend in Portugal who makes full use of fruits in season. We use vacuum-packed dry-cured ham, because it comes in convenient even-sized slices.

Roasted figs with Parma ham and goat cheese

Serves 6

2 x 3.5oz rolls firm goat cheese, such as Capricorn
6 fresh figs
12 slices Parma ham

arugula or salad leaves, to serve
balsamic vinegar, to serve
olive oil, to serve

Serves 12

4 x 3.5oz rolls firm goat cheese, such as Capricorn
12 fresh figs
24 slices Parma ham

arugula or salad leaves, to serve
balsamic vinegar, to serve
olive oil, to serve

1 Pop the goat cheese in the freezer for about an hour or until firm.

2 Preheat the oven to 425°F (220°C). Cut off the pointed stem at the top of each fig, then stand the figs upright on a board. Cut a cross in the top of each one, but don't cut right down to the base.

3 Trim the ends off the cheese and discard, then cut each roll into three slices. Cut each slice in half to give semi-circles. Cut half the semi-circles in half again to give quarters.

4 Lie each slice of ham out flat and trim off any excess fat.

5 Put a semi-circle of cheese into each fig where you've made the cross. Use the quarters to fit in either side, so the complete cross is filled with goat cheese.

6 Wrap each fig in a piece of ham, then wrap it in another piece, working in the other direction. Squeeze the ham together at the top.

7 Roast for 8 minutes (10 minutes for 12) or until the cheese has melted and the ham is crisp.

8 Arrange the figs on serving plates with some arugula or salad leaves, drizzle with a little balsamic vinegar and olive oil, and serve at once.

Great for a crowd... Replace the goat cheese with a blue cheese such as Stilton. You can simply grate this and use it to fill the cross in the figs.

VARIATION

When figs are not in season, we use skinned, medium-sized, slightly under-ripe tomatoes prepared in the same way. Spoon a teaspoon of pesto over the cheese and tomato before wrapping it in the Parma ham.

PREPARE AHEAD
You can prepare the figs up to the end of step 6 up to 12 hours ahead. Not suitable for freezing.

This is such an easy first course for when asparagus is plentiful and at its best in the months of May and June.

Asparagus with Parmesan and mustard sauce

Serves 6

1lb 10oz (750g) asparagus spears, woody ends removed
salt and freshly ground black pepper
1¾oz (50g) Parmesan cheese, freshly grated

For the mustard sauce

2 tsp Dijon mustard
2 tsp white wine vinegar
¼ cup sunflower oil
2 tbsp mayonnaise
juice of ½ lemon
1 tsp superfine sugar

Serves 12

3lb 3oz (1.5kg) asparagus spears, woody ends removed
salt and freshly ground black pepper
3½oz (100g) Parmesan cheese, freshly grated

For the mustard sauce

1 heaped tbsp Dijon mustard
1½ tbsp white wine vinegar
½ cup sunflower oil
¼ cup mayonnaise
juice of 1 lemon
2 tsp superfine sugar

1 Preheat the oven to 425°F (220°C). Meanwhile, put the asparagus spears into a shallow pan of boiling salted water and bring back up to a boil. Boil for 3 minutes, then drain, refresh in cold water, and dry on paper towels.

2 Arrange six bundles of asparagus on a large baking sheet lined with parchment paper (12 bundles on two baking sheets for 12), season with salt and freshly ground black pepper, and sprinkle with the cheese.

3 Bake for 8 minutes (12 minutes for 12) or until the cheese has melted and browned and the asparagus is piping hot.

4 Meanwhile, make the sauce: put all the ingredients into a bowl and whisk with a hand whisk until well combined, then season with salt and freshly ground black pepper.

5 Carefully transfer the bundles on to hot plates and serve with the mustard sauce.

VARIATION
We like to cook the asparagus on a baking sheet and serve them in individual portions, but you can bake them in a large ovenproof dish and take it to the table if you prefer.

PREPARE AHEAD
The asparagus can be prepared up to the end of step 2 up to 1 day ahead. The sauce can be made up to 4 days ahead. Not suitable for freezing.

These make a delicious creamy starter. Serve them in ramekins with crusty bread to mop up all the sauce.

Roquefort and parsley mousseline creams

Serves 6

Special equipment 6 x size 5fl oz(150ml) ramekins, greased

3 tbsp butter
3 tbsp all-purpose flour
10fl oz (300ml) hot milk
3 large eggs, separated

3½oz (100g) Roquefort, coarsely grated
1 tbsp freshly chopped parsley
salt and freshly ground black pepper
dash of Tabasco

Serves 12

Special equipment 12 x size 5fl oz (150ml) ramekins, greased

5 tbsp butter
5 tbsp all-purpose flour
2 cups hot milk
6 large eggs, separated

8oz (225g) Roquefort, coarsely grated
2 tbsp freshly chopped parsley
salt and freshly ground black pepper
dash of Tabasco

1 Preheat the oven to 375°F (190°C). Meanwhile, melt the butter in a large saucepan, add the flour and then the milk, and whisk until the mixture thickens to a smooth white sauce. Remove from the heat and allow to cool slightly.

2 Meanwhile, whisk the egg whites in a bowl with an electric hand whisk until stiff.

3 Stir the cheese and parsley into the warm sauce and season with salt and freshly ground black pepper (not too much salt, because the cheese is salty). Add the egg yolks and Tabasco and stir to combine.

4 Mix a spoonful of the egg whites into the sauce until smooth, then fold in the rest so the mixture is light and combined. Spoon evenly into the ramekins and sit on a baking sheet.

5 Bake for 15–20 minutes (20–25 minutes for 12) or until risen and golden.

PREPARE AHEAD
The creams can be made up to the end of step 4 up to 6 hours ahead. Not suitable for freezing.

A warming first course that's full of flavor. The bruschette are also perfect for a light lunch. Serve with dressed arugula leaves.

Bruschette with Reblochon and roasted vegetables

Serves 6

2 yellow peppers, halved, seeded, and chopped into 1in (2.5cm) pieces
1 red onion, sliced into wedges
3 small zucchini, cut into ½in (1cm) slices
¼ cup olive oil
salt and freshly ground black pepper

2 tsp balsamic vinegar
small bunch of basil, roughly chopped
½ ciabatta or white baguette
2 garlic cloves, crushed
7oz (200g) Reblochon de Savoie
paprika, to dust

Serves 12

4 yellow peppers, halved, seeded, and chopped into 1in (2.5cm) pieces
2 red onions, sliced into wedges
6 small zucchini, cut into ½in (1cm) slices
½ cup olive oil
salt and freshly ground black pepper

4 tsp balsamic vinegar
large bunch of basil, roughly chopped
1 ciabatta or white baguette
4 garlic cloves, crushed
14oz (400g) Reblochon de Savoie
paprika, to dust

1 Preheat the oven to 425°F (220°C). Mix the vegetables in a roasting pan (two pans for 12), add half the oil, and season with salt and freshly ground black pepper. Toss together well, then roast for 30 minutes (45 minutes for 12) or until soft and tinged golden brown. Remove from the oven and stir in the vinegar and basil.

2 Meanwhile, cut the ciabatta or baguette into six slices (12 slices for 12). Mix the remaining oil with the garlic in a small bowl, then brush both sides of the bread with it. Place on a baking sheet and bake on a shelf under the vegetables, turning them halfway through, for 10–12 minutes or until lightly golden and crisp.

3 Remove the crispy bruschette from the oven and top with the vegetables. Keeping the rind on, slice the cheese into six wedges (12 wedges for 12), put one on top of each pile of vegetables, then dust lightly with paprika.

4 Return to the oven for 10–12 minutes (12–15 minutes for 12) or until the cheese has melted. If some runs off the sides of the bread, quickly scoop it back on top. Serve hot.

VARIATION

Reblochon de Savoie is a French cheese from the Alps. It is aged in cellars or caves in the mountains and is similar to Brie, but with a nuttier flavor. You can use Brie or goat's cheese instead, if you prefer.

PREPARE AHEAD
The ciabatta can be baked up to 3 days ahead. The vegetables can be roasted up to 8 hours ahead. Assemble up to the end of step 3 up to 3 hours ahead. Not suitable for freezing.

You can prepare this attractive starter ahead and have it ready and waiting in the fridge. Serve with lightly buttered brown bread.

Shrimp and crawfish cocktail

Serves 6

½ cup mayonnaise

juice of ½ lemon

2 tbsp tomato ketchup

2 tsp creamed horseradish sauce

3 tbsp capers, drained, rinsed, dried, and roughly chopped

salt and freshly ground black pepper

11oz (300g) small cooked peeled shrimp

6oz (175g) tub cooked crawfish tails, drained

4 Baby Gem lettuces or romaine hearts

2 tbsp freshly chopped parsley

Serves 12

1 cup mayonnaise

juice of 1 lemon

4 tbsp tomato ketchup

1 heaped tbsp creamed horseradish sauce

6 tbsp capers, drained, rinsed, dried, and roughly chopped

salt and freshly ground black pepper

1lb 5oz (600g) small cooked peeled shrimp

2 x 6oz (175g) tubs cooked crawfish tails, drained

8 Baby Gem lettuces or similar

4 tbsp freshly chopped parsley

1 Mix the first five ingredients together in a bowl and season with salt and freshly ground black pepper.

2 Dry the shrimp and crawfish tails on paper towels and stir into the sauce.

3 Peel the lettuce leaves from the heart and arrange 18 leaves (36 for 12) on a platter or on individual plates, allowing three leaves per person. Spoon the shrimp mixture into the leaves and sprinkle with a little of the parsley.

PREPARE AHEAD

The sauce can be made up to 4 days ahead.

The dish can be assembled up to 6 hours ahead.

Not suitable for freezing.

A first course with wow factor, yet it is surprisingly easy to make. Serve cold with warm brown rolls or some good brown bread.

Smoked salmon and shrimp in dill mayonnaise

Serves 6

7oz (200g) peeled cooked shrimp
7oz (200g) sliced smoked salmon
small bunch of fresh dill
5½oz tub sour cream
finely grated zest of 1 lemon
juice of ½ lemon
dash of Tabasco
freshly ground black pepper

mâche or watercress, a little
  vinaigrette, and 6 lemon
  wedges, to serve

Serves 12

14oz (400g) peeled
  cooked shrimp
14oz (400g) sliced
  smoked salmon
large bunch of fresh dill
2 x 5½oz tubs sour cream
finely grated zest of 2 lemons
juice of 1 lemon

generous dash of Tabasco
freshly ground black pepper
mâche or watercress, a little
  vinaigrette, and 12 lemon
  wedges, to serve

1 Lay the shrimp on paper towels and squeeze out any excess liquid.

2 Cut one long strip, about ½ x 2in (1 x 5cm), per serving from the salmon slices and put to one side. Cut the remaining smoked salmon into small pieces about ½in (1cm) in size.

3 Set aside a sprig of dill per serving, then chop the rest of the bunch finely and put into a mixing bowl. Add the sour cream, lemon zest, lemon juice, Tabasco, and some freshly ground black pepper and stir to combine.

4 Add the shrimp and chopped salmon pieces.

5 Arrange the mâche on individual plates, drizzle with vinaigrette, then pile the shrimp mixture in the center.

6 Twist the reserved pieces of salmon into half-bow shapes and arrange on the top. Garnish with a sprig of dill and a wedge of lemon.

Great for a crowd... These are perfect for a crowd because they are individual servings, so you'll always know you have the right number.

VARIATION

For very special occasions, arrange a fresh king prawn in the shell on the top of each portion. This recipe was given to us by Rosie, a private caterer, and we have adapted it to make it our own.

PREPARE AHEAD

The shrimp and salmon mixture can be made up to the end of step 4 up to 8 hours ahead—the flavors will actually improve. The plates can be arranged up to 3 hours ahead. Not suitable for freezing.

A delicious and impressive starter, which looks stunning at a dinner party, wedding, or other celebration. Serve with dressed salad leaves, lemon wedges, and buttered brown bread.

Crab, avocado, and smoked salmon tians

Serves 6

Special equipment 6 x 2¾in (7cm) metal cooking rings arranged on a baking sheet lined with plastic wrap

11oz (300g) fresh crab meat
3½oz (100g) cream cheese
bunch of dill, finely chopped
juice of 1 lemon
dash of Tabasco

½ tsp Dijon mustard
salt and freshly ground
   black pepper
3 small ripe avocados, halved,
   stoned, and peeled
6 handfuls of salad leaves such
   as watercress, arugula, or
   lamb's lettuce, to garnish
6 slices smoked salmon

Serves 12

Special equipment 12 x 2¾in (7cm) metal cooking rings arranged on a baking sheet lined with plastic wrap

1lb 5oz (600g) fresh crab meat
7oz (200g) cream cheese
large bunch of dill, finely chopped
juice of 2 lemons
generous dash of Tabasco

1 tsp Dijon mustard
salt and freshly ground
   black pepper
6 small ripe avocados, halved,
   stoned, and peeled
12 handfuls of salad leaves such
   as watercress, arugula, or
   lamb's lettuce, to garnish
12 slices smoked salmon

1 Mix the crab meat, cream cheese, dill, half the lemon juice, the Tabasco, and mustard in a bowl and season with salt and freshly ground black pepper.

2 Mash one avocado with a fork until smooth (two avocados for 12) and cut the remaining avocados into small pieces. Mix the mashed and chopped avocado together, stir in the remaining lemon juice, and season with salt and freshly ground black pepper.

3 Spoon the avocado mixture into the base of each cooking ring and press down with the back of a spoon.

4 Divide the crab mixture among the rings and spread to the edges to cover the avocado entirely. Cover with plastic wrap and chill in the fridge for a few hours.

5 When ready to serve, arrange a handful of salad leaves on each plate, invert a ring on top, then carefully remove the ring and plastic wrap. Top each tian with smoked salmon.

PREPARE AHEAD
The tians can be made up to 6 hours ahead.
Not suitable for freezing.

IMPROVISING
If you don't have metal cooking rings to shape the tians, don't worry—you can use ramekins lined with plastic wrap. Lift the tians out carefully before serving and remove the plastic wrap.

This is ideal for any occasion—buffet, picnic, even a smart dinner party. Serve it with toast or on individual plates with dressed arugula leaves.

Double salmon and egg terrine

Serves 6

Special equipment 1lb (450g) loaf pan lined with plastic wrap

3½oz (100g) fresh salmon filet, skinned

a pat of butter, plus 1 tbsp, at room temperature

salt and freshly ground black pepper

3½oz (100g) smoked salmon trimmings

3½oz (100g) cream cheese

3 tbsp light mayonnaise

1 tbsp freshly chopped chives

2 tbsp lemon juice

4 large hard-boiled eggs, chopped fairly finely

cress, to garnish

Serves 12

Special equipment 2lb (900g) loaf pan lined with plastic wrap

8oz (225g) fresh salmon filet, skinned

a large pat of butter, plus 3 tbsp, at room temperature

salt and freshly ground black pepper

6oz smoked salmon trimmings

7oz (200g) cream cheese

6 tbsp light mayonnaise

2 tbsp freshly chopped chives

juice of ½ lemon

8 large hard-boiled eggs, chopped fairly finely

cress, to garnish

1 Preheat the oven to 350°F (180°C). Place the salmon on some foil, spoon the pat of butter on top, and season with salt and freshly ground black pepper. Scrunch the sides of the foil together at the top to make a parcel, place on a baking sheet, and bake for 12–15 minutes (15–20 minutes for 12) or until just cooked. Set aside to cool in the foil.

2 Pick out the nicest pieces of smoked salmon (around half) and put the rest into a food processor with the cream cheese, the remaining butter, mayonnaise, chives, and lemon juice. Break up the cold salmon in the foil and add to the processor with the juices. Season with salt and freshly ground black pepper, then whiz until smooth. Spoon into a mixing bowl.

3 Add the eggs and stir until combined. Scatter the remaining smoked salmon trimmings (chopped, if necessary) on top of the plastic wrap in the base of the loaf pan.

4 Spoon the mousse mixture on top and level the surface. Cover with plastic wrap and chill in the fridge for at least 6 hours to firm up.

5 To serve, pop the terrine in the freezer for about 30 minutes to make slicing easier, then turn it out of the pan and cut into slices. Scatter with cress and serve.

PREPARE AHEAD
The terrine can be made up to the end of step 4 up to 2 days ahead. Not suitable for freezing.

A quick-to-prepare starter served with smoked trout. You'll find it in the chiller cabinets at the supermarket. Serve with warm rolls.

Smoked mackerel and watercress pâté

Serves 6

Special equipment 7½in (19cm) square cake pan, lined with plastic wrap

7 tbsp butter, at room temperature
6oz (175g) cream cheese
1 tbsp creamed horseradish
juice of ½ lemon

11oz (300g) smoked mackerel, skin removed
a few drops of Tabasco
scant 1oz (25g) fresh watercress, plus a little extra to garnish
freshly ground black pepper
6 small slices smoked trout
6 lemon wedges, to garnish

Serves 12

Special equipment 9 x 12in (23 x 30cm) traybake or roasting pan, lined with plastic wrap

2 sticks butter, at room temperature
12oz (350g) cream cheese
2 tbsp creamed horseradish
juice of 1 lemon

1lb 5oz (600g) smoked mackerel, skin removed
a few drops of Tabasco
1¾oz (50g) fresh watercress, plus a little extra to garnish
freshly ground black pepper
12 small slices smoked trout
12 lemon wedges, to garnish

1 Put the butter, cream cheese, horseradish, and lemon juice into a processor and whiz until completely smooth.

2 Remove any tiny bones from the mackerel, then break the flesh into pieces and add to the processor. Add the Tabasco and watercress, season with freshly ground black pepper, and whiz again until just blended.

3 Spoon into the pan and level the top. Cover with plastic wrap and chill overnight.

4 To serve, pop the pâté in the freezer for about 30 minutes to make slicing easier, then turn it out and cut into squares, triangles, slices, or rounds. Arrange a piece on each plate, top with a slice of smoked trout in a swirl, then garnish with watercress and a lemon wedge.

PREPARE AHEAD
The pâté can be made up to the end of step 3 up to 2 days ahead. Not suitable for freezing.

Mary made this as part of a New Year's Eve potluck supper party. The tray was quick to prepare and easy to bundle into the car with a plate of brown bread and butter.

Celebratory fish platter

Serves 6

For the gravadlax

1lb 2oz (500g) piece salmon filet, from the thick end, skin on
2 tbsp dried dill
2 tbsp coarse sea salt
2 tbsp superfine sugar
salt and freshly ground black pepper
6 tbsp mayonnaise
1 tsp Dijon mustard
2 tsp freshly chopped dill

For the shrimp cocktail

11oz (300g) small cooked peeled shrimp

6 tbsp light mayonnaise
juice of ½ lemon
2 tbsp tomato ketchup
2 tbsp creamed horseradish sauce

To serve

2½oz (75g) mâche or arugula
6 large Little Gem lettuce leaves
6 large cooked shrimp, shell and head on
8oz (225g) smoked eel, cut into ¾in (2cm) pieces
lemon wedges

Serves 12

For the gravadlax

2¼lb (1kg) piece salmon filet, from the thick end, skin on
4 tbsp dried dill
4 tbsp coarse sea salt
4 tbsp superfine sugar
salt and freshly ground black pepper
12 tbsp mayonnaise
1 tbsp Dijon mustard
1 tbsp freshly chopped dill

For the shrimp cocktail

1lb 5oz (600g) small cooked peeled shrimp

12 tbsp light mayonnaise
juice of 1 small lemon
¼ cup tomato ketchup
¼ cup creamed horseradish sauce

To serve

6oz (175g) mâche or arugula
12 large Little Gem lettuce leaves
12 large cooked shrimp, shell and head on
14oz (400g) smoked eel, cut into ¾in (2cm) pieces
lemon wedges

1 To make the gravadlax, place the salmon skin side down on a large piece of foil, then pull out any bones with tweezers or a small knife. Sprinkle over the dill, salt, sugar, and some freshly ground black pepper, making sure all the salmon is covered. Wrap in the foil and place on a tray or baking sheet. Place another baking sheet on top and put some heavy weights or canned food on it to weigh the fish down. Transfer to the fridge for 12 hours or overnight.

2 Take the salmon from the fridge and pour away any juices. Place in the freezer for 30 minutes to make slicing easier. Then, using a sharp knife, cut into thin slices (see right).

3 To make the shrimp cocktail, dry the shrimp thoroughly with paper towels. Mix the mayonnaise, lemon juice, ketchup, and horseradish in a bowl, add the shrimp, and season with salt and freshly ground black pepper.

4 To serve, scatter the mâche or arugula over the base of a platter. Spoon the shrimp cocktail into the lettuce leaves, garnish with a large shrimp, then arrange around the edge. Put the smoked eel in a pile at the opposite end, arrange the gravadlax in the center, then place the lemon wedges alongside. Mix the mayonnaise for the gravadlax with the mustard and dill, season with salt and freshly ground black pepper, and serve in a bowl.

SLICING THE SALMON

Cut the salmon into thin slices. Keep the knife angled at about 45° so the slices are wide. Discard the skin.

PREPARE AHEAD AND FREEZE

The gravadlax can be made up to 2 days ahead. Freeze for up to 1 month. The cocktail sauce can be made up to 12 hours ahead. Not suitable for freezing. The platter can be assembled up to 4 hours ahead.

This is so easy to make in a food processor. It requires no oven-baking—instead, it's cooked on the stove top. Serve with toast.

Rustic mushroom liver pâté

Serves 6

Special equipment 1lb (450g) loaf pan, lined with plastic wrap

½oz (15g) dried porcini mushrooms

2 tbsp olive oil

1 onion, roughly chopped

1¾oz (50g) smoked bacon, snipped into small pieces

1 garlic clove, crushed

1¾oz (50g) chestnut mushrooms, thinly sliced

1 tsp each freshly chopped parsley and thyme leaves

7oz (200g) fresh chicken livers

scant 1oz (25g) fresh white breadcrumbs

3 tbsp butter, at room temperature

3½oz (100g) cream cheese

2 tsp Worcestershire sauce

salt and freshly ground black pepper

a little freshly chopped parsley, to garnish

Serves 12

Special equipment 2lb (900g) loaf pan, lined with plastic wrap

scant 1oz (25g) dried porcini mushrooms

4 tbsp olive oil

1 large onion, roughly chopped

3½oz (100g) smoked bacon, snipped into small pieces

2 garlic cloves, crushed

3½oz (100g) chestnut mushrooms, thinly sliced

2 tsp each freshly chopped parsley and thyme leaves

14oz (400g) fresh chicken livers

1¾oz (50g) fresh white breadcrumbs

6 tbsp butter, at room temperature

7oz (200g) cream cheese

1 tbsp Worcestershire sauce

salt and freshly ground black pepper

a little freshly chopped parsley, to garnish

1 Put the porcini into a bowl and pour over just enough boiling water to cover. Set aside to soften for about 30 minutes, then drain and dry well with paper towels.

2 Heat half the oil in a frying pan, add the onion, bacon, and porcini, and fry for 1 minute. Cover with a lid and cook over a low heat for 10 minutes or until the bacon is cooked. Add the garlic, mushrooms, parsley, and thyme and fry for 5 minutes or until the mushrooms are just cooked. Transfer to a mixing bowl.

3 Heat the remaining oil in the unwashed pan and fry the chicken livers for 1–2 minutes on each side or until brown on the outside and still pink in the center. Add to the bowl with the porcini mixture and leave to cool.

4 Spoon half the cold chicken liver mixture into a processor, add the breadcrumbs, butter, cream cheese, and Worcestershire sauce, and whiz until smooth. Season with salt and freshly ground black pepper and whiz again until smooth and combined. Place in a bowl.

5 Chop the remaining cold chicken liver mixture coarsely, then add to the bowl with the smooth pâté and stir to combine. Spoon into the prepared pan and level the top. Cover with plastic wrap and chill for a minimum of 6 hours or overnight.

6 To serve, turn the pan upside down on to a serving plate and remove the plastic wrap. Press some chopped parsley on top, cut the pâté in fairly thick slices, and serve.

PREPARE AHEAD
The pâté can be made up to 3 days ahead. Not suitable for freezing.

A very sociable first course that's also a bit of a cheat. If you are serving 12, arrange the food on two platters or tart plates.

Express Mediterranean platter

Serves 6

8 pepperdew peppers, drained and sliced

1 tbsp freshly chopped parsley

7oz prepared hummus

salt and freshly ground black pepper

6 stuffed vine leaves

7oz (200g) feta cheese, cut into bite-sized cubes

7oz (200g) marinated artichokes in oil, drained and oil reserved

7oz (200g) Kalamata olives in oil, drained and oil reserved

6 pita breads

Serves 12

16 pepperdew peppers, drained and sliced

2 tbsp freshly chopped parsley

14oz prepared hummus

salt and freshly ground black pepper

12 stuffed vine leaves

14oz (400g) feta cheese, cut into bite-sized cubes

14oz (400g) marinated artichokes in oil, drained and oil reserved

14oz (400g) Kalamata olives in oil, drained and oil reserved

12 pita breads

1 Take a large flat platter or round tart plate and put a small bowl in the center. Mix the pepperdew pepper slices and parsley with the hummus, season with salt and freshly ground black pepper, and spoon into the bowl.

2 Arrange the vine leaves, feta, artichokes, and olives in piles around the platter.

3 Toast the pitta and slice into fingers, then arrange in a pile next to the artichokes.

4 Drizzle the feta with some of the oil from the olives or artichokes and serve chilled or at room temperature.

KALAMATA OLIVES

We love the sweetness and rich flavor of Kalamata olives, but you can use your favorite olives instead.

PREPARE AHEAD

The hummus can be mixed with the parsley and peppers up to 4 days ahead. The platter can be assembled up to 8 hours ahead.

When you're serving numbers at a smart dinner party, it's always a good feeling to know the first course is made and waiting in the fridge. This recipe is perfect for that. Serve with brown bread rolls.

Filet of beef with beet and horseradish dressing

Serves 6

11oz (300g) middle-cut filet steak, trimmed

1 tbsp olive oil, plus a little extra to serve

salt and freshly ground black pepper

4 medium-sized cooked red beets, peeled and thinly sliced

1¾oz (50g) arugula

1¾oz (50g) piece Parmesan cheese

For the horseradish dressing

2 tbsp creamed horseradish sauce

3 tbsp light mayonnaise

2 tbsp lemon juice

Serves 12

2 x 11oz (300g) middle-cut filet steaks, trimmed

2 tbsp olive oil, plus a little extra to serve

salt and freshly ground black pepper

8 medium-sized cooked red beets, peeled and thinly sliced

3½oz (100g) arugula

3½oz (100g) piece Parmesan cheese

For the horseradish dressing

4 tbsp creamed horseradish sauce

6 tbsp light mayonnaise

4 tbsp lemon juice

1 Rub the steak with the oil and season with salt and freshly ground black pepper.

2 Heat a frying pan until very hot, then fry the filet for 2½ minutes on each side (fry each filet separately for 12). This will give you a rare steak. If you prefer medium, cook for another minute on each side. Remove from the pan and leave to cool.

3 To make the dressing, put the ingredients into a small bowl and whisk with a hand whisk until smooth and combined. Season with salt and freshly ground black pepper.

4 When the steak is cold, carve into very thin slices—you're aiming to get 30 slices per filet. Arrange five thin slices in a star shape on each plate. Arrange five slices of beet in the middle of the plate in a spiral shape, then drizzle with the horseradish dressing.

5 Gather together a little bundle of arugula leaves for each plate and place on top of the beets. Using a potato peeler, shave little shavings of Parmesan over the top.

6 Drizzle with a little olive oil and serve straightaway.

MIDDLE-CUT FILET

When you carve the filet, you want the slices to be long and thin rather than round. Which is why we use two middle-cut filets to serve 12 instead of one whole filet, which would be thinner at one end. The middle-cut filets give you the correct shape.

PREPARE AHEAD

The plates can be prepared up to the end of step 5 up to 6 hours ahead. Drizzle with oil just before serving. Not suitable for freezing.

You can use any variety of sliced meats you like for this appetizing selection of roasted vegetables with an eggplant and mint dip. Serve with chunky bread, flat bread, or toasted pita bread.

Moroccan platter

Serves 6

For the eggplant and mint dip

2 large eggplants
2 tbsp olive oil
3 fat garlic cloves (unpeeled)
3½fl oz (100ml) Greek yogurt
juice of ½ lemon
3 tbsp freshly chopped mint, plus a sprig to garnish
salt and freshly ground black pepper

For the roasted vegetables

4 zucchini, thickly sliced
1 yellow pepper, halved, seeded, and sliced into large chunks
1 red pepper, halved, seeded, and sliced into large chunks
2 tbsp olive oil
2 tbsp balsamic vinegar

Sliced meats

6 slices Parma ham
6 slices salami
6 slices dried chorizo

Serves 12

For the eggplant and mint dip

4 large eggplants
¼ cup olive oil
6 fat garlic cloves (unpeeled)
7fl oz (200ml) Greek yogurt
juice of 1 lemon
6 tbsp freshly chopped mint, plus 2 sprigs to garnish
salt and freshly ground black pepper

For the roasted vegetables

8 zucchini, thickly sliced
2 yellow peppers, halved, seeded, and sliced into large chunks
2 red peppers, halved, seeded, and sliced into large chunks
¼ cup olive oil
¼ cup balsamic vinegar

Sliced meats

12 slices Parma ham
12 slices salami
12 slices dried chorizo

1 Preheat the oven to 425°F (220°C).

2 To make the eggplant and mint dip, slice the eggplants in half lengthwise, arrange cut side up in a roasting pan, and drizzle with the oil. Add the garlic to the pan and roast for 30–35 minutes or until the eggplant flesh is soft.

3 Scoop the flesh out of the eggplants and place in a processor. Discard the skins. Squeeze the garlic from their skins and add to the eggplant, then whiz together until smooth. Add the yogurt, lemon juice, and mint, season with salt and freshly ground black pepper, and whiz again until combined. Spoon into a serving bowl (two bowls for 12) and set aside to cool.

4 Meanwhile, make the roasted vegetables. Arrange the zucchini, yellow pepper, and red pepper in a roasting pan, drizzle over the oil, and roast in the preheated oven for 30–35 minutes or until just cooked. Drizzle over the vinegar, season with salt and freshly ground black pepper, and set aside to cool.

5 To assemble the dish, arrange the cold meats in piles on a platter (two platters for 12), garnish the dip with mint and place in the center, then arrange the roasted vegetables and the bread of your choice at the ends.

PREPARE AHEAD
The dip can be made up to 3 days ahead. The vegetables can be roasted up to 1 day ahead. The platter can be assembled up to 8 hours ahead. Not suitable for freezing.

SERVING PITA BREAD

Pita bread goes really well with this platter. Toast until lightly golden and handle with care—it gets very hot.

"A platter of tasty ingredients passed around the table makes a sociable starter. If you're serving 12, prepare two identical platters. If your guests are going to be standing up to eat, dot several platters around the room so they can help themselves."

Moroccan platter (see overleaf) ●●●>

Special main courses

There are often times when we want our guests to sit together at a table and eat. To give such events a real sense of occasion, we like to serve a main course that's that little bit special.

Special main courses

Main courses don't have to be tricky to be special—it's presentation that's key. Guests couldn't fail to be impressed by a whole side of salmon served on a platter with a glistening tarragon butter sauce, yet it's relatively straightforward to make. The same is true of duck breasts roasted until golden on the outside and pink in the middle, then sliced and arranged in a fan with a piquant lime and ginger sauce.

The other recipes in this chapter all follow suit. They are low on effort, but high on impact—just what you want when you're cooking for a crowd.

Special side dishes

Special main courses call for special side dishes, so on pages 123–129 we've included a selection of potato dishes and vegetable dishes for supper parties, dinner parties, or lunch. These are so delicious, they could almost be served as a course by themselves.

● If you want to keep the main course lighter, however, stick with some simply cooked vegetables or a green salad. Buy what's in season and pick out the freshest you can.

● In general, serve one or two side dishes. If you're cooking for large numbers, you might want to restrict it to just one—too much choice can quickly translate into too much preparation and too many dishes to serve hot.

"Our special main course recipes are low on effort, but high on impact—just what you want when you're cooking for a crowd."

Serving the main course

We like to serve our guests with the main course at a sit-down meal and always bear in mind the size of their appetites—you can generally count on a farmer or tree surgeon being famished, for instance, but our girlfriends usually aren't. The side dishes we bring to the table so people can help themselves.

Gently does it

Although you don't want to keep your guests hanging around, you don't want to hurry proceedings either.

● If you're not serving a starter, seat people before you bring out your main course.

● If you are serving a starter and your main course needs reheating, do it while you're eating the first course. Remember to allow 15–20 minutes for roast meats to rest before you carve them.

● Reheat your dessert, if necessary, while you're eating the main course.

● Don't rush to clear people's plates as soon as they've finished. Keep the atmosphere leisurely and relaxed. You might even encourage guests to swap places around the table before you serve the next course.

TABLE TALK *Since you're pulling out the stops with the food, it makes sense to go to a little extra effort with the table decorations. Use your most impressive china, arrange fresh flowers in a vase, and light the candles before your guests come to the table to sit down.*

The tomato in the vegetable stock gives the sauce a wonderful color. To allow the flavors to infuse, prepare it the day before. Serve with new potatoes and fresh green vegetables or salad.

Salmon filet with tarragon butter sauce

Serves 6

1 onion, finely chopped
1 carrot, finely chopped
1 celery stalk, finely chopped
1 large tomato, cut in half
1½ cups water
1 heaped tbsp freshly chopped tarragon (stems reserved)

a little olive oil, to grease
salt and freshly ground black pepper
1lb 10oz–2lb (750–900g) side of salmon filet in one piece, skin on
11 tbsp cold butter (straight from the fridge), cut into cubes

Serves 12

2 onions, finely chopped
2 carrots, finely chopped
2 celery stalks, finely chopped
2 large tomatoes, cut in half
3 cups water
2 heaped tbsp freshly chopped tarragon (stems reserved)

a little olive oil, to grease
salt and freshly ground black pepper
4lb (1.8kg) side of salmon or 2 x 1lb 10oz–2lb (750–900g) sides of salmon
2¾ sticks of cold butter (straight from the fridge), cut into cubes

1 Put the onion, carrot, celery, tomato, and water into a saucepan. Add the reserved tarragon stems and bring to a boil. Cover with a lid and simmer over low heat for 10 minutes. Set aside for a minimum of 1 hour (ideally overnight) for the flavors to infuse.

2 Preheat the oven to 350°F (180°C). Line a baking sheet with foil, oil it lightly, and sprinkle with salt and freshly ground black pepper.

3 Lay the salmon skin side down on a board. Using a sharp knife, divide it into equal serving portions, cutting through the flesh until the knife touches the skin, but not cutting through it. Lay skin side up on the foil and bake for 20 minutes (25–30 minutes for 12) or until matte pink and just done. The precise timing will depend on the thickness.

4 To make the sauce, strain the vegetable stock into a saucepan, then boil rapidly until it reduces by half. Put the butter into a heatproof bowl, pour over the boiling stock, and whiz with a hand blender or in a processor until smooth.

5 Peel the skin from the fish and discard (if it doesn't peel easily, it isn't quite cooked, so pop it back into the oven for a few minutes). Transfer the fish portions to a platter or plates. Add the tarragon to the hot sauce, pour over the fish, and serve.

VARIATION

You can cook individual salmon filets if you like, but we prefer doing it this way, because the fish doesn't dry out.

PREPARE AHEAD

The sauce can be made up to 2 days ahead. Add the tarragon while reheating. The salmon can be cooked the day before and served cold. Not suitable for freezing.

Salmon filets, cooked simply and slowly, are complemented by a rich sauce of asparagus, cream, and pesto. Serve with baby new potatoes.

Salmon and asparagus with a basil sauce

Serves 6

6 x 5½oz (150g) center-cut
   salmon filets, skinned
salt and freshly ground
   black pepper
12 asparagus spears

1¼ cups heavy cream
juice of ½ lemon
¼ cup pesto

Serves 12

12 x 5½oz (150g) center-cut
   salmon filets, skinned
salt and freshly ground
   black pepper
24 asparagus spears

2 cups heavy cream
juice of 1 lemon
½ cup pesto

1 Preheat the oven to 275°F (140°C). Line a roasting pan with a large piece of foil and arrange the salmon filets on top in a single layer. Season with salt and freshly ground black pepper, then scrunch the sides of the foil at the top so the filets are enclosed.

2 Cook in the oven for 50 minutes (1 hour for 12) or until the salmon is matte pink and just done. Don't let it overcook or it will become dry.

3 Meanwhile, trim the woody ends from the asparagus spears and discard, then cut off 2in (5cm) from each tip and put to one side. Finely shred the stalks, cutting them diagonally into thin slices.

4 Bring a pan of salted water to a boil, add the asparagus tips and shredded stalks, then bring back to a boil and cook for 3 minutes. Drain, separate the tips from the stalks, and keep warm.

5 Heat the cream, lemon juice, and pesto in a pan until hot. Add the cooked shredded stalks and season with salt and freshly ground black pepper.

6 To serve, arrange the hot salmon filets on a serving plate. Pour over the sauce and garnish each filet with two asparagus tips. Serve any leftover sauce separately.

Great for a crowd... Don't be tempted to pile the filets on top of each other to cook them—bake in a single layer in separate roasting pans.

PREPARE AHEAD
The asparagus can be cooked up to 8 hours ahead, then drained, refreshed in cold water, and drained again. Plunge the asparagus tips into boiling water for 30 seconds to warm through. The sauce can be made up 8 hours ahead. Not suitable for freezing.

Salmon and asparagus with a basil sauce (see overleaf) •••>

So many people love fishcakes, which is why we always invent a new recipe for them for each of our books.

Double salmon fishcakes with horseradish sauce

Serves 6

12oz (350g) cooked salmon, skin and bones removed

3½oz (100g) hot-smoked salmon

1lb (450g) mashed potato

3 tbsp mayonnaise

2 tbsp creamed horseradish

2 heaped tbsp freshly snipped chives

2 heaped tbsp freshly chopped parsley

salt and freshly ground black pepper

1 egg, beaten

1¾oz (50g) fresh breadcrumbs

1 tbsp olive oil

1 lemon, cut into 6 wedges, to garnish

For the horseradish sauce

5fl oz (150ml) sour cream or crème fraîche

3 tbsp creamed horseradish

2 tbsp mayonnaise

2 tbsp freshly snipped chives

Serves 12

1lb 9oz (700g) cooked salmon, skin and bones removed

7oz (200g) hot-smoked salmon

2lb (900g) mashed potato

6 tbsp mayonnaise

¼ cup creamed horseradish

¼ cup freshly snipped chives

¼ cup freshly chopped parsley

salt and freshly ground black pepper

1 egg, beaten

3½oz (100g) fresh breadcrumbs

2 tbsp olive oil

2 lemons, each cut into 6 wedges, to garnish

For the horseradish sauce

10fl oz (300ml) sour cream or crème fraîche

6 tbsp creamed horseradish

¼ cup mayonnaise

¼ cup freshly snipped chives

1 Put both kinds of salmon, the mashed potato, mayonnaise, horseradish, and herbs into a mixing bowl, season with salt and freshly ground black pepper, and stir well to combine.

2 Divide the mixture into 12 (24 for 12) and shape into fishcakes. They shouldn't be too thick. Brush with beaten egg, coat with breadcrumbs, and chill for a minimum of an hour.

3 Meanwhile, make the sauce: put all the ingredients into a bowl, season with salt and freshly ground black pepper, and mix together well. Set aside.

4 Heat the oil in a non-stick frying pan and fry the fishcakes for 3–4 minutes on each side or until golden on the outside and hot in the middle. You may need to do this in batches and keep them warm in the oven.

5 Serve the fishcakes hot with a spoonful of the cold sauce and a lemon wedge.

PREPARE AHEAD AND FREEZE
The fishcakes can be made up to the end of step 2 up to 1 day ahead. Alternatively, fry them the day before and reheat. The sauce can be made up to 3 days ahead. Freeze the fishcakes at the end of step 2 for up to 2 months.

A wonderful all-in-one dish—new potatoes, onions, and zucchini with lightly cooked trout filets and a fresh sauce.

Trout filets with roasted vegetables and lemon sauce

Serves 6

1lb 10oz (750g) baby new
   potatoes, halved lengthwise
3 medium onions, peeled and
   cut into 8 wedges
salt and freshly ground
   black pepper
3 tbsp olive oil
4 small zucchini, thinly sliced
6 trout filets, skin on

For the sauce

6 tbsp freshly chopped parsley
finely grated zest and juice of
   1 large lemon
6 tbsp butter, melted

Serves 12

3lb 3oz (1.5kg) baby new
   potatoes, halved lengthwise
5 large onions, peeled and cut
   into 8 wedges
salt and freshly ground
   black pepper
6 tbsp olive oil
8 small zucchini, thinly sliced
12 trout filets, skin on

For the sauce

large bunch of parsley, chopped
finely grated zest and juice of
   2 large lemons
1½ sticks of butter, melted

1 Preheat the oven to 400°F (200°C). Put the potatoes and onions in a pan, cover with cold salted water, bring to a boil, and cook for 10 minutes or until just tender.

2 Drain, toss in half the oil, season with black pepper, and arrange in a single layer in a large roasting pan or ovenproof dish (two pans or dishes for 12). Roast for 20 minutes (30 minutes for 12) or until the potatoes and onions are just tender.

3 Toss the zucchini in a bowl with the remaining oil and season with salt and freshly ground black pepper.

4 Season the flesh side of the trout with salt and freshly ground black pepper. Stir the contents of the roasting pan, then lay the trout skin side up in a single layer on top of them. Scatter the zucchini around the fish. Return to the oven and cook for 12–15 minutes (20–30 minutes for 12) or until the fish is tender.

5 Meanwhile, make the sauce: mix the parsley, lemon zest, and lemon juice together in a bowl. Stir in the butter and season with salt and freshly ground black pepper.

6 Peel the skin from the fish and discard. Transfer to a serving plate with the vegetables, then spoon some of the hot sauce over the top. Serve the rest of the sauce separately.

SKINNING THE TROUT

If the skin doesn't come off easily, the trout is not quite cooked, so pop it back into the oven for a few minutes.

PREPARE AHEAD

The vegetables can be cooked up to the end of step 2 up to 6 hours ahead. The sauce can be made up to 1 day ahead. Not suitable for freezing.

An impressive centerpiece for a dinner party or buffet table. Cooking the trout with the skin on gives it a fresher flavor and keeps it moist.

Hot baked trout with tomato and basil salsa

Serves 6

a little olive oil

salt and freshly ground
   black pepper

1lb 10oz (750g) trout filet,
   skin on

For the salsa

1lb 2oz (500g) tomatoes

½ cucumber

3 spring onions, finely chopped

3 tbsp freshly shredded basil

3 tbsp olive oil

1 tsp superfine sugar

a good dash of Tabasco

1 tbsp lemon juice

Serves 12

a little olive oil

salt and freshly ground
   black pepper

3lb (1.35kg) trout filet or
   2 x 1lb 10oz (750g) trout
   filets, skin on

For the salsa

2¼lb (1kg) tomatoes

1 cucumber

6 spring onions, finely chopped

6 tbsp freshly shredded basil

6 tbsp olive oil

2 tsp superfine sugar

a good dash of Tabasco

2 tbsp lemon juice

1 Preheat the oven to 400°F (200°C). Line a baking sheet with foil, then brush it with a little olive oil and sprinkle with salt and freshly ground black pepper.

2 Lay the trout skin side down on a board. Using a sharp knife, cut it into equal serving portions, taking care not to cut through the skin. Lay it skin side up on the baking sheet and bake for 15–20 minutes (30 minutes for 12) or until just cooked.

3 Meanwhile, make the salsa: skin the tomatoes (see right), then slice in half, remove the seeds, and cut the flesh into small dice. Peel the cucumber with a vegetable peeler, then slice in half lengthwise. Discard the seeds and cut the flesh into dice the size of the tomatoes.

4 Mix the tomatoes, cucumber, onions, and half the basil in a bowl. Whisk the oil, sugar, Tabasco, lemon juice, and some salt and freshly ground black pepper in a separate bowl, then pour over the tomatoes and stir to combine.

5 Peel the skin from the trout and discard (if it does not peel off easily, it is not quite cooked, so pop it back in the oven for a few minutes). Arrange on a serving platter.

6 Spoon the salsa down the center of the fish and scatter the remaining basil over it. If you have any salsa leftover, serve it in a separate bowl. Serve the trout hot or warm with the cold salsa.

PREPARE AHEAD
The salsa can be made up to 8 hours ahead.
Not suitable for freezing.

SKINNING TOMATOES

STEP 1 Place the tomato in boiling water for 20 seconds or until the skin splits, then remove.

STEP 2 When cool enough to handle, carefully peel the skin from the tomato with a paring knife.

These look impressive, yet are so easy. Buy pieces of haddock that are roughly the same shape. Serve with salad and new potatoes.

Haddock mousseline parcels

Serves 6

12 x 2½oz (75g) pieces of unsmoked haddock
salt and freshly ground black pepper
6oz (175g) undyed smoked haddock filet, roughly chopped
1¾oz (50g) baby spinach
a little freshly grated nutmeg
2 tbsp freshly chopped parsley
finely grated zest of 1 lemon

16oz tub crème fraîche
1 egg
6 sheets filo pastry
melted butter, for brushing

For the spinach sauce

pat of butter
6oz (175g) baby spinach
juice of 1 lemon

Serves 12

24 x 2½oz (75g) pieces of unsmoked haddock
salt and freshly ground black pepper
12oz (350g) undyed smoked haddock filet, roughly chopped
3½oz (100g) baby spinach
a little freshly grated nutmeg
¼ cup freshly chopped parsley
finely grated zest of 2 lemons

2 x 16oz tubs crème fraîche
2 eggs
12 sheets filo pastry
melted butter, for brushing

For the spinach sauce

pat of butter
12oz (350g) baby spinach
juice of 2 lemons

1 Preheat the oven to 400°F (200°C). Pop a baking sheet in to get very hot (two sheets for 12). Arrange the unsmoked haddock pieces in pairs on a board and season well with salt and freshly ground black pepper.

2 Put the smoked haddock into a processor and whiz for 1 minute or until finely chopped. Add the spinach, nutmeg, parsley, lemon zest, and 2 tablespoons of the crème fraîche (4 tablespoons for 12) and season well with freshly ground black pepper. Separate the egg(s), add the white(s) to the processor, and reserve the yolk(s) for the sauce. Whiz until fairly smooth.

3 Divide the mousseline mixture into six equal portions (12 portions for 12) and spoon on top of half the unsmoked haddock pieces. Sit another piece of haddock on top of each one.

4 Brush the sheets of filo with butter. Place half of them side by side on a board, then place the other half directly on top. Cut each into four lengthwise to give 12 strips (24 strips for 12).

5 Sit each haddock sandwich in the middle of a strip of filo, then bring the sides up to meet at the top. Lay another strip of filo over the top in the opposite direction and tuck the sides underneath, so the haddock is wrapped in filo on all sides. Repeat with the others.

6 Brush the tops of the filo with melted butter and sit the parcels on the hot baking sheet(s). Bake for 15 minutes (25 minutes for 12) or until golden and crisp.

7 To make the sauce, melt the butter in a pan and cook the spinach for 2 minutes or until wilted. Add the rest of the crème fraîche, some salt and freshly ground black pepper, and bring to a boil. Transfer to a processor and whiz till smooth. Stir in the yolk(s) and lemon juice and reheat.

8 To serve, cut each haddock parcel in half diagonally to make two triangles. Spoon the hot sauce on to dinner plates and sit two triangles of haddock upright in the center of each one.

PREPARE AHEAD

The parcels can be made up to the end of step 5 up to 5 hours ahead. The sauce can be made up to 8 hours ahead. Add the yolk(s) and lemon juice just before serving. Not suitable for freezing.

Fresh and healthy, this dish is great for garden parties. Marinate it overnight for maximum flavor. Serve with salad and new potatoes.

Marinated chicken with summer salsa

Serves 6

1 jalepeño seeded, and finely diced
4 garlic cloves, crushed
6 tbsp freshly chopped parsley
zest and juice of 1 large lemon
¼ cup olive oil
2 tbsp honey
4 tsp paprika
6 skinless boneless chicken breasts

½ cucumber, peeled, halved, seeded, and diced
6 scallions, finely sliced
small bunch of cilantro, roughly chopped
finely grated zest and juice of 1 lime
2 tsp balsamic vinegar
2 tbsp olive oil
1 tsp superfine sugar
salt and freshly ground black pepper

For the salsa

2 large tomatoes, cut in half, seeded, and diced

Serves 12

2 jalepeños, seeded, and finely diced
8 garlic cloves, crushed
bunch of parsley, chopped
zest and juice of 2 lemons
½ cup olive oil
¼ cup honey
2 heaped tbsp paprika
12 skinless boneless chicken breasts

1 cucumber, peeled, halved, seeded, and diced
12 scallions, finely sliced
large bunch of cilantro, roughly chopped
finely grated zest and juice of 2 limes
1 tbsp balsamic vinegar
¼ cup olive oil
2 tsp superfine sugar
salt and freshly ground black pepper

For the salsa

4 large tomatoes, cut in half, seeded, and diced

1 Mix the first seven ingredients together in a large bowl. Add the chicken breasts and turn to coat. Leave to marinate in the fridge for 1–2 hours or overnight.

2 Preheat the oven to 425°F (220°C). Heat a griddle pan until hot, add the chicken, and brown for 20–30 seconds on each side or until griddle marks are left. You may need to do this in batches. Arrange on a baking sheet lined with non-stick baking parchment.

3 Roast for 25 minutes (35 minutes for 12) or until golden and cooked through. Remove from the oven and allow to rest for 5 minutes.

4 Meanwhile, make the salsa: mix all the ingredients in a large bowl and season with salt and freshly ground black pepper.

5 Carve the chicken into thick slices and serve with the salsa.

PREPARE AHEAD
The chicken can be prepared up to the end of step 2 up to 1 day ahead. The salsa ingredients can be prepared up to 1 day ahead and mixed together 1 hour ahead. Not suitable for freezing.

This is truly scrumptious. It's also quick to make. Homemade pesto is best, but you can use good-quality pesto from a jar if you're short of time. Serve with potatoes and salad.

Chicken with pesto, Taleggio, and roasted tomatoes

Serves 6

6 skinless boneless
 chicken breasts
salt and freshly gound
 black pepper
6oz (175g) Taleggio cheese
 (straight from the fridge),
 cut into small cubes
3 tbsp pesto

2 tbsp freshly chopped basil
3 tbsp cream cheese
1¾oz (50g) fresh breadcrumbs
a pinch of paprika
14oz (400g) cherry tomatoes
 on the vine
2 tbsp olive oil
1 tbsp balsamic vinegar

Serves 12

12 skinless boneless
 chicken breasts
salt and freshly gound
 black pepper
11oz (300g) Taleggio cheese
 (straight from the fridge),
 cut into cubes
5 tbsp pesto

¼ cup freshly chopped basil
5 tbsp cream cheese
2½oz (75g) fresh breadcrumbs
a pinch of paprika
2lb (900g) cherry tomatoes
 on the vine
3 tbsp olive oil
2 tbsp balsamic vinegar

1 Preheat the oven to 425°F (220°C). Arrange the chicken breasts in a single layer in an ovenproof dish or roasting pan and season with salt and freshly ground black pepper.

2 Mix the Taleggio, pesto, basil, and cream cheese in a bowl and season with salt and freshly ground black pepper. Spoon on to the chicken breasts, spreading the mixture out to cover them completely. Sprinkle with the breadcrumbs and dust with a little paprika.

3 Bake for 20 minutes, then arrange the tomatoes around the chicken, pour the oil and vinegar over them, and return to the oven for a further 10 minutes (30 minutes for 12) or until the chicken is just cooked through. Be careful not to overcook it.

4 To serve, arrange a chicken breast on each plate with a few tomatoes, then spoon over some of the juices from the dish.

PREPARE AHEAD AND FREEZE
The chicken can be prepared up to the end of step 2 up to 12 hours ahead. Freeze at the end of step 2 for up to 2 months.

MAKING PESTO

STEP 1 Put a large bunch of basil, 2 crushed garlic cloves, 1 tbsp pine nuts, and 2 tbsp freshly grated Parmesan cheese in a blender.

STEP 2 With the motor running, slowly pour in 3½fl oz (100ml) extra virgin olive. Season to taste.

A quick recipe that you can either prepare ahead or at the last minute. Serve with new potatoes and green vegetables or salad.

Sun-dried tomato and herb chicken

Serves 6

1 tbsp freshly chopped parsley
3 tbsp freshly snipped chives
1 tbsp freshly chopped basil
7oz cream cheese
1 egg yolk
2 tsp lemon juice
1¾oz (50g) sun-dried tomatoes, snipped into small pieces
salt and freshly ground black pepper

6 boneless chicken breasts, skin on
a little honey

For the sauce

5fl oz (150ml) dry white wine
2½ cups heavy cream
1 tbsp freshly chopped parsley

Serves 12

2 tbsp freshly chopped parsley
6 tbsp freshly snipped chives
2 tbsp freshly chopped basil
14oz cream cheese
2 egg yolks
1 tbsp lemon juice
3½oz (100g) sun-dried tomatoes, snipped into small pieces
salt and freshly ground black pepper

12 boneless chicken breasts, skin on
a little honey

For the sauce

10fl oz (300ml) dry white wine
5 cups heavy cream
2 tbsp freshly chopped parsley

1 Preheat the oven to 400°F (200°C). Put the first seven ingredients into a bowl, season with salt and freshly ground black pepper, and stir until combined.

2 Loosen the skin from the chicken breasts, but keep it attached at one side. Spoon the filling underneath and replace the skin.

3 Arrange the chicken breasts in a roasting pan, season with salt and freshly ground black pepper, then drizzle with a little honey.

4 Roast for 25–30 minutes (35–40 minutes for 12) or until golden and cooked through.

5 Meanwhile, make the sauce: put the wine into a pan (use a wide-based pan for 12, to make the reduction quicker) and boil over high heat until it has reduced to about 3 tablespoons (6 tablespoons for 12). Add the cream and boil for a couple of minutes to thicken. Season with salt and freshly ground black pepper.

6 Allow the chicken breasts to rest for a few minutes after roasting, then add any juices from the pan to the sauce. Carve each breast into three or serve whole. Add the parsley to the hot sauce and serve with the chicken.

SUN-DRIED TOMATOES
Sun-dried tomatoes are sold dry-packed or packed in oil. Either type will work for this recipe, although drain the oil-packed variety on paper towels before using.

PREPARE AHEAD
The chicken can be prepared up to the end of step 2 up to 1 day ahead. The sauce can be made up to 2 days ahead. Not suitable for freezing.

This is one of Lucy's fail-safe recipes that can be rustled up quickly while everyone is enjoying a glass of wine. Serve with plain rice.

Pan-fried chicken with mushrooms and tarragon

Serves 6

1 tbsp olive oil

5 small skinless boneless chicken breasts, cut into thin strips

salt and freshly ground black pepper

1 large onion, finely chopped

2 medium zucchini, cut into thick matchsticks

12oz (350g) button mushrooms, quartered

2 large garlic cloves

7fl oz (200ml) dry white wine

¾ cup heavy cream

juice of ½ lemon

1 heaped tbsp freshly chopped tarragon

Serves 12

This dish is not suitable for more than six because the sauce would not reduce to a thick consistency and be wet from the large quantity of vegetables.

1 Heat the oil in a deep frying pan, add half the chicken strips, season with salt and freshly ground black pepper, and brown over high heat until golden all over. Remove with a slotted spoon and set aside on a plate. Cook the rest of the chicken strips in the same way.

2 Add the onion and fry over high heat for a few minutes or until golden. Cover with a lid, lower the heat, and cook for 15 minutes or until tender. Turn up the heat, add the zucchini, mushrooms, and garlic, and fry for 3 minutes or until the vegetables start to soften. Remove from the pan and set aside with the chicken.

3 Add the wine to the pan and boil over high heat until it has reduced in volume to about 4 tablespoons. Stir in the cream and boil again for a few minutes until the sauce thickens. Stir in the lemon juice and season with salt and freshly ground black pepper. Return the chicken and vegetables to the pan for a couple of minutes to heat through.

4 Add the tarragon and serve immediately.

PREPARE AHEAD

This is best cooked to serve. Not suitable for freezing.

This is such a simple yet classy dish, easy to cook for a crowd on formal occasions. Serve with new potatoes and green vegetables.

Boursin-stuffed chicken with garlic and mint sauce

Serves 6

5.2oz package Poivre Boursin cheese

2½oz (75g) mature Cheddar cheese, grated

6 skinless boneless chicken breasts

salt and freshly ground black pepper

2 tbsp honey

a pinch of paprika

7fl oz (200ml) dry white wine

2 large garlic cloves, sliced in half

1¼ cups heavy cream

7oz (200g) French beans, trimmed and sliced into three

11oz (300g) frozen fava beans

11oz (300g) frozen baby peas

a pat of butter

2 tbsp freshly chopped mint

Serves 12

2 x 5.2oz package Poivre Boursin cheese

6oz (175g) mature Cheddar cheese, grated

12 skinless boneless chicken breasts

salt and freshly ground black pepper

¼ cup honey

a pinch of paprika

14fl oz (400ml) dry white wine

4 large garlic cloves, sliced in half

2½ cups heavy cream

14oz (400g) French beans, trimmed and sliced into three

1lb 5oz (600g) frozen fava beans

1lb 5oz (600g) frozen baby peas

a large pat of butter

¼ cup freshly chopped mint

1 Preheat the oven to 425°F (220°C). Mash the Boursin and Cheddar together with a fork in a small bowl. Make three diagonal slashes in the top of each chicken breast, cutting about half the way through. Season with salt and freshly ground black pepper, then spoon the cheese into the gaps. Arrange in a flat ovenproof dish.

2 Drizzle with the honey and sprinkle with paprika. Roast in the oven for 20–25 minutes or until cooked, then remove from the oven and leave to rest for 5 minutes.

3 Meanwhile, put the wine and garlic into a saucepan and boil until reduced by half. Add the cream and boil until reduced by one-third or until the sauce has thickened to a pouring consistency. Remove the garlic and season with salt and freshly ground black pepper.

4 Bring a pan of salted water to a boil. Add the French beans, fava beans, and baby peas and boil for 4 minutes or until just cooked. Drain and toss with the butter.

5 Reheat the sauce and add the mint. Spoon the vegetables on to plates and place a chicken breast on top of each one. Serve with a little of the sauce.

POIVRE BOURSIN

You'll find this in packages in the cheese section of the supermarket. Be sure to get the full-fat cheese and not the "light" version.

PREPARE AHEAD

The chicken breasts can be prepared up to the end of step 1 up to 1 day ahead. The sauce can be made up to 3 days ahead. Add the mint just before serving. Not suitable for freezing.

A warming dish that's perfect for sharing with friends when game is in season. Serve with mash or red cabbage and green vegetables.

Pheasant breasts with mushrooms and Madeira

Serves 6

2 onions, sliced

3 thyme sprigs

3 young pheasants

2½ cups hot chicken stock

3 tbsp butter

9oz (250g) small chestnut mushrooms, quartered

¼ cup all-purpose flour

¼ cup cold water

5fl oz (150ml) Madeira

1 tbsp balsamic vinegar

1 tbsp freshly chopped thyme leaves

1 tbsp crème fraîche

salt and freshly ground black pepper

Serves 12

4 onions, sliced

6 thyme sprigs

6 young pheasants

1 quart hot chicken stock

6 tbsp butter

1lb 2oz (500g) small chestnut mushrooms, quartered

½ cup all-purpose flour

½ cold water

10fl oz (300ml) Madeira

2 tbsp balsamic vinegar

2 tbsp freshly chopped thyme leaves

2 tbsp crème fraîche

salt and freshly ground black pepper

1 Preheat the oven to 400°F (200°C). Line a large roasting pan with foil and scatter the onions over the base.

2 Put a sprig of thyme in the cavity of each bird. Arrange them breast side down on top of the onions in the pan.

3 Pour over the hot stock, cover with foil, and roast for 50 minutes (1 hour for 12) or until the breasts are tender. Remove from the pan and allow to rest. Reserve the stock.

4 Melt the butter in a saucepan, add the mushrooms, and fry over high heat for a few minutes or until soft. Strain the stock from the roasting pan into a measuring glass until you have 15fl oz/450ml (3 cups/900ml for 12).

5 Mix the flour to a runny paste with the cold water, then stir in with the mushrooms and fry for 1 minute. Gradually add the measured stock and Madeira, stirring until blended. Bring to a boil, add the vinegar, thyme, and crème fraîche, and season with salt and freshly ground black pepper.

6 Using a sharp knife, detach the pheasant breasts from the carcass and cut each into three diagonally. Arrange in an ovenproof dish and pour over the hot sauce. If the thighs are tender, they can also be served. If tough, use to make game stock with the carcass.

PREPARE AHEAD

The dish can be cooked up to the end of step 6 up to 1 day ahead. Not suitable for freezing.

This is an easy way to cook duck breasts, as you brown them well ahead. You then cook them at the last minute, without the worry about whether they will be golden or not. Serve with green beans.

Duck breasts with a piquant lime and ginger sauce

Serves 6

6 duck breasts, skinned
salt and freshly ground
  black pepper
1 tbsp olive oil
2 tsp freshly grated ginger root
1 cup crème fraîche

juice of 1 lime
small pat of butter, at
  room temperature
3 tbsp lime marmalade
chives, to garnish

Serves 12

12 duck breasts, skinned
salt and freshly ground
  black pepper
2 tbsp olive oil
4 tsp freshly grated ginger root
2 cups crème fraîche

juice of 2 limes
large pat of butter, at
  room temperature
6 tbsp lime marmalade
chives, to garnish

1 Season the duck breasts with salt and freshly ground black pepper, then heat the oil in a frying pan and brown each one on its skinned side for a minute or so or until golden. Set aside. Add the ginger to the pan and heat over low heat for 1 minute. Whisk in the crème fraîche and lime juice until smooth and combined. Set aside until needed.

2 Mix the butter and marmalade together in a bowl, then spread over the browned side of the cold duck breasts. Arrange in a roasting pan browned side up.

3 When ready to serve, preheat the oven to 425°F (220°C). Roast the duck for 12–15 minutes (15–20 minutes for 12) or until cooked but still pink. Set aside to rest.

4 Meanwhile, place the roasting pan on the stove top, add the lime and ginger sauce, and heat until hot, scraping up any sticky bits from the bottom of the pan.

5 Carve each duck breast diagonally into three and serve on the hot sauce with a garnish of chives.

PREPARE AHEAD
You can prepare the duck up to the end of step 2 up to 1 day ahead. Not suitable for freezing.

This is a joy because it can be prepared ahead and reheated just before serving. Lucy often cooks it at her demonstrations, where it goes down a treat. Serve with new potatoes and a green vegetable.

Filet steak with a creamy mushroom sauce

Serves 6

8oz (225g) cremini mushrooms, thinly sliced

2 tbsp brandy

1¼ cups heavy cream

salt and freshly ground black pepper

6 x 5½oz (150g) middle-cut filet steaks

1 tbsp olive oil

8oz (225g) baby spinach

1¾oz (50g) fresh white breadcrumbs

a little paprika, to dust

Serves 12

1lb (450g) cremini mushrooms, thinly sliced

¼ cup brandy

2 cups heavy cream

salt and freshly ground black pepper

12 x 5½oz (150g) middle-cut filet steaks

2 tbsp olive oil

1lb (450g) baby spinach

2½oz (75g) fresh white breadcrumbs

a little paprika, to dust

1 Put the mushrooms and brandy into a wide-based pan and toss over high heat for 2–3 minutes or until the liquid has reduced slightly. Scoop out the mushrooms with a slotted spoon, add the cream, and boil for 5 minutes or until it has reduced by half and reached a coating consistency. Return the mushrooms to the pan, season with salt and freshly ground black pepper, then set aside to cool completely.

2 Heat a large non-stick frying pan over high heat. Brush each steak with a little oil and season with salt and freshly ground black pepper. Pan-fry each steak for 1–2 minutes on each side or until golden and sealed. Transfer to a baking sheet. You will need to do this in batches.

3 Add the spinach to the pan and cook for a few minutes or until just wilted. Place a mound on top of each steak. Spoon the cold mushroom sauce on top of the spinach (just enough to cover—you should have some sauce left over to reheat and serve with the steaks).

4 Preheat the oven to 425°F (220°C). Sprinkle the steaks with the breadcrumbs and a dusting of paprika and bake for 8 minutes (11 minutes for 12) or until piping hot but just rare in the middle. Add 2 minutes for medium and 4 minutes for medium to well done. Rest for a couple of minutes before serving. Reheat the remaining mushroom sauce in a pan.

5 Serve the steaks piping hot with the sauce alongside.

PREPARE AHEAD
The steaks can be prepared up to the end of step 3 up to 12 hours ahead. Not suitable for freezing.

Apart from the marinating—which is vital for the flavor of the sauce to come through—this is a very quick dish. Buy steaks of the same thickness, so they cook at the same rate. Serve with noodles.

Teriyaki steak

Serves 6

3½fl oz (100ml) mirin
3 tbsp soy sauce
2 tbsp light brown sugar
1 garlic clove, crushed
6 x 5½oz (150g) sirloin steaks
   or rump steaks

2 tbsp olive oil
8oz (225g) mixed wild
   mushrooms, such as oyster,
   shiitake, and cremini, sliced

Serves 12

This dish is not suitable for more than six people because you would have to cook it in two batches, which would mean some steaks would end up being overcooked.

1 Put the mirin, soy sauce, sugar, and garlic into a wide shallow dish and stir together.

2 Add the steaks and turn to coat. Leave to marinate for a minimum of 30 minutes and up to 8 hours.

3 Heat half the oil in a non-stick frying pan. Remove the steaks from the marinade (reserving the marinade) and fry for 2½ minutes on each side—they should be medium rare. Transfer to a hot plate to rest. You may need to do this in batches.

4 Heat the remaining oil in the pan, add the mushrooms, and fry over high heat for a few minutes or until just cooked. Pour in the reserved marinade and bring to a boil.

5 Serve the steaks whole or in slices with the mushrooms and sauce spooned on top.

MIRIN

You'll find mirin in a bottle in the Asian section of the supermarket. It is a traditional Japanese rice seasoning, similar to rice wine or sake, but with a low alcohol content.

PREPARE AHEAD
The marinade can be made up to 4 days ahead.
The steaks can be marinated for up to 8 hours.
Not suitable for freezing.

The advantage of using center-cut beef filet is that it's the same diameter all along, which means it roasts evenly and won't overcook at one end. This is delicious with our Thai green rice on page 116.

Thai beef with lime and chili

Serves 6

2lb (900g) center-cut beef filet
1 tbsp olive oil
1 jalepeño, seeded
 and roughly chopped
1in (2.5cm) fresh ginger root,
 peeled and roughly chopped
1 fat garlic clove, roughly
 chopped
small bunch of mint,
 stems removed

finely grated zest and juice
 of 1 lime
3½oz (100g) coconut cream
6oz crème fraîche
1 tbsp sweet chili dipping sauce
1 tbsp sugar
½ tbsp fish sauce
3 heaped tbsp light mayonnaise

Serves 12

4lb (1.8kg) center-cut beef filet
2 tbsp olive oil
2 jalepeños, seeded
 and roughly chopped
2in (5cm) fresh ginger root,
 peeled and roughly chopped
2 fat garlic cloves, roughly
 chopped
large bunch of mint,
 stems removed

finely grated zest and juice
 of 2 limes
7oz carton coconut cream
12oz crème fraîche
2 tbsp sweet chili dipping sauce
2 tbsp sugar
1 tbsp fish sauce
6 heaped tbsp light mayonnaise

1 Preheat the oven to 425°F (220°C). Rub the beef with the oil and brown quickly on all sides in a large pan.

2 Transfer to a roasting pan and roast for 20 minutes (30 minutes for 12)—it should be medium rare—then cover loosely with foil and leave to rest for 15–20 minutes.

3 Meanwhile, put the chili, ginger, garlic, mint, lime zest, and lime juice into a processor and whiz until finely chopped. Add the six remaining ingredients and whiz again.

4 Carve the beef, allowing 2–3 slices per person, and arrange on a platter with the Thai green rice, if serving. Place the sauce alongside in a bowl.

PREPARE AHEAD
The sauce can be made up to 3 days ahead.
The beef can be browned up to 12 hours
ahead. Not suitable for freezing.

This brightly colored side dish is full of flavor. It is the perfect accompaniment to our Thai beef with lime and chili on page 114.

Thai green rice

Serves 6

24 asparagus spears
3½oz (100g) baby corn
salt
8oz (225g) frozen baby peas
3½oz (100g) easy cook
   long-grain rice

4 scallions, finely sliced
2 tbsp soy sauce
2 tbsp sweet chili dipping sauce
a little olive oil, to fry

Serves 12

48 asparagus spears
7oz (200g) baby corn
salt
1lb (450g) frozen baby peas
7oz (200g) easy cook
   long-grain rice

8 scallions, finely sliced
¼ cup soy sauce
¼ cup sweet chili dipping sauce
a little olive oil, to fry

1 Trim the tough ends from the asparagus spears diagonally and discard, then cut the stalks into diagonal slices and set the tips to one side. Cut the corn into 3–4 diagonal slices, depending on their size.

2 Cook the asparagus stalks and corn in boiling salted water for 4 minutes or until just cooked, then drain and refresh in cold water.

3 Cook the asparagus tips and baby peas in boiling salted water for 2 minutes, then drain and refresh in cold water. Cook the rice in boiling salted water according to the package instructions, then drain.

4 Mix the rice with the cooked vegetables and scallions, then toss with the soy sauce and chili dipping sauce.

5 Heat the olive oil in a wok or non-stick frying pan and stir-fry the rice for 5 minutes or until hot. Serve at once—if kept hot, the vegetables will lose their vibrant green color.

PREPARE AHEAD
The rice can be prepared up to the end of step
4 up to 12 hours ahead. Not suitable for freezing.

Light and fresh, this stir-fry is the perfect dish to rustle up as a speedy supper for up to six people. Serve with noodles or rice.

Sirloin steak and vegetable stir-fry

Serves 6

12oz (350g) thin sirloin steak or filet steak, sliced into very thin strips
1 tbsp honey
salt and freshly ground black pepper
2 tbsp olive oil
2 carrots, sliced into matchsticks

6 scallions, sliced
5½oz (150g) baby corn, cut into thick slices
5½oz (150g) sugarsnap peas, sliced in half lengthwise
9oz (250g) bok choy, white and green separated and cut into thick slices

For the sauce

3 tbsp mirin
2 tbsp soy sauce
2 tbsp hoisin sauce
2 tbsp water
2 tsp corn starch

Serves 12

This dish is not suitable for more than six people because the vegetables would release too much water and make the stir-fry soggy.

1 Toss the steak in the honey and season well with salt and freshly ground black pepper.

2 Heat the oil in a large frying pan or wok over high heat, add the steak, and stir-fry for 1–2 minutes or until brown and just cooked. Transfer to a plate with a slotted spoon.

3 Add the carrots, scallions, and corn and stir-fry over high heat for 3 minutes. Add the sugarsnap peas and the white part of the pak choi and stir-fry for 3 minutes.

4 Put the mirin, soy sauce, and hoisin sauce in a small bowl. Mix the water and corn starch to a smooth paste in another bowl, then add to the sauce. Pour the sauce into the frying pan with the steak and the green leaves of the bok choy and fry for 1–2 minutes or until the green leaves have just wilted.

5 Season with salt and freshly ground black pepper and serve at once.

PREPARE AHEAD
You can prepare all the ingredients up to 4 hours ahead. The sauce can be made up to 1 day ahead. Not suitable for freezing.

Lamb loin filet is lean, tender, and very quick to cook. It's also quite expensive, so this recipe is for extra special occasions. Serve with creamy mashed potatoes and a green vegetable.

Marinated marmalade and whiskey lamb filet

Serves 6

3 large lamb loin filets, trimmed
3 heaped tbsp thin-cut Seville orange marmalade
finely grated zest of ½ lemon
1 garlic clove, crushed
2 tbsp whiskey
2 tbsp olive oil
salt and freshly ground black pepper

For the sauce

1¼ cups chicken stock
1½ tbsp soy sauce
2 tsp balsamic vinegar
2 level tsp corn starch
1 tbsp cold water

Serves 12

6 large lamb loin filets, trimmed
6 heaped tbsp thin-cut Seville orange marmalade
finely grated zest of 1 lemon
2 garlic cloves, crushed
4 tbsp whiskey
4 tbsp olive oil
salt and freshly ground black pepper

For the sauce

2 cups chicken stock
3 tbsp soy sauce
4 tsp balsamic vinegar
4 level tsp corn starch
2 tbsp cold water

1 Arrange the lamb filets in a flat dish. Put the marmalade, lemon zest, garlic, and whiskey into a small bowl and mix together. Pour over the lamb, cover, and leave to marinate in the fridge for about an hour or up to 6 hours.

2 Preheat the oven to 425°F (220°C). Heat the oil in large frying pan. Scrape the marinade off the filets and reserve for the sauce. Season the lamb with salt and freshly ground black pepper, then fry quickly until brown on all sides. You may need to do this in batches. Arrange on a baking sheet.

3 Roast for 8 minutes (12 minutes for 12) or until cooked but still pink in the middle. Set aside to rest.

4 Meanwhile, rinse the frying pan, add the reserved marinade along with the stock, soy sauce, and balsamic vinegar, and bring to a boil. Put the corn starch into a cup, add the cold water, and mix until smooth. Add a little of the hot sauce and mix again, then stir into the frying pan and bring to a boil to thicken it slightly.

5 Carve the lamb into slices, strain the sauce, and serve alongside.

PREPARE AHEAD AND FREEZE
The lamb can be marinated for up to 6 hours.
The sauce can be made up to 3 days ahead.
Freeze the sauce for up to 3 months.

Slow-roasted lamb is ideal for a crowd—it looks after itself in the oven, it's tender, and easy to carve. No wonder it's Mary's family lunch most Sundays. Serve with mint sauce and red currant jelly.

Slow-roast leg of lamb

Serves 6

3lb 3oz (1.5kg) half-boned
   leg of lamb
8 garlic cloves, thinly sliced
bunch of fresh thyme
2 red onions, roughly chopped
1 tbsp olive oil
salt and freshly ground
   black pepper

2½ cups water mixed with
   1 beef stock cube
1 heaped tbsp all-purpose flour
3 tbsp water
1 heaped tbsp red currant jelly
a little gravy browning (optional)

Serves 12

2 x 3lb 3oz (1.5kg) half-boned
   legs of lamb
16 garlic cloves, thinly sliced
large bunch of fresh thyme
4 red onions, roughly chopped
2 tbsp olive oil
salt and freshly ground
   black pepper

5½ cups water mixed with
   2 beef stock cubes
2 heaped tbsp all-purpose flour
6 tbsp water
2 heaped tbsp red currant jelly
a little gravy browning
   (optional)

1 Preheat the oven to 220°C (425°F). Lay the lamb on a board and use a small sharp knife to make holes in the flesh. Push the garlic and thyme into the holes.

2 Arrange the onions in the base of a large roasting pan. Sit a grill rack over the onions and place the lamb on top. Drizzle over the oil and season with salt and freshly ground black pepper.

3 Roast for 30–40 minutes (40–50 minutes for 12) or until brown. Remove the pan from the oven and reduce the oven temperature to 275°F (140°C).

4 Pour the stock around the lamb, cover the pan with foil, and return to the oven for 4 hours (4½ hours for 12) or until the meat is tender and just falling off the bone.

5 Transfer the lamb to a board, cover with foil, and leave to rest while you make the gravy.

6 Put the flour into a cup and mix to a smooth runny paste with the water. Heat the roasting pan on the stove, whisk in the flour mixture and the red currant jelly, and bring to a boil, stirring all the time until smooth. Check the seasoning and add a little gravy browning if you'd like the gravy to be a rich brown color.

7 Carve the lamb and serve with the hot gravy.

PREPARE AHEAD
The lamb can be prepared up to the end of step 2 up to 1 day ahead. Not suitable for freezing.

VARIATIONS

If you're cooking on a budget, use shoulder of lamb, which is much more reasonably priced, although it can be a little fatty. Make sure you skim off any fat at the end of cooking. If you prefer thin gravy, leave out the flour—just use the juices in the pan.

As a team, we like to go to the pub occasionally, to chat and have a moment off from cooking. One evening we had a recipe similar to this—delicious and beautifully presented. Serve with spinach.

Mini pork en croûtes

Serves 6

2½oz (75g) mature Cheddar cheese, grated
1¾oz (50g) fresh white breadcrumbs
2 tbsp freshly chopped parsley
1 tsp freshly chopped thyme
1 egg
salt and freshly ground black pepper

dash of Tabasco
2 x 12oz (350g) pork filets, trimmed
8 slices Parma ham
a little all-purpose flour, to dust
1 sheet ready-rolled puff pastry
1 egg, beaten with a little milk

Serves 12

5oz (150g) mature Cheddar cheese, grated
3½oz (100g) fresh white breadcrumbs
¼ cup freshly chopped parsley
2 tsp freshly chopped thyme
2 eggs
salt and freshly ground black pepper

generous dash of Tabasco
4 x 12oz (350g) pork filets, trimmed
16 slices Parma ham
a little all-purpose flour, to dust
2 x 1 sheet ready-rolled puff pastry
1 egg, beaten with a little milk

1 Put the cheese, breadcrumbs, herbs, and egg into a small bowl. Season with salt and freshly ground black pepper, add the Tabasco, and mix well.

2 Slice each pork filet in half horizontally, then cover with plastic wrap and bash with a rolling pin until they are slightly thinner. Spread the cheese mixture on top of the halved filets, then put the filet halves together again, with the cheese mixture in the middle.

3 Arrange four slices of the ham side by side on a board. With the edges overlapping slightly, they should be about as wide as one of the pork filets. Sit a filet across the ham at one end and roll it up so the pork is encased in the ham. Do the same with the other filet(s).

4 On a lightly floured work surface, roll the pastry out into a 13 x 16in (33 x 40cm) rectangle (two rectangles for 12). Slice in half widthwise and brush with egg. Wrap each filet in pastry and place join side down on a baking sheet. Brush with egg and chill for an hour.

5 Preheat the oven to 425°F (220°C). Bake the parcels for 25–30 minutes (45 minutes for 12) or until golden and crisp. Allow to rest for 5–10 minutes before carving. Meanwhile, make the apple gravy (see right).

6 Slice each en croûte in three, then slice each piece in half diagonally and stand them on a dinner plate. Serve hot with the apple gravy. Serve any extra gravy separately.

PREPARE AHEAD AND FREEZE
The pork can be prepared up to the end of step 3 up to 12 hours ahead. Not suitable for freezing. The gravy can be made up to 2 days ahead. Freeze for up to 1 month.

FOR THE APPLE GRAVY
For six, heat a pat of butter in a saucepan, add 1 finely chopped large onion, and fry for 2 minutes. Cover with a lid and cook over a low heat for 15 minutes or until the onion is soft. Sprinkle in ¼ cup all-purpose flour, blend in 1¾ cup chicken stock and the same quantity of unsweetened apple juice, and bring to a boil, stirring. Season with salt and freshly ground black pepper, add 2 tbsp Worcestershire sauce and a little gravy browning as well if you'd like the gravy to be a rich brown color. Push through a sieve and discard the onion. For 12, double the quantities, so you need a large pat of butter, 2 large onions, ½ cup flour, 2½ cups each of chicken stock and apple juice, and ¼ cup Worcestershire sauce.

A variation on one of Mary's best-loved pork recipes. Lucy's family adores it and always puts in a request for it on special occasions. Serve with mashed potatoes and green vegetables.

Paprika pork filet

Serves 6

2 tbsp olive oil

2lb (900g) pork filet, trimmed and cut into ½in (1cm) slices

1½ tbsp butter

1 large onion, roughly chopped

1 level tbsp paprika

2 level tbsp all-purpose flour

1¼ cups chicken stock

5 tbsp sherry

1 tsp tomato purée

6oz (175g) button mushrooms, halved

salt and freshly ground black pepper

7oz crème fraîche

Serves 12

¼ cup olive oil

4lb (1.8kg) pork filet, trimmed and sliced into ½in (1cm) slices

3 tbsp butter

2 large onions, roughly chopped

2 level tbsp paprika

¼ cup all-purpose flour

2 cups chicken stock

5fl oz (150ml) sherry

2 tsp tomato purée

12oz (350g) button mushrooms, halved

salt and freshly ground black pepper

14oz crème fraîche

1 Heat the oil in a large non-stick frying pan or casserole. Add the pork and brown quickly on all sides. Remove with a slotted spoon and set aside. You may need to do this in batches.

2 Add the butter and onion to the pan, cover with a lid, and leave to soften over low heat for 15 minutes or until tender.

3 Stir in the paprika and flour and fry over high heat for 1 minute. Add the stock and sherry and bring to a boil, stirring all the time, to thicken slightly. Add the tomato purée and mushrooms.

4 Return the pork to the pan, season with salt and freshly ground black pepper, cover with a lid, and simmer over low heat for 15 minutes (25–30 minutes for 12) or until the pork is tender.

5 Stir in the crème fraîche and serve piping hot.

Great for a crowd... When cooking larger quantities, use just enough oil to coat the bottom of the pan and take care not to overcook the pork or it will be dry. Freezes well.

PREPARE AHEAD AND FREEZE

The dish can be prepared up to the end of step 4 up to 1 day ahead. Freeze at the end of step 4 for up to 1 month.

This is one Mary's favorite ways of serving potatoes. She's been cooking them for over 25 years and they're as popular now as they were then. Serve with chops, grilled meat, or fish.

Heavenly potato gratin

Serves 6

Special equipment 1 quart shallow ovenproof dish, buttered

2lb (900g) even-sized waxy red-skinned potatoes

1 tsp salt

freshly ground black pepper

3 tbsp butter, melted, plus a little extra to grease

¾ cup half and half

Serves 12

Special equipment 2 quart shallow ovenproof dish, buttered

4lb (1.8kg) even-sized waxy red-skinned potatoes

1 tsp salt

freshly ground black pepper

5 tbsp butter, melted, plus a little extra to grease

1¼ cups half and half

1 Preheat the oven to 400°F (220°C). Rub off any excess dirt from the potatoes and put them unpeeled into a pan. Cover with cold water and add the salt. Cover with a lid, bring to a boil, and cook until just tender. The timing will depend on their size, but they should be soft around the edges and slightly firm in the center. Set aside for them to cool completely.

2 Peel the skins from the potatoes and discard. Using a coarse grater, grate the potatoes into the buttered dish, seasoning between the layers with salt and freshly ground black pepper. Do not press down—they should be light and fluffy.

3 Pour over the melted butter and cream, then bake for 20–25 minutes (40 minutes for 12) or until crisp and golden brown.

THE RIGHT DISH

Make sure you use an ovenproof dish that's wide and shallow, so you get more of the delicious crispy golden crust.

PREPARE AHEAD

The potatoes can be made up to the end of step 2 up to 1 day ahead. Not suitable for freezing.

These are best prepared a day ahead. Make more than you need and freeze them for another occasion—they're great when there are just two or four of you. Serve with chops, grilled meat, or fish.

Cheese-topped dauphinois potatoes

Serves 6

Special equipment *7in (18cm) square shallow metal pan lined with non-stick paper and greased*

1lb 10oz (750g) large Yukon Gold potatoes or other floury potatoes

¾ cup chicken stock or vegetable stock

½ cup heavy cream

salt and freshly ground black pepper

pat of butter

scant 1oz (25g) mature Cheddar cheese, grated

Serves 12

Special equipment *9 x 12in (23 x 30cm) roasting pan lined with non-stick paper and greased*

3lb (1.35kg) large Yukon Gold potatoes or other floury potatoes

1½ cups chicken stock or vegetable stock

¾ cup heavy cream

salt and freshly ground black pepper

1½ tbsp butter

1¾oz (50g) mature Cheddar cheese, grated

1 Preheat the oven to 425°F (220°C). Peel the potatoes and rinse under cold water, then dry and slice very thinly by hand or with the slicer attachment on a processor. Put the stock into a large bowl and mix with the cream.

2 Arrange a layer of potato over the base of the pan, season with salt and freshly ground black pepper, then pour over a little of the stock mixture. Continue in the same way until the potato and liquid are used up. Dot the butter over the top and cover tightly with foil.

3 Bake for 30 minutes (45 minutes for 12) or until soft around the edges but still firm in the middle. Remove the foil and cook for a further 25–30 minutes (35–45 minutes for 12) or until golden and tender. Leave to cool, then chill—overnight is best.

4 Choose a lipped board or tray that's bigger than the roasting pan (so it will catch any juices) and place on a worktop. Carefully turn the roasting pan upside down on to it and remove the paper. Cut the potatoes into even-sized servings, arrange on a greased or paper-lined baking sheet, and sprinkle the cheese on top.

5 Reheat in an oven preheated to 400°F (200°C) for 25–30 minutes (35 minutes for 12) or until golden and piping hot.

PREPARE AHEAD AND FREEZE
The dish can be made up to the end of step 3 up to 1 day ahead or up to the end of step 4 up to 8 hours ahead. Freeze for up to 2 months.

These are great all year round, but are especially good in the summer months when the flavor of fresh thyme is at its best. Serve with barbecued meats or fish.

Roast potatoes with chile and thyme

Serves 6

6 large old potatoes, peeled and cut into 2in (5cm) cubes

salt and freshly ground black pepper

3 tbsp olive oil

juice of ½ lemon

2 tsp freshly chopped thyme leaves

2–3 garlic cloves, crushed

1–2 jalepeños (depending on preference), seeded and finely chopped

2 tbsp freshly chopped parsley

Serves 12

12 large old potatoes, peeled and cut into 2in (5cm) cubes

salt and freshly ground black pepper

6 tbsp olive oil

juice of 1 lemon

4 tsp freshly chopped thyme leaves

5 fat garlic cloves, crushed

3–4 jalepeños (depending on preference), seeded and finely chopped

¼ cup freshly chopped parsley

1 Preheat the oven to 425°F (220°C). Meanwhile, cook the potatoes in boiling salted water for 4–5 minutes or until they are just soft around the edges but still have a little bite in the middle. Drain and transfer to a bowl.

2 Put all the other ingredients except the parsley into a small bowl and lightly whisk to combine. Pour over the potatoes and season with salt and freshly ground black pepper.

3 Pop a roasting pan (two pans for 12) into the oven for a few minutes to get very hot. Spoon the potatoes and dressing into the pan(s) and roast for 25–30 minutes (45–55 minutes for 12) or until golden and crispy. Garnish with the parsley and serve.

PREPARE AHEAD

The potatoes can be prepared up to the end of step 2 up to 1 day ahead. Not suitable for freezing.

Roasted vegetables make a wonderful side dish for so many meats and fish. The secret is to cook the vegetables in a single layer, so they chargrill rather than steaming and becoming soggy.

Roasted Mediterranean vegetables

Serves 6

2 tbsp olive oil

1 small eggplant, sliced into 2in (5cm) chunks

2 small zucchini, thickly sliced

1 red pepper, halved, seeded, and cut into 2in (5cm) chunks

1 onion, quartered

3 garlic cloves (unpeeled)

2 sprigs of fresh rosemary

3 sprigs of fresh thyme

salt and freshly ground black pepper

Serves 12

¼ cup olive oil

2 small eggplants, sliced into 2in (5cm) chunks

4 small zucchini, thickly sliced

2 red peppers, halved, seeded, and cut into 2in (5cm) chunks

2 onions, quartered

6 garlic cloves (unpeeled)

4 sprigs of fresh rosemary

6 sprigs of fresh thyme

salt and freshly ground black pepper

1 Preheat the oven to 425°F (220°C). Put the oil into a large roasting pan (two pans for 12) and pop in the oven for a few minutes to get hot.

2 Add the vegetables and toss in the hot oil. Scatter over the garlic and herbs.

3 Roast for 40–45 minutes (1 hour for 12) or until tender and golden. Turn halfway through cooking.

4 Transfer to a serving bowl with a slotted spoon. Squeeze the garlic from their skins and mix in with the vegetables. Discard the herbs if woody. Season with salt and freshly ground black pepper, toss, and serve.

USING LEFTOVERS

If you have any vegetables left over, toss them with a little balsamic vinegar and some olive oil and serve them as a salad.

PREPARE AHEAD

The vegetables can be prepared up to the end of step 4 up to 1 day ahead. Not suitable for freezing.

We love recipes that you can do much of the preparation for up to a day ahead and that require little last-minute attention. These carrots can be popped into the oven while you're doing the roast.

Orange-glazed carrots

Serves 6

2¼lb (1kg) carrots, sliced
   thickly diagonally
salt and freshly ground
   black pepper

1½ tbsp butter, melted
½ orange
freshly chopped parsley,
   to garnish

Serves 12

4½lb (2kg) carrots, sliced
   thickly diagonally
salt and freshly ground
   black pepper

3 tbsp butter, melted
1 orange
freshly chopped parsley,
   to garnish

1 Preheat the oven to 400°F (200°C). Immerse the carrots in a pan of boiling salted water for 4 minutes to blanch them, then drain and refresh in cold water.

2 Pour over the melted butter, season with salt and freshly ground black pepper, and stir to coat well.

3 Arrange in a roasting pan or ovenproof dish. Squeeze over the juice from the orange and pop the shell in the pan for extra flavor.

4 Cover with foil and bake for 30 minutes (40 minutes for 12) or until tender.

5 To serve, remove the orange shell and discard. Sprinkle over the parsley and toss lightly.

PREPARE AHEAD
The carrots can be blanched up to 1 day ahead.
Coat in the butter and orange juice and roast
to serve. Not suitable for freezing.

This is an unusual vegetable dish, best served alongside more conventional vegetables such as broccoli or green beans. Serve as an accompaniment to meat or fish.

Roasted endive with garlic butter

Serves 6

salt and freshly ground black pepper
12 endive heads, sliced in half lengthwise
1½ tbsp butter

2 garlic cloves, crushed
1¾oz (50g) mature Cheddar cheese, grated
a little paprika, to dust

Serves 12

salt and freshly ground black pepper
24 endive heads, sliced in half lengthwise
3 tbsp butter

4 garlic cloves, crushed
3½oz (100g) mature Cheddar cheese, grated
a little paprika, to dust

1 Preheat the oven to 425°F (220°C). Bring a pan of cold salted water to a boil, add the endive, and bring back up to a rolling boil. Cook for 3 minutes, then drain. Arrange the endive in a single layer in an ovenproof dish.

2 Add the butter and garlic to the empty pan and melt over the heat. Spoon over the endive in the dish and season with salt and freshly ground black pepper. Sprinkle over the cheese and a light dusting of paprika.

3 Bake for 15–20 minutes (25–30 minutes for 12) or until lightly golden.

PREPARE AHEAD
The endive can be prepared up to the end of step 1 up to 6 hours ahead. Not suitable for freezing.

Potluck parties

Potluck parties, where various people bring along a contribution, are huge fun and a lot less work than doing it all yourself. The all-in-one dishes in this chapter are portable and ideal for preparing ahead.

Potluck parties

There are lots of occasions when a potluck party (sometimes called a safari supper or shared party) fits the bill—a charity event or function at the children's school, a New Year's Eve celebration or family get-together. And though they aren't exactly new, they're all the rage right now because people are leading increasingly busy lives. For a potluck party to be a success, organization and coordination are called for—you don't want everyone turning up with a fish pie! Here's our guide to organizing or contributing to a potluck party.

Organizing a potluck party

● **The occasion** Let people know the reason for the party and what kind of event you'd like it to be—formal or casual? Will guests be able to sit or will they stand, plate in hand?

● **The guests** How many people are you inviting? What sort of age will most people be? Will there be children or teenagers? All these factors can affect what you cook.

● **The venue** Are you hosting the party in your home or will people meet in the church hall, in someone's backyard, or on the beach? If you're hosting the party in your home, find out if dishes will require reheating or cooking. And make a note of how many dishes will need to be reheated so you can work out if there'll be enough space in your oven and on your stovetop. If you're hosting the party at a venue, check what cooking facilities there are—oven, range, or microwave. Is there enough counter space to lay dishes out on? Find out if there's a fridge or freezer, then let people know so they can plan accordingly.

● **The food** Ask people what dish they'd like to bring along. Listen to their suggestion—some may have strengths they'd like to capitalize on. They might be excellent with pastry, for instance. But keep the selection of recipes balanced. It might mean twisting the occasional arm, so someone brings along a dish that wasn't necessarily their first choice.

"For a potluck party to be a success, organization and coordination are called for—you don't want everyone turning up with a fish pie!"

● **The drinks** You might be planning to supply the drinks and glasses yourself. Alternatively, you could appoint one person or several people to take care of them. You could even ask everyone to bring what they enjoy themselves.

● **The equipment** If you don't have enough plates and cutlery, make sure you ask people to bring some with them. Will you need to provide platters, baskets, and cooking utensils? Will you need folding chairs? And don't forget the cleaning up—pack a few garbage bags, as well as some plastic containers or plastic bags for leftovers.

Contributing to a potluck party

When you're invited to contribute to a potluck party, your favorite recipe might spring instantly to mind. This might not be ideal, however. These are the points to consider.

● **The time of day** Is it brunch, lunch, or supper?

● **The time of year** A casserole would hit the spot in midwinter, but it might be less enthusiastically received on a blisteringly hot summer's day.

● **The occasion** Is the party in honor of a special occasion or is it a more casual affair?

● **The guestlist** How many people are coming and who are they? Check, too, if there are guests with special dietary requirements.

● **The food** Will your dish need reheating? And how? Does it require chilling? Ask about the facilities at the other end.

● **The equipment** Presenting food in the dish it was cooked in is perfectly okay at a casual get-together, and foil containers are ideal when you intend to serve food straight on to plates, but, for a more formal occasion, you might need to take a serving dish. Don't forget any cooking utensils or serving implements you'll need. And stick your name on everything or you may never see them again.

● **Garnishes** Remember to take any last-minute ingredients, garnishes, or decorations.

● **Leftovers** Make provisions for leftovers by taking plastic containers and plastic bags with you. And pack an extra-large bag to bring your dirty cooking dish home in.

This recipe is ideal for preparing the day before. Shelled crawfish tails can be bought in all good supermarkets or fishmongers. They come in tubs of brine. Serve the pie with steamed broccoli or salad.

Salmon and crawfish pie

Serves 6

Special equipment *2 quart shallow wide-based ovenproof dish*

1lb 10oz (750g) Yukon Gold potatoes or other floury potatoes, cut into 2in (5cm) pieces

salt and freshly ground black pepper

a pat of butter

1 cup milk

For the pie

5 tbsp butter

1 onion, finely chopped

2 leeks, finely sliced

½ cup all-purpose flour

2 cups hot milk

juice of ½ lemon

2 tbsp freshly chopped dill

2 tbsp freshly chopped parsley

2 tbsp capers, drained

1lb 2oz (500g) skinned salmon filet, cut into 2in (5cm) cubes

9oz (250g) cooked crawfish tails in brine, drained

2½oz (75g) Cheddar cheese, grated

lemon wedges, to serve

Serves 12

Special equipment *2 x 2 quart shallow wide-based ovenproof dishes or 1 x 3 quart dish*

3lb 3oz (1.5kg) Yukon Gold potatoes or other floury potatoes, cut into 2in (5cm) pieces

salt and freshly ground black pepper

a large pat of butter

1¼ cup milk

For the pie

10 tbsp butter

2 onions, finely chopped

4 leeks, finely sliced

¾ cup all-purpose flour

1 quart hot milk

juice of 1 lemon

¼ cup freshly chopped dill

¼ cup freshly chopped parsley

¼ cup capers, drained

2¼lb (1kg) skinned salmon filet, cut into 2in (5cm) cubes

1lb 2oz (500g) cooked crawfish tails in brine, drained

6oz (175g) Cheddar cheese, grated

lemon wedges, to serve

1 Preheat the oven to 425°F (220°C). Put the potatoes in a pan of cold salted water, cover with a lid, bring to a boil, and cook for 15 minutes or until tender. Drain, add the butter and milk, season with salt and freshly ground black pepper, and mash until smooth. You may need a little more milk to get the right consistency.

2 Meanwhile, melt the butter for the pie in a large saucepan. Stir in the onion and leeks, cover with a lid, and cook over a low heat for 15 minutes or until the onion is soft. Stir in the flour and, over high heat, gradually add the milk, stirring all the time until the sauce is smooth and thick.

3 Remove from the heat, add all the remaining ingredients (except the cheese), and season with salt and freshly ground black pepper. Spoon into the ovenproof dish and level the top. Cover with the mash and fluff up the surface with a fork. Sprinkle over the cheese.

4 Bake for 35 minutes (50 minutes for 12) or until golden brown and piping hot. Serve at once with wedges of lemon.

PREPARE AHEAD
The pie can be made up to the end of step 3 up to 1 day ahead. Not suitable for freezing.

Named after the area of Scotland famous for its fish and seafood, this pie is quick to make. It's also unusual in that the potatoes are in the bake and not mashed on top. Serve with peas or salad.

Loch Fyne haddock bake

Serves 6

Special equipment *2 quart shallow wide-based ovenproof dish*

12oz (350g) Yukon Gold potatoes or other floury potatoes, peeled and cut into ¾in (2cm) cubes

salt and freshly ground black pepper

1lb 2oz (500g) baby spinach

1 tbsp olive oil

9oz (250g) small cremini mushrooms, sliced in half

pat of butter

3 eggs, hardboiled, peeled, and sliced into quarters

1lb 2oz (500g) undyed smoked haddock, skinned and cut into 2in (5cm) pieces

1¼ cups heavy cream

2 tsp wholegrain mustard

2½oz (75g) mature Cheddar cheese, grated

Serves 12

Special equipment *2 x quart shallow wide-based ovenproof dishes or 1 x 3 quart dish*

1lb 10oz (750g) Yukon Gold potatoes or other floury potatoes, peeled and cut into ¾in (2cm) cubes

salt and freshly ground black pepper

2¼lb (1kg) baby spinach

2 tbsp olive oil

1lb 2oz (500g) small cremini mushrooms, sliced in half

pat of butter

6 eggs, hardboiled, peeled, and sliced into quarters

2¼lb (1kg) undyed smoked haddock, skinned and cut into 2in (5cm) pieces

2 cups heavy cream

4 tsp wholegrain mustard

6oz (175g) mature Cheddar cheese, grated

1 Preheat the oven to 400°F (200°C). Meanwhile, put the potatoes into a pan of cold salted water, cover with a lid, bring to a boil, and cook for 10–15 minutes or until just cooked. Drain well and set aside.

2 Heat a large frying pan, add the spinach, and cook for a few minutes or until just wilted but still holding its shape. Drain well in a colander, squeezing to remove excess liquid, then set aside. You may need to do this in batches.

3 Heat the oil in the frying pan, add the mushrooms, and fry for 3 minutes or until just cooked.

4 Grease the ovenproof dish(es) with the butter, then arrange the potatoes, spinach, and mushrooms in the base. Scatter the eggs and haddock over the dish and season with salt and freshly ground black pepper.

5 Mix the cream and mustard in a bowl with some salt and freshly ground black pepper, then pour over the fish mixture, and sprinkle with the cheese.

6 Bake for 20–25 minutes (30–35 minutes for two dishes for 12 or 40–45 minutes for one dish for 12) or until golden on top and cooked through.

SMOKED HADDOCK
Make sure you buy undyed smoked haddock – the dyed fillets are bright yellow and very unnatural-looking.

PREPARE AHEAD
The bake can be made up to the end of step 4 up to 8 hours ahead. Not suitable for freezing.

Guests of all ages will enjoy this tasty tuna, macaroni, and cheese bake. And it really is extremely economical to make. Serve with crusty bread or dressed salad.

Macaroni tuna bake

Serves 6

Special equipment 1½ quart shallow wide-based ovenproof dish

12oz (350g) macaroni
salt and freshly ground
    black pepper
5½oz (150g) frozen peas
5 tbsp butter
½ cup all-purpose flour
3 cups hot milk
1 tbsp Dijon mustard
juice of ½ lemon

2½oz (75g) strong Cheddar
    cheese, grated
2½oz (75g) Parmesan cheese,
    freshly grated
2 x 6.5oz cans tuna in
    springwater, drained
4 large tomatoes, cut in
    quarters, seeded, and
    roughly chopped

Serves 12

Special equipment 2 quart shallow wide-based ovenproof dish

1lb 10oz (750g) macaroni
salt and freshly ground
    black pepper
10oz (300g) frozen peas
1½ sticks butter
1½ cups plain flour
6 cups hot milk
2 tbsp Dijon mustard
juice of 1 lemon

6oz (175g) strong Cheddar
    cheese, grated
6oz (175g) Parmesan cheese,
    freshly grated
4 x 6.5oz cans tuna in
    springwater, drained
8 large tomatoes, cut in
    quarters, seeded, and
    roughly chopped

1 Preheat the oven to 400°F (200°C). Cook the macaroni in boiling salted water according to the package instructions. Add the peas 3 minutes before the end. Drain, refresh in cold water, and set aside.

2 Melt the butter in a saucepan, add the flour, and stir over the heat for 1 minute. Add the hot milk slowly, whisking until the sauce is smooth and thick.

3 Add the mustard, lemon juice, and two-thirds of each cheese. Add the pasta and peas and lots of salt and freshly ground black pepper. Stir in the tuna and mix together. Spoon into the ovenproof dish, scatter over the tomatoes, and sprinkle over the remaining cheese.

4 Bake for 20–25 minutes (30–35 minutes for 12) or until lightly golden and crispy.

PREPARE AHEAD
The dish can be made up to the end of step 3 up to 1 day ahead. Not suitable for freezing.

This is an old-fashioned pie, perfect for a winter Sunday lunch. If you're cooking for 12, we think it is easier to make two pies rather than one really large one, but it's up to you.

Traditional chicken, leek, and mushroom pie

Serves 6

Special equipment *2 quart ovenproof pie dish*

5 tbsp butter

3 large leeks, sliced

½ cup all-purpose flour, plus a little extra to dust

1¼ cups apple juice

2 cups chicken stock

9oz (250g) portabella mushrooms, sliced

1 tbsp Dijon mustard

1 tbsp freshly chopped thyme leaves

3 tbsp crème fraîche

1lb 10oz (750g) cooked chicken, sliced

salt and freshly ground black pepper

1 sheet all-butter puff pastry

1 egg, beaten with a little milk

Serves 12

Special equipment *2 x 2 quart ovenproof pie dishes or 1 x 3 quart dish*

1½ sticks butter

6 leeks, sliced

1 cup all-purpose flour, plus a little extra to dust

2 cups apple juice

3 cups chicken stock

1lb (450g) portabella mushrooms, sliced

2 tbsp Dijon mustard

2 tbsp freshly chopped thyme leaves

6 tbsp crème fraîche

3lb 3oz (1.5kg) cooked chicken, sliced

salt and freshly ground black pepper

2 sheets all-butter puff pastry

2 eggs, beaten with a little milk

1 Preheat the oven to 400°F (200°C). Meanwhile, melt the butter in a large frying pan, add the leeks, and fry over high heat for 2 minutes. Cover with a lid, lower the heat, and cook for 10 minutes or until tender.

2 Turn up the heat, stir in the flour, then blend in the apple juice and stock. Bring to a boil, stirring all the time, then add the mushrooms, mustard, thyme, and crème fraîche. Add the chicken, season with salt and freshly ground black pepper, and simmer for 5 minutes. Spoon into the pie dish and set aside to cool.

3 Meanwhile, make the pastry top. On a worktop lightly dusted with flour, roll out the pastry until it is a little bigger than the dish. Cut strips of pastry to the size of the lip of the dish, then wet the lip with water and attach the strips on top. Wet the top of the strips with water, then lay the pastry lid on them and press to seal the edges. Crimp the edges with your fingers.

4 Brush the pastry with the egg and bake in the oven for 35 minutes (1 hour for a large pie for 12—cover it with foil if it begins to get too brown) or until the pastry is crisp and golden and the filling is piping hot.

PREPARE AHEAD AND FREEZE
The pie can be made up to the end of step 3 up to 1 day ahead. Freeze at the end of step 3 for up to 2 months.

A whole lamb shank can look too filling. Our recipe gives guests the option of having half. Serve with mashed potato and cabbage.

Winter lamb shanks

Serves 6

Special equipment *2 quart shallow ovenproof dish*

2 tbsp olive oil
6 lamb shanks, trimmed of any excess fat
2 medium onions, thinly sliced
3 garlic cloves, crushed
¼ cup all-purpose flour
2 cups cold chicken stock
3 tbsp sun-dried (or regular) tomato paste
5fl oz (150ml) red wine or Port
3 tbsp soy sauce
1 tbsp freshly chopped thyme leaves
salt and freshly ground black pepper
1½ tbsp balsamic vinegar

Serves 12

Special equipment *2 x 2 quart shallow ovenproof dishes*

¼ cup olive oil
12 lamb shanks, trimmed of any excess fat
4 medium onions, thinly sliced
6 garlic cloves, crushed
¾ cup all-purpose flour
4 cups cold chicken stock
6 tbsp sun-dried (or regular) tomato paste
10fl oz (300ml) red wine or Port
6 tbsp soy sauce
2 tbsp freshly chopped thyme leaves
salt and freshly ground black pepper
3 tbsp balsamic vinegar

1 Preheat the oven to 325°F (160°C). Heat half the oil in a large deep saucepan or casserole. Brown the shanks all over until golden. Remove and set aside. You may need to do this in batches.

2 Add the remaining oil to the pan, add the onions and garlic, and cook over high heat for 5 minutes or until starting to soften. Put the flour into a pitcher and slowly whisk in the cold stock until smooth. Add to the pan with the tomato paste and red wine or Port and bring to a boil.

3 Return the lamb to the pan, add the soy sauce and thyme, and season with salt and freshly ground black pepper. Stir well, cover with a lid, and transfer to the oven for 3–4 hours (4 hours for 12) or until the meat is tender and starting to fall off the bone. Stir in the vinegar.

4 Remove the shanks from the sauce, wrap in foil, and set aside to cool. Pour the sauce into a 2 quart shallow ovenproof dish (two dishes for 12), cool, and cover with foil. When the sauce and shanks are completely cold, transfer to the fridge overnight.

5 To serve, preheat the oven to 350°F (180°C). Using a spoon, remove the fat from the surface of the sauce and discard. Remove the meat from the bone in one piece, then cut each piece in half. Add to the sauce and cover with foil.

VARIATION
If you don't want to do the second stage of cooking and are happy to present the shanks whole, serve at the end of step 3.

PREPARE AHEAD AND FREEZE
This is best made the day before and reheated.
Freeze for up to six weeks.

This variation on the classic shepherd's pie has a layered topping of potato and cream instead of mash. Serve with a green vegetable.

GREAT FOR A CROWD

Shepherd's pie dauphinois

Serves 6

Special equipment 2 quart shallow wide-based ovenproof dish

2lb (900g) raw ground lamb
2 onions, chopped
2 large carrots, finely diced
½ cup all-purpose flour
10fl oz (300ml) red wine
1¼ cups beef stock
1 tbsp Worcestershire sauce
1 tbsp tomato purée
dash of gravy browning (optional)

salt and freshly ground
   black pepper

For the topping

2lb (900g) Yukon Gold or other
   floury potatoes, cut into
   ⅛in (3mm) slices
1¼ cup heavy cream
2½oz (75g) mature Cheddar
   cheese, grated

Serves 12

Special equipment 2 x 2 quart shallow wide-based ovenproof dishes

4lb (1.8kg) raw ground lamb
4 onions, chopped
4 large carrots, finely diced
½ cup all-purpose flour
20fl oz (600ml) red wine
2 cups beef stock
2 tbsp Worcestershire sauce
2 tbsp tomato purée

dash of gravy browning (optional)
salt and freshly ground
   black pepper

For the topping

4lb (1.8kg) Yukon Gold potatoes
   or other floury potatoes, cut
   into ⅛in (3mm) slices
1¼ cups heavy cream
6oz (175g) mature Cheddar
   cheese, grated

1 Preheat the oven to 325°F (160°C). Meanwhile, put the lamb, onions, and carrots into a deep frying pan or casserole and fry over high heat, stirring frequently, for 5 minutes or until the meat is brown. Drain away any fat.

2 Stir in the flour and, over high heat, add the wine, stock, Worcestershire sauce, and tomato purée (add the gravy browning, too, if you want the sauce to be a rich dark color). Stir until blended, then bring to a boil. Season with salt and freshly ground black pepper, cover with a lid, and transfer to the oven for 1–1½ hours or until the meat is tender.

3 Check the seasoning, then place the meat into the ovenproof dish(es) and set aside to cool. Increase the oven temperature to 425°F (220°C).

4 Put the potatoes in a pan of boiling salted water for 4–5 minutes to blanch them. Drain, refresh in cold water, and dry well with paper towels.

5 Arrange a layer of potato on top of the cold meat, then pour over half the cream and season with salt and freshly ground black pepper. Arrange the remaining potatoes on top, pour over the remaining cream, and sprinkle over the cheese.

6 Bake for 30 minutes (45–50 minutes for 12) or until golden and bubbling.

Great for a crowd... At the end of step 5, brown under the broiler before baking so you'll know the pie is already golden on top. Freezes well.

CHEAT

Liquid gravy browning in bottles can be difficult to track down in the stores these days, but it's well worth the hunt. Not only does it make a sauce or gravy an appetizing rich brown, it saves you time, too, as you don't have to brown the onions for so long. We use it the all of the time.

PREPARE AHEAD AND FREEZE

The pie can be prepared up to the end of step 5 up to 1 day ahead. Freeze for up to 2 months.

Shepherd's pie dauphinois (see overleaf) ●●●>

Although there are many trendy new lasagnas out there, we are often asked for a classic lasagna. This is a recipe we've perfected over the years. Leave it to stand for six hours before cooking.

GREAT FOR A CROWD

Classic beef lasagna

Serves 6

Special equipment *2 quart shallow wide-based ovenproof dish*

1 tbsp sunflower oil
2lb (900g) raw ground beef
2 onions, roughly chopped
4 celery stalks, diced
2 garlic cloves, crushed
2 level tbsp all-purpose flour
2 x 14oz cans chopped tomatoes
¾ cup beef stock
3 tbsp tomato purée
1 tsp sugar
1 tbsp freshly chopped
  thyme leaves

For the white sauce

3 tbsp butter
3 tbsp all-purpose flour
3 cups hot milk
2 tsp Dijon mustard
1¾oz (50g) Parmesan cheese,
  freshly grated
salt and freshly ground
  black pepper

18–24 lasagna noodles
  (pre-cooked or no-boil variety)
85g (3oz) mature Cheddar
  cheese, grated

Serves 12

Special equipment *2 x 2 quart shallow wide-based ovenproof dishes or 1 x 3 quart dish*

1 tbsp sunflower oil
4lb (1.8kg) raw ground beef
4 onions, roughly chopped
8 celery stalks, diced
4 garlic cloves, crushed
¼ cup all-purpose flour
4 x 14oz cans chopped tomatoes
1¼ cups beef stock
6 tbsp tomato purée
2 tsp sugar
2 tbsp freshly chopped
  thyme leaves

For the white sauce

6 tbsp butter
6 tbsp all-purpose flour
5½ cups hot milk
1 heaped tbsp Dijon mustard
3½oz (100g) Parmesan cheese,
  freshly grated
salt and freshly ground
  black pepper

36–48 lasagna noodles
  (pre-cooked or no-boil variety)
6oz (175g) mature Cheddar
  cheese, grated

1 Preheat the oven to 325°F (160°C). Heat the oil in a large frying pan until hot, then add the beef and cook until brown all over. Stir in the onions, celery, and garlic.

2 Add the flour and stir to coat the vegetables and beef, then blend in the tomatoes, stock, tomato purée, sugar, and thyme. Bring to a boil, cover with a lid, then transfer to the oven for 1–1½ hours or until the beef is tender.

3 Meanwhile, make the white sauce. Melt the butter in a saucepan, add the flour, and cook over the heat for 1 minute. Slowly add the hot milk, whisking until the sauce is thick and smooth. Add the mustard and Parmesan cheese and season well with salt and freshly ground black pepper.

4 Remove the meat sauce from the oven and put one-third into the base of the ovenproof dish (two dishes for 12). Spoon one-third of the white sauce on top and arrange a layer of noodles on top of that. Season with salt and freshly ground black pepper.

5 Spoon half the remaining meat sauce on top, then half the remaining white sauce. Put another layer of noodles on top and season with salt and freshly ground black pepper. Add the rest of the meat sauce followed by the rest of the white sauce.

6 Sprinkle over the Cheddar cheese, then transfer to the fridge for a minimum of 6 hours before cooking so the pasta has chance to soften.

7 To serve, preheat the oven to 400°F (200°C), then cook the lasagna in the middle of the oven for 45 minutes (1 hour for 12) or until golden brown on top, bubbling around the edges, and the pasta is soft.

Great for a crowd... Make a batch of meat sauce, using just enough oil to coat the bottom of the pan. Make a batch of white sauce, then assemble the lasagnas. Freezes well.

PREPARE AHEAD AND FREEZE
The lasagna can be made up to the end of step 6 up to 2 days ahead. Freeze the lasagna at the end of step 6 for up to 2 months.

"It's good to have a few of these lasagnas ready and waiting in the freezer. They are wonderful for big events like buffets and pot luck parties and are always a huge success."

MAKING THE WHITE SAUCE

STEP 1 Melt the butter in a fairly large saucepan, add the flour, and cook for 1 minute, stirring.

STEP 2 Gradually blend in the hot milk, whisking all the time until the mixture bubbles and thickens.

A lasagna with wow factor. The secret ingredient is butternut squash. Prepare the dish the day before if you can, so the lasagna sheets have time to soften in the sauce. Serve with salad and crusty bread.

Butternut squash lasagna

Serves 6

Special equipment *2 quart shallow wide-based ovenproof dish*

1 tbsp olive oil

8oz (225g) butternut squash (peeled weight), chopped into small cubes (see page 229)

1 red pepper, halved, seeded, and diced

1 onion, roughly chopped

2 garlic cloves, crushed

8oz (225g) cremini mushrooms, sliced

2 x 14oz cans chopped tomatoes

1 tbsp tomato purée

2 tsp sugar

1 tbsp freshly chopped thyme

salt and freshly ground black pepper

3½oz (100g) spinach, chopped

24–30 no-cook lasagna noodles

For the white sauce

5 tbsp butter

5 tbsp all-purpose flour

3 cups hot milk

2 tsp Dijon mustard

3½oz (100g) Gruyère cheese, grated

9oz (250g) mozzarella, chopped into small cubes

Serves 12

Special equipment *2 x 2 quart shallow wide-based ovenproof dishes or 1 x 3 quart shallow wide-based ovenproof dish*

2 tbsp olive oil

1lb 2oz (500g) butternut squash (peeled weight), chopped into small cubes (see page 229)

2 red peppers, halved, seeded, and diced

2 onions, roughly chopped

4 garlic cloves, crushed

1lb 2oz (500g) cremini mushrooms, sliced

4 x 14oz cans chopped tomatoes

2 tbsp tomato purée

1 heaped tbsp sugar

2 tbsp freshly chopped thyme

salt and freshly ground black pepper

7oz (200g) spinach, chopped

40–50 no-cook lasagna noodles

For the white sauce

1½ sticks butter

¾ cup all-purpose flour

6 cups hot milk

1 heaped tbsp Dijon mustard

7oz (200g) Gruyère cheese, grated

1lb 2oz (500g) mozzarella, chopped into small cubes

1 Heat the oil in a large deep frying pan. Add the squash, pepper, onion, and garlic and fry over moderate heat for 4–5 minutes or until the onion is starting to soften. Add the mushrooms, tomatoes, tomato purée, sugar, thyme, and some salt and freshly ground black pepper. Cover with a lid and simmer over low heat for 20–30 minutes (35–40 minutes for 12) or until the vegetables are tender. Add the spinach and toss together until just wilted.

2 Meanwhile, make the white sauce. Melt the butter in a saucepan, add the flour, and stir over the heat for 1 minute. Slowly whisk in the hot milk until the sauce is smooth and thick. Season with salt and freshly ground black pepper, then stir in the mustard and half the Gruyère.

3 Spoon one-third of the tomato sauce over the base of the ovenproof dish, then spoon one-third of the white sauce on top. Arrange a single layer of lasagna noodles over the white sauce and scatter over half the mozzarella. Spoon half the remaining tomato sauce on top, followed by half the remaining white sauce. Arrange another layer of lasagna on top and scatter over the remaining mozzarella. Spread the rest of the tomato sauce on top, followed by the rest of the white sauce, then sprinkle with the remaining Gruyère.

4 Transfer to the fridge for at least 6 hours or overnight so the lasagna starts to soften.

5 To serve, preheat the oven to 400°F (200°C), then bake the lasagna for 45 minutes (1–1¼ hours for 12) or until golden brown and bubbling around the edges.

PREPARE AHEAD AND FREEZE
The lasagna can be made up to the end of step 3 up to 2 days ahead. Freeze for up to 2 months.

Buy mozzarella in a brick rather than a ball for this—it is far easier to cut into small pieces. You can use rigatoni or penne for this recipe. Serve with dressed salad.

Pasta and meatball bake with tomato and basil sauce

Serves 6

Special equipment 2 quart shallow wide-based ovenproof dish

For the sauce

1 tbsp olive oil
1 large onion, finely chopped
1 red chile, halved, seeded, and finely chopped
2 garlic cloves, crushed
28oz can chopped tomatoes
2 tbsp tomato purée
salt and freshly ground black pepper
2 tbsp coarsely chopped fresh basil
a dash of sugar (optional)

For the meatballs

1lb (450g) good-quality bulk sausagemeat
scant 1oz (25g) fresh fine breadcrumbs
1¾oz (50g) freshly grated Parmesan cheese
2 tbsp finely chopped fresh basil
1¾oz (50g) mozzarella, cut into about 30 cubes

1 tbsp olive oil
8oz (225g) rigatoni pasta
1¾oz (50g) Parmesan cheese, freshly grated
1¾oz (50g) mozzarella, chopped into small pieces

Serves 12

Special equipment 2 x 2 quart shallow wide-based ovenproof dishes or 1 x 3 quart dish

For the sauce

2 tbsp olive oil
2 large onions, finely chopped
2 red chiles, halved, seeded, and finely chopped
4 garlic cloves, crushed
2 x 28oz cans chopped tomatoes
3 tbsp tomato purée
salt and freshly ground black pepper
3 tbsp coarsely chopped fresh basil
a dash of sugar (optional)

For the meatballs

2lb (900g) good-quality bulk sausagemeat
1¾oz (50g) fresh fine breadcrumbs
3½oz (100g) freshly grated Parmesan cheese
¼ cup finely chopped fresh basil
3½oz (100g) mozzarella, cut into about 60 cubes

1 tbsp olive oil
1lb (450g) rigatoni pasta
3½oz (100g) Parmesan cheese, freshly grated
3½oz (100g) mozzarella, chopped into small pieces

1 Preheat the oven to 400°F (200°C). Meanwhile, put the oil for the sauce into a deep saucepan, add the onion, and fry over high heat for a few minutes or until softened slightly but not colored.

2 Add the chile and garlic and fry over high heat for a few minutes. Add the tomatoes and tomato purée, then season with salt and freshly ground black pepper. Bring to a boil, cover with a lid, then lower the heat and simmer for 15 minutes. Add the basil and taste—if it is a little sharp, add a dash of sugar.

3 Meanwhile, make the meatballs. Put the sausagement, breadcrumbs, Parmesan, and basil into a mixing bowl. Mix together with your hands, season with salt and freshly ground black pepper, and shape into 30 balls (60 for 12). Using your finger, make a hole in the middle of each meatball, then push a cube of mozzarella into the center and reshape so the mozzarella is hidden inside.

4 Heat the oil in a large frying pan and fry the meatballs for 4 minutes or until they are golden brown all over and just cooked through. You may need to do this in batches.

5 Meanwhile, cook the pasta in boiling salted water according to the package instructions until just tender. Drain, refresh in cold water, and dry well with paper towels.

6 Stir the pasta into the sauce and season with salt and freshly ground black pepper. Stir in the meatballs, then spoon into the ovenproof dish and sprinkle the Parmesan cheese and mozzarella on top.

7 Bake for 20–25 minutes (45 minutes for 12) or until golden brown on top and piping hot in the center.

Great for a crowd... Make a batch of tomato sauce. Make the meatballs, but leave out the mozzarella in the center, as it will take too long to do. Cook the pasta, then assemble the bakes.

PREPARE AHEAD
You can make the bake up to the end of step
6 up to 8 hours ahead. Not suitable for freezing.

"This is a perfect all-in-one dish of pasta, meatballs, and tomato sauce. Each meatball is stuffed with mozzarella to give a lovely surprise when you bite into it. Enjoy!"

CHOPPING BASIL LEAVES

STEP 1 Gather the basil leaves together in two small piles. Roll one pile of leaves up tightly into a ball.

STEP 2 Slice across to make shreds. Gather together, turn 90° and chop small. Repeat with the other pile.

Half a small butternut squash per person is ideal at lunchtime or even as a main meal. Serve with dressed salad and bread.

Butternut squash with spinach and bacon

Serves 6

3 x 14oz (400g) butternut squash, halved lengthwise through the stalk and seeds and fibers discarded (see page 229)

2 tbsp olive oil

½ cup of water

salt and freshly ground black pepper

7oz smoked slab bacon, cut into small pieces

2 leeks, sliced

9oz (250g) cremini mushrooms, quartered

3½oz (100g) baby spinach

½ cup heavy cream

2½oz (75g) Parmesan cheese, freshly grated

freshly chopped parsley, to garnish

Serves 12

6 x 14oz (400g) butternut squash, halved lengthwise through the stalk and seeds and fibers discarded (see page 229)

¼ cup olive oil

¾ cup water

salt and freshly ground black pepper

14oz smoked smoked slab bacon, cut into small pieces

4 leeks, sliced

1lb 2oz (500g) cremini mushrooms, quartered

7oz (200g) baby spinach

1 cup heavy cream

6oz (175g) Parmesan cheese, freshly grated

freshly chopped parsley, to garnish

1 Preheat the oven to 400°F (200°C). Put the squash cut side up in a large roasting pan (two pans for 12) and drizzle over the oil. Pour the water around them, season with salt and freshly ground black pepper, and roast in the oven for 45 minutes (1 hour for 12) or until the flesh is soft. Set aside and allow to cool slightly.

2 Meanwhile, put the bacon into a dry frying pan and stir over medium heat until the fat comes out. Add the leeks and cook slowly for 10 minutes or until soft. Add the mushrooms and spinach and stir together over high heat for 10 minutes or until the spinach has wilted and the mushrooms are nearly cooked.

3 Remove the pan from the heat and stir in the cream, some salt and freshly ground black pepper, and half the cheese. Scoop out some of the cooked squash, leaving a ¾in (2cm) border inside each squash case, and stir into the spinach mixture. Spoon the mixture into the squash cases and sprinkle over the remaining cheese.

4 Bake for 20–25 minutes (55 minutes for 12) or until golden on top and heated through. Garnish with a sprinkle of parsley and serve.

PREPARE AHEAD
The squash can be prepared up to the end of step 3 up to 1 day ahead. Not suitable for freezing.

This is a winning recipe for vegetarians and perfect for a summer lunch with a green salad and crusty bread.

Eggplant baked with feta and chickpeas

Serves 6

3 medium eggplants, sliced in half lengthwise

2 tbsp olive oil

salt and freshly ground black pepper

1 large onion, roughly chopped

2 garlic cloves, crushed

14oz can chopped tomatoes

14oz can chickpeas, drained and rinsed

2 tbsp sun-dried tomato paste

1¾oz (50g) pitted black or green olives, sliced in half

small bunch of fresh mint, chopped

3½oz (100g) feta cheese, crumbled

Serves 12

6 medium eggplants, sliced in half lengthwise

4 tbsp olive oil

salt and freshly ground black pepper

2 large onions, roughly chopped

4 garlic cloves, crushed

2 x 400g cans chopped tomatoes

2 x 400g cans chickpeas, drained and rinsed

4 tbsp sun-dried tomato paste

100g (3½oz) pitted black or green olives, sliced in half

large bunch of fresh mint, chopped

200g (7oz) feta cheese, crumbled

1 Preheat the oven to 400°F (200°C). Put the eggplant cut side up in a roasting pan. Drizzle over half the oil, season with salt and freshly ground black pepper, and bake for 25 minutes (40 minutes for 12) or until the flesh is tender. Remove from the oven and leave to cool.

2 Heat the remaining oil in a frying pan. Add the onion and garlic and cook for 10 minutes or until soft. Add the tomatoes, chickpeas, tomato paste, and olives, and simmer for 5 minutes.

3 Meanwhile, scoop out a little of the flesh from the eggplant halves, leaving a ½in (1cm) border inside the eggplant cases. Add the flesh to the chickpea mixture and mix together. Add the mint and half the feta and season with salt and freshly ground black pepper. Spoon the mixture into the eggplant cases and top with the remaining feta.

4 Bake in the oven for 20 minutes (35 minutes for 12) or until the feta is tinged brown and the eggplants are hot.

PREPARE AHEAD

The dish can be assembled up to the end of step 3 up to 1 day ahead. Not suitable for freezing.

Use your favorite sausages for this smokey casserole. We like pork and leek. Serve with a green vegetable.

Smokey sausage cassoulet

Serves 6

3 tbsp olive oil

12 sausages

4 large onions, sliced

2 tsp paprika

1¾oz (50g) chorizo, very finely chopped

2 x 14oz cans chopped tomatoes

2 tbsp tomato purée

2 tbsp Worcestershire sauce

2 tsp balsamic vinegar

salt and freshly ground black pepper

14oz can butter beans, drained and rinsed

Serves 12

5 tbsp olive oil

24 sausages

7 large onions, sliced

4 tsp paprika

3½oz (100g) chorizo, very finely chopped

4 x 14oz cans chopped tomatoes

¼ cup tomato purée

¼ cup Worcestershire sauce

1 tbsp balsamic vinegar

salt and freshly ground black pepper

2 x 14oz cans butter beans, drained and rinsed

1 Heat 1 tablespoon of the oil in a large non-stick frying pan or casserole dish over high heat, then brown the sausages until golden on all sides. Remove with a slotted spoon and set aside. You may need to do this in batches.

2 Add the remaining oil to the pan and fry the onions for a few minutes or until lightly golden. Add the remaining ingredients (except the butter beans and sausages) and season with salt and freshly ground black pepper.

3 Simmer over a gentle heat for 20–25 minutes or until the onions are nearly soft. Add the butter beans and stir.

4 Arrange the sausages on top, cover with a lid, and cook for 20 minutes (35–40 minutes for 12) or until the sausages are completely cooked.

VARIATION

The dish is especially popular with the young. If you know they like baked beans, you can substitute them for the butter beans.

PREPARE AHEAD

The cassoulet can be made up to the end of step 3 up to 1 day ahead. Alternatively, cook it completely and reheat to serve. Not suitable for freezing.

All Italian

In Italy, eating is such a relaxed communal affair, centered around family and friends. Here, we've brought together some of the best-loved dishes Italians serve when they're cooking for a crowd.

All Italian

There's something so wonderful about Italian cooking. Maybe it's because the dishes are so simple, honest, and straightforward. Or perhaps it's because the Italians use only the finest ingredients and never overload them with fussy sauces.

Lunch is the most important meal of the day—so much so that at noon the country almost comes to a standstill. Pasta or risotto is eaten as a first course, followed by a second course of meat or fish served with salad or vegetables.

We are less traditional about this and offer one of these courses as a main meal—either in the evening or at lunchtime. Served in slightly larger portions, an Italian "first course" of pasta or risotto makes an elegant and crowd-pleasing dish—likewise a "second course" of chicken stuffed with pork sausagemeat or chicken casseroled in a gutsy tomato sauce.

Dried pasta vs. fresh pasta

Pasta is so endlessly versatile, teaming well with almost every ingredient under the sun. In the recipes in this chapter, we serve it with fish, seafood, cheese, and tomatoes, as well as with a classic bolognese sauce.

We always use dried pasta—as the Italians do—it's so convenient to have in the house. But you can use fresh pasta if you prefer, although its texture is not always so good. Our pasta of choice is a trusted Italian brand, made from 100 percent durum wheat ("semola di grano duro"). It keeps for several months in a tightly closed package.

"Pasta is so endlessly versatile, teaming well with almost every ingredient under the sun. In this chapter, we serve it with fish, seafood, cheese, and tomatoes."

Perfect pasta every time

The golden rule when cooking pasta is to use a very large pan and plenty of water and salt—at least 2 liters (4½ pints) water and 2 tsp salt for every 8oz (225g) pasta. It's important to get it right at this stage because you can't season pasta once it's cooked. Some people also swear by a splash of oil to stop the pasta sticking, but in our experience it makes no difference at all because it simply makes its way to the surface, where it floats.

● Start by bringing the salted water to a boil. Add the pasta and stir to separate. If you are cooking spaghetti, let the ends soften, then push the strands slowly against the side of the pan, twisting and lowering them into the water as you do so.

● Cover the pan with a lid so the water returns to a boil as quickly as possible, then reduce the heat so it is bubbling briskly. Remove the lid and cook, uncovered, according to the timings on the package.

● To test if the pasta is cooked, lift a piece out and bite it—it should be tender but still a little firm. The Italians call this "al dente".

● Pour the contents of the pan into a large colander and shake it to drain the pasta well. It is now ready to serve, with or without a sauce.

● If you're preparing the pasta ahead of time, cook it until "al dente", then drain and refresh first under running warm water and then under cold water. Don't leave it sitting in the water in the pan or it will disintegrate. To reheat, plunge it into boiling water for a minute or until heated through, then drain.

Adding the sauce

● If you're serving the pasta with a sauce, make sure the frying pan or saucepan you're making the sauce in is large enough to accommodate the pasta as well.

● Add the pasta to the sauce and not the sauce to the pasta. That way, you can work it in gradually without it sticking.

Risottos are popular with everyone, and this version, full of flavor and bright healthy vegetables, is great for vegetarians. Serve hot with fresh salad leaves.

Roasted vegetable risotto

Serves 6

8oz (225g) butternut squash, peeled and cut into ¾in (2cm) cubes (see page 229)

1 onion, coarsely chopped

1 small eggplant, cut into ½in (1cm) cubes

1 small red pepper, halved, seeded, and cut into ½in (1cm) cubes

3 tbsp olive oil

salt and freshly ground black pepper

2 tsp freshly chopped thyme leaves

11oz (300g) risotto rice

8oz (225g) cremini mushrooms, sliced

1 quart hot vegetable stock

1¾oz (50g) Parmesan cheese, made into small shavings with a vegetable peeler

2 tbsp freshly snipped chives

Serves 12

1lb (450g) butternut squash, peeled and cut into ¾in (2cm) cubes (see page 229)

2 onions, coarsely chopped

2 small eggplants, cut into ½in (1cm) cubes

2 small red peppers, halved, seeded, and cut into ½in (1cm) cubes

6 tbsp olive oil

salt and freshly ground black pepper

1 heaped tbsp freshly chopped thyme leaves

1lb 5oz (600g) risotto rice

1lb (450g) cremini mushrooms, sliced

2 quarts hot vegetable stock

3½oz (100g) Parmesan cheese, made into small shavings with a vegetable peeler

¼ cup freshly snipped chives

1 Preheat the oven to 400°F (200°C). Put the squash, onion, eggplant, and pepper into a large roasting pan (two pans for 12) in a single layer.

2 Pour over a third of the oil and toss well with your hands. Season with salt and freshly ground black pepper, then sprinkle over the thyme.

3 Roast for 30 minutes (35 minutes for 12) or until tender and golden.

4 Heat the remaining oil in a deep saucepan, add the rice, then stir in the mushrooms and gradually add the stock (see right).

5 When all the stock has been absorbed and the rice is cooked, stir in the roasted vegetables and half the Parmesan. Transfer to a serving dish and sprinkle with the remaining Parmesan and the chives.

PREPARE AHEAD
The vegetables can be roasted up to 8 hours ahead. Not suitable for freezing.

MAKING A RISOTTO

STEP 1 Heat the oil in a deep pan over high heat, add the rice, and stir to coat. Add the mushrooms.

STEP 2 Add the hot stock a ladleful at a time. Stir continuously and only add more when it's been absorbed.

Mary's sister-in-law, Margaret, made this for 90 people for a charity lunch recently and it was a triumph. Serve with new potatoes.

Sardinian chicken

Serves 6

2 tbsp olive oil

2½oz (75g) pancetta, cut into strips

6 large chicken thighs (bone in), skinned

1 large onion, chopped

1 small red pepper, halved, seeded, and diced

3 garlic cloves, crushed

8oz (225g) button mushrooms, quartered

4fl oz (120ml) red wine

1 level tbsp all-purpose flour

14oz can chopped tomatoes

5 tbsp tomato purée

salt and freshly ground black pepper

1 tsp freshly chopped thyme leaves

grated zest of 1 lemon

2 tbsp capers, drained and chopped

Serves 12

¼ cup olive oil

6oz (175g) pancetta, cut into strips

12 large chicken thighs (bone in), skinned

2 large onions, chopped

1 large red pepper, halved, seeded and diced

6 garlic cloves, crushed

1lb (450g) button mushrooms, quartered

8fl oz (250ml) red wine

1 heaped tbsp all-purpose flour

2 x 14oz cans chopped tomatoes

¾ cup tomato purée

salt and freshly ground black pepper

2 tsp freshly chopped thyme leaves

grated zest of 2 lemons

¼ cup capers, drained and chopped

1 Preheat the oven to 350°F (180°C). Heat half the oil in a large deep frying pan or casserole, add the pancetta and chicken, and cook over high heat for a few minutes or until the pancetta is crisp and the chicken golden all over. You may need to do this in batches. Remove with a slotted spoon and set aside.

2 Add the remaining oil to the pan, followed by the onion, pepper, garlic, and mushrooms, and fry for a few minutes or until starting to soften.

3 Put the wine into a pitcher and blend to a smooth paste with the flour.

4 Add the tomatoes and tomato purée to the pan, then blend in the wine mixture, season with salt and freshly ground black pepper, and bring to a boil. Return the chicken and pancetta to the pan, add the thyme, lemon zest, and capers, and bring to a boil.

5 Cover with a lid and transfer to the oven for 1 hour (1¼ hours for 12) or until the chicken is tender. Serve piping hot.

Great for a crowd... This is perfect for making in one large batch if you have a pan or casserole big enough. Brown the chicken in batches beforehand. And make sure it is completely tender when you take it out of the oven.

VARIATION

You can use boned thighs if you prefer. They'll take about 30 minutes less to cook.

PREPARE AHEAD AND FREEZE

The casserole can be made up to 2 days ahead.

Freeze for up to 2 months.

If time is short, you can use peppers from a jar for this. Serve with rice or mashed potatoes and a green vegetable.

Italian farmhouse chicken

Serves 6

1 tbsp olive oil
1 large onion, coarsely chopped
2 garlic cloves, crushed
2 x 14oz cans chopped tomatoes
2 tbsp tomato purée
1 tsp sugar
salt and freshly ground
    black pepper
3 red peppers, cut in half
    and seeded

For the stuffing

1lb (450g) pork sausagemeat
finely grated zest of ½ lemon
small bunch of basil leaves, torn
1 tbsp Dijon mustard

12 boneless skinless
    chicken thighs

Serves 12

2 tbsp olive oil
2 large onions, coarsely chopped
4 garlic cloves, crushed
4 x 14oz cans chopped tomatoes
¼ cup tomato purée
2 tsp sugar
salt and freshly ground
    black pepper
6 red peppers, cut in half
    and seeded

For the stuffing

2lb (900g) pork sausagemeat
finely grated zest of 1 lemon
large bunch of basil leaves, torn
2 tbsp Dijon mustard

24 boneless skinless
    chicken thighs

1 Preheat the oven to 400°F (200°C). Heat the oil in a frying pan, add the onion and garlic, and fry over high heat for a few minutes or until lightly golden. Stir in the tomatoes, tomato purée, and sugar, season with salt and freshly ground black pepper, and bring to a boil. Cover with a lid and simmer for 25 minutes or until the onion is tender.

2 Meanwhile, arrange the peppers cut side down on a baking sheet and bake for 20 minutes or until the skin has started to blacken. Transfer to a plastic bag, seal the top, and set aside (this makes it easier to remove the skin). Once cool, peel and cut each half in two.

3 To make the stuffing, put the sausagemeat into a mixing bowl, add the lemon zest, basil, and mustard, season with salt and freshly ground black pepper, and mix well. Divide the mixture into 12 (24 for 12) and shape into little sausages.

4 Place the chicken thighs skinned side down on a board, open them up flat, and bash with a rolling pin to make them a little thinner (see right). Make sure each thigh is the same thickness. Season with salt and freshly ground black pepper.

5 Place a slice of pepper on each thigh, add one of the sausages, and roll the thigh up. Repeat with the other thighs. Arrange join side down in a single layer in a shallow ovenproof dish and pour over the tomato sauce.

6 Bake for 40–45 minutes (45–50 minutes for 12) or until bubbling and the chicken is cooked.

PREPARING THE THIGHS

Place the chicken thigh on a cutting board between sheets of plastic wrap and flatten with a rolling pin.

PREPARE AHEAD AND FREEZE

The chicken thighs can be prepared up to the end of step 5 up to 12 hours ahead. Freeze the uncooked stuffed rolled chicken thighs for up to 2 months.

These look so lovely and the soft-yolked quail's eggs on top are an extra treat. Marinated and grilled eggplants may be available from the deli counter of the supermarket.

Mini eggplant and arugula pizzas

Serves 6

Special equipment 4in (10cm) round cutter

2 x 5½oz frozen pizza crusts, thawed

½ cup tomato purée

2 tbsp tomato paste

salt and freshly ground black pepper

7oz marinated and grilled eggplant, drained (oil reserved) and sliced

3½oz (100g) Gruyère cheese, grated

6 quail's eggs

1¾oz (50g) arugula

Serves 12

Special equipment 4in (10cm) round cutter

4 x 5½oz frozen pizza crusts, thawed

1 cup tomato purée

¼ cup tomato paste

salt and freshly ground black pepper

14oz marinated and grilled eggplant, drained (oil reserved) and sliced

8oz (225g) Gruyère cheese, grated

12 quail's eggs

3½oz (100g) arugula

1 Preheat the oven to 400°F (200°C). Using a 4in (10cm) round cutter, cut three circles from each pizza crust and arrange on a baking sheet (two baking sheets for 12).

2 Put the tomato purée into a bowl, add the tomato paste, season with salt and freshly ground black pepper, and mix well. Spread over the base of each dough circle.

3 Arrange the eggplant slices over the tomato and sprinkle with the cheese. Using the back of a tablespoon, make a well in the center of each pizza, ready for the egg to sit in.

4 Bake for 8 minutes (10 minutes for 12) or until the pizzas are very hot, then carefully crack an egg into the well in each one, keeping the yolk intact. Return to the oven for 3 minutes or until the pizza is lightly golden, the egg white completely cooked, and the yolk just set.

5 Transfer to serving plates, arrange some arugula on top of each pizza, and drizzle with a little of the reserved eggplant oil. Serve at once.

PIZZA CRUST

Look for pre-formed unbaked pizza crusts in the freezer section of the supermarket. Thaw the crusts before using.

PREPARE AHEAD AND FREEZE

The pizzas can be made up to the end of step 3 up to 8 hours ahead. Freeze at the end of step 3 for up to 2 months.

This is a traditional bolognese sauce, with chicken livers for a lovely depth of flavor. It's well worth making double the quantity, so you can freeze a batch for another day.

Classic spaghetti bolognese

Serves 6

1 tbsp sunflower oil

7oz (200g) fresh chicken livers, trimmed of any sinew and cut into small pieces

2lb (900g) raw lean ground beef

2 onions, finely chopped

2 garlic cloves, crushed

3½fl oz (100ml) Port

2 x 14oz cans chopped tomatoes

3 tbsp tomato purée

1 tsp sugar

salt and freshly ground black pepper

11oz (300g) spaghetti

Serves 12

2 tbsp sunflower oil

1lb (450g) fresh chicken livers, trimmed of any sinew and cut into small pieces

4lb (1.8kg) raw lean ground beef

4 onions, finely chopped

4 garlic cloves, crushed

7fl oz (200ml) Port

4 x 14oz cans chopped tomatoes

6 tbsp tomato purée

2 tsp sugar

salt and freshly ground black pepper

1lb 5oz (600g) spaghetti

1 Preheat the oven to 325°F (160°C). Heat the oil in a large non-stick frying pan over high heat, add the chicken livers, and brown quickly all over. Remove with a slotted spoon and set aside.

2 Add the ground beef in batches and brown all over, adding a little more oil if the pan is getting dry. Return the chicken livers to the pan along with all the beef.

3 Add the onions and garlic and fry for 2 minutes. Stir in the Port, tomatoes, tomato purée, and sugar and bring to a boil. Season with salt and freshly ground black pepper, cover with a lid, and transfer to the oven for 1–1¼ hours or until tender.

4 To serve, cook the spaghetti in boiling salted water according to the package instructions. Drain well, transfer to a serving bowl, and top with the bolognese sauce.

PREPARE AHEAD AND FREEZE

The sauce can be made up to 2 days ahead.
Freeze for up to 3 months.

We usually buy ready-peeled shrimp for this, but if you can only find them with their shells on, buy a few extra and do it yourself—they're very easy to peel. Serve with dressed salad.

Seafood linguine

Serves 6

8oz (225g) dried linguine

salt and freshly ground black pepper

small pat of butter

5½oz (150g) (shelled weight) raw tiger shrimp

5½oz (150g) raw squid, sliced

5½oz (150g) raw sea scallops, sliced in half horizontally

1 large shallot, finely chopped

8fl oz (250ml) dry white wine

7fl oz (200ml) heavy cream

juice of 1 large lemon

small bunch of dill, chopped

Serves 12

1lb (450g) dried linguine

salt and freshly ground black pepper

large pat of butter

11oz (300g) (shelled weight) raw tiger shrimp

11oz (300g) raw squid, sliced

11oz (300g) raw sea scallops, sliced in half horizontally

2 large shallots, finely chopped

20fl oz (600ml) dry white wine

15fl oz (450ml) heavy cream

juice of 2 large lemons

large bunch of dill, chopped

1 Cook the linguine in boiling salted water according to package instructions. Drain well.

2 Heat the butter in a large frying pan, add the shrimp, squid, and scallops, and fry for 3–4 minutes or until the shrimp have turned pink and the squid and scallops are just cooked. Remove with a slotted spoon and set aside.

3 Add the shallot and wine to the pan, bring to a boil, and allow to bubble over high heat until the wine has reduced by half. Add the cream and return to a boil.

4 Add the cooked seafood and toss together. Season with salt and freshly ground black pepper, stir in the pasta, lemon juice, and dill, heat through thoroughly, and serve.

PREPARE AHEAD

The dish is best prepared and served immediately. Not suitable for freezing.

PEELING SHRIMP

STEP 1 Start by pulling off the head of the shrimp, then peel off the shell and legs with your fingers.

STEP 2 If the shrimp are large, slice along the back and remove the dark intestinal vein. This step is optional.

This is a budget recipe. A sort of upmarket macaroni cheese—perfect for a crowd of hungry teenagers—and one they could very easily cook for themselves. Serve with dressed salad.

Penne alla parmigiana

Serves 6

Special equipment *1½ quart shallow ovenproof dish*

12oz (350g) penne
salt and freshly ground black pepper
3 tbsp butter
3 tbsp all-purpose flour
1 quart hot milk

1 tbsp Dijon mustard
3½oz (100g) strong Cheddar cheese, grated
3½oz (100g) Parmesan cheese, freshly grated
6 tomatoes, halved, seeded, and roughly chopped

Serves 12

Special equipment *2 quart shallow ovenproof dish*

1lb 5oz (600g) penne
salt and freshly ground black pepper
6 tbsp butter
¾ cup all-purpose flour
6 cups hot milk

2 tbsp Dijon mustard
6oz (175g) strong Cheddar cheese, grated
6oz (175g) Parmesan cheese, freshly grated
8 large tomatoes, halved, seeded, and roughly chopped

1 Preheat the oven to 400°F (200°C). Cook the penne in boiling salted water according to the package instructions. Drain and refresh in cold water.

2 Melt the butter in a large saucepan, add the flour, and stir over the heat for 1 minute. Gradually add the milk, whisking all the time, until the sauce is smooth and thick.

3 Add the mustard and two-thirds of the Cheddar and Parmesan, then add the penne and some salt and freshly ground black pepper.

4 Spoon into the ovenproof dish, arrange the tomatoes on top, and sprinkle over the remaining cheese.

5 Bake for 20–25 minutes (35–40 minutes for 12) or until lightly golden and crispy.

PREPARE AHEAD
The dish can be made up to the end of step 4 up to 1 day ahead. Not suitable for freezing.

PREPARING TOMATOES

STEP 1 Halve the tomato, loosen the seeds with a teaspoon, then gently squeeze them out into a bowl.

STEP 2 Place cut side down on a board and slice into strips. Cut across the strips if you want dice.

This full-flavored tomato and garlic sauce with a hint of chili is excellent with spaghetti. The breadcrumbs give a lovely crispy texture—make sure they are very fine. Serve with dressed salad.

Spaghetti with jumbo shrimp and tomatoes

Serves 6

11oz (300g) spaghetti

salt and freshly ground black pepper

¼ cup olive oil

1¾oz (50g) very fine fresh brown breadcrumbs

finely grated zest and juice of 1 lemon

1 large shallot, finely chopped

4 garlic cloves, crushed

1 red chile, halved, seeded, and finely diced

11oz (300g) peeled cooked jumbo shrimp

6 large ripe tomatoes, halved, seeded, and roughly chopped

1 large bunch of flat-leaf parsley, chopped

freshly grated Parmesan cheese, to serve

Serves 12

1lb 5oz (600g) spaghetti

salt and freshly ground black pepper

7 tbsp olive oil

3½oz (100g) very fine fresh brown breadcrumbs

finely grated zest and juice of 2 lemons

2 large shallots, finely chopped

8 garlic cloves, crushed

2 red chiles, halved, seeded, and finely diced

1lb 5oz (600g) peeled cooked jumbo shrimp

12 large ripe tomatoes, halved, seeded, and roughly chopped

1 very large bunch of flat-leaf parsley, chopped

freshly grated Parmesan cheese, to serve

1 Cook the spaghetti in boiling salted water according to package instructions. Drain well.

2 Heat 1 tablespoon of the oil (1½ tablespoons for 12) in a deep frying pan, add the breadcrumbs and lemon zest, and fry for 1 minute or until crispy. Remove with a slotted spoon and set aside.

3 Add the remaining oil to the pan, stir in the shallot, garlic, and chile and fry for 3–4 minutes or until starting to soften.

4 Stir in the shrimp and tomatoes, then add the parsley and lemon juice.

5 Stir in the spaghetti, season with salt and freshly ground black pepper, and heat through thoroughly. Stir in the breadcrumbs and serve immediately with the Parmesan.

PREPARE AHEAD

This is best prepared and served immediately.
Not suitable for freezing.

Spaghetti with jumbo shrimp and tomatoes (see overleaf) •••>

Penne are one of our favorite kinds of pasta because sauces cling really well to the quill shape. But you can use spaghetti if you prefer. Serve with dressed salad.

Penne with asparagus and dolcelatte

Serves 6

12oz (350g) asparagus spears

12oz (350g) penne

salt and freshly ground black pepper

1 tbsp olive oil

9oz (250g) small portabella mushrooms, sliced

1 garlic clove, crushed

¾ cup heavy cream

3½oz (100g) dolcelatte cheese, cut into small cubes

small bunch of basil, chopped

Serves 12

1lb 5oz (600g) asparagus spears

1lb 5oz (600g) penne

salt and freshly ground black pepper

2 tbsp olive oil

1lb 2oz (500g) small portabella mushrooms, sliced

2 garlic cloves, crushed

1¼ cups heavy cream

8oz (225g) dolcelatte cheese, cut into small cubes

large bunch of basil, chopped

1 Cut off the tips of the asparagus about 2in (5cm) from the top and set aside. Cut the rest of the spears into small slices.

2 Cook the penne in boiling salted water according to the package instructions. Add the sliced asparagus 5 minutes before the end of cooking. Add the asparagus tips 3 minutes before the end of cooking. Drain and refresh in cold water.

3 Heat the oil in a large frying pan, add the mushrooms and garlic, and fry for 2 minutes. Add the cream and cheese, season with salt and freshly ground black pepper, and stir well.

4 Add the pasta and asparagus to the pan, bring to a boil, and reheat until piping hot. Stir in half the basil and transfer to a serving bowl.

5 Garnish with the remaining basil and serve at once.

PREPARE AHEAD

The penne and asparagus can be cooked up to the end of step 2 up to 6 hours ahead and kept in a colander covered in plastic wrap. Not suitable for freezing.

A delicious creamy pasta dish that's also quick to cook—it takes barely 15 minutes once you've prepared the ingredients. You can use bacon instead of pancetta if you prefer. Serve with salad.

Pasta with pancetta, fava beans, and mascarpone

Serves 6

11oz (300g) conchiglie shell pasta

salt and freshly ground black pepper

5½oz (150g) frozen small fava beans

7oz (200g) green beans, trimmed and sliced into three

5oz package pancetta cubes

8oz mascarpone cheese

2½oz (75g) freshly grated Parmesan cheese

juice of 1 small lemon

small bunch of basil, roughly chopped

Serves 12

1lb 5oz (600g) conchiglie shell pasta

salt and freshly ground black pepper

11oz (300g) frozen small fava beans

14oz (400g) green beans, trimmed and sliced into three

2 x 5oz package pancetta cubes

1lb mascarpone cheese

6oz (175g) freshly grated Parmesan cheese

juice of 1 large lemon

large bunch of basil, roughly chopped

1 Cook the pasta in boiling salted water according to the package instructions. Add the fava beans and green beans 5 minutes before the end of cooking.

2 Meanwhile, heat a large frying pan, add the pancetta, and fry until crisp. Stir in the mascarpone and two-thirds of the Parmesan and stir until melted.

3 Drain the pasta and beans, leaving a little of the cooking water in the saucepan. Add the pasta and beans to the frying pan along with ¾ cup of the cooking water (1¼ cup for 12). Add the lemon juice and basil, toss together well, and season with salt and freshly ground black pepper.

4 Sprinkle with the remaining Parmesan and serve at once.

PREPARE AHEAD

The pasta and beans can be cooked, drained, and refreshed in cold water up to 6 hours ahead. Remember to reserve a little of the cooking water. Not suitable for freezing.

To make the cannelloni easier to serve, arrange them in neat rows in a rectangular dish. Serve with dressed salad and crusty bread.

Mushroom and spinach cannelloni

Serves 6

Special equipment *1½ quart wide-based ovenproof dish*

1 tbsp olive oil
1lb 2oz (500g) mixed mushrooms, such as shiitake, cremini, and button, roughly chopped
3 garlic cloves, crushed
8oz (225g) baby spinach, roughly chopped
salt and freshly ground black pepper
14oz can tomatoes, drained and juice discarded

2 tbsp pesto
2½oz (75g) freshly grated Parmesan cheese
12 cannelloni tubes, boiled

For the sauce

5 tbsp butter
5 tbsp all-purpose flour
3 cups hot milk
½ cup heavy cream
2 heaped tbsp pesto

Serves 12

Special equipment *2 x 1½ quart wide-based ovenproof dishes or 1 x 3 quart dish*

2 tbsp olive oil
2¼lb (1kg) mixed mushrooms, such as shiitake, cremini, and button, roughly chopped
6 garlic cloves, crushed
1lb 2oz (500g) baby spinach, roughly chopped
salt and freshly ground black pepper
2 x 14oz cans tomatoes, drained and juice discarded

¼ cup pesto
6oz (175g) freshly grated Parmesan cheese
24 cannelloni tubes, boiled

For the sauce

1½ sticks butter
1¼ cups all-purpose flour
6 cups hot milk
1 cup heavy cream
¼ cup pesto

1 Heat the oil in a frying pan, add the mushrooms, and fry over high heat for 2 minutes or until just cooked. Add the garlic and spinach and toss together until the spinach is just wilted. Season with salt and freshly ground black pepper and set aside to cool.

2 To make the sauce, melt the butter in a saucepan, whisk in the flour, and cook for 1 minute. Whisking all the time, gradually blend in the hot milk and the cream and bring to a boil. Season with salt and freshly ground black pepper, remove from the heat, and stir in the pesto.

3 Put the tomatoes into a mixing bowl, add the cooled mushroom mixture, the pesto, and one-third of the Parmesan. Stir to combine.

4 Preheat the oven to 400°F (200°C). Meanwhile, fill the cannelloni tubes with the mushroom and spinach filling, dividing it equally among them.

5 Spoon one-third of the sauce into the base of the ovenproof dish and arrange the filled cannelloni on top in neat rows. Pour the remaining sauce over the top and sprinkle with the rest of the Parmesan.

6 Bake for 30–35 minutes (45 minutes for 12) or until golden brown and bubbling.

PREPARE AHEAD
The cannelloni can be made up to the end of step 5 up to 8 hours ahead. Not suitable for freezing.

Buffets
and bowls

Buffets probably need no introduction, but "bowls" might. Bowl food is 21st-century party fare, as substantial as lunch or supper, but served in a bowl and designed to be eaten standing up.

Buffets and bowls

When it comes to informal gatherings, the two of us have rather different ideas—it's probably a generation thing. Mary likes buffets because guests can help themselves and sit down at the table or perch somewhere to chat and eat. For Lucy, buffets are still way too formal. Space is also at a premium in her house, so her guests have to cram together and pitch in. The ideal way for her to entertain her family and friends is with one choice of main course presented in bowls, which people eat standing up.

Buffet or bowls?

For Mary, the advantages of buffets are simple.

● You can invite more people than for a sit-down meal. Some can stand and some can sit and everyone is free to mix and chat.

● Your guests can see what's on offer and choose their favorites, serving themselves as much or as little as they like.

● Less help is needed when serving.

While for Lucy the plus points of bowl food are:

● Just a bowl and fork are needed, so it's easy for guests to stand and eat.

● You don't need to worry about not having enough chairs, and there's no need to bother with setting the table, either.

● You can offer just one dish—unlike at a buffet.

● So long as the food is easy to eat from a bowl with a fork, you can serve almost anything—a curry, casserole and dumplings, lasagna, or a hearty stew.

● You have the option of serving food straight into the bowls or putting it out for people to help themselves.

So, that's us. But the choice of styles is entirely yours.

"The beauty of bowl parties is that you can cram all your friends into one room and don't have to worry about where they'll sit."

Bowl food

● Avoid anything you need to eat with a knife and fork.

● If you decide to offer a choice, make life easier for yourself by mixing cold dishes with hot. That way, you only have to worry about serving one dish hot, rather than several.

● Serve accompaniments such as sauces, raita, and chutneys on a side table. Put them in bowls with a teaspoon for guests to help themselves.

● Deep white bowls are ideal for serving bowl food, but you could also use cereal bowls or dessert bowls with a large rim. It doesn't matter if you mix and match.

● For an Asian theme, use Asian food boxes—they're made of cardboard and are foldable. You can buy them online and in specialty stores.

Buffets

A buffet usually consists of one or two main courses, with a selection of side dishes and a choice of desserts.

● Cold buffets are easier because almost everything can be prepared ahead. However, we always serve warm new potatoes or baked potatoes, even at a cold buffet.

● Prepare all the dishes to serve the number of people you have coming. If you make them any smaller, there's the risk that some will run out. People will go back for second helpings, and any leftovers can be kept in the fridge for a few days or frozen.

● Make portions attractive and small. With guests tucking into more than one dish, you don't want to overwhelm them. We score suggested serving portions on the top of large dishes such as pies and lasagnas.

● Take care what dishes you serve together—most guests will want to sample everything, and poached salmon might not be the perfect partner for chicken tikka masala.

● If you're serving a whole ham, carve a few slices to get people going.

● If you're offering a first course at a formal meal, serve it at the tables where guests will sit.

For our guide to setting a buffet table, turn the page.

How to set a buffet table

Put the table against a wall, with just enough room behind it for you to squeeze in and replace the dishes at the back or carve a ham. Depending on the layout of your room, display the food from right to left (as here) or left to right, and in the order guests will put it on their plates, so main dishes should come before sauces or side dishes. Keep any meat dishes together and any fish dishes together. Presenting food in a logical order like this makes it quicker and easier for your guests. Here, we've shown you how to set a buffet table for a bowl party.

Side dish
Place side dishes of potatoes, pasta, or rice after the sauces.

Salad
Have the bowl of salad at the end.

Sauces
Place any sauces after the main dishes.

Bread basket
Cut the bread into even-sized pieces and place it next to the side dishes.

Butter
Put cubes of butter in a small dish near the bread.

Napkins
Place a pile of paper or fabric napkins at the end.

Cutlery
Arrange forks in a jar or glass. If your guests need knives and forks, wrap them in napkins and place at the end of the table.

Seasonings
Serve salt and ready-ground black pepper in shallow dishes that guests can take a pinch from.

Finish <·········

<·········

"Indoors or out, a buffet is such an easy way to entertain a crowd. If you've invited more than 30 people and have enough room, set two buffet tables, with the same food on each."

Serving platters

Position the main dish(es) up front and make sure there are serving implements next to each one.

Bowls or plates

These are the very first thing your guests will need. Place them in a pile at the start.

The traditional Italian salsa verde sauce gives an amazing flavor and a wonderful green layer. Pastry aside, this is a very healthy recipe.

Salmon salsa verde en croûte

Serves 6

For the salsa verde

3 tbsp flat-leaf parsley
2 tbsp fresh basil leaves
2 tbsp fresh mint leaves
1 garlic clove, halved
3 anchovy filets
2 tbsp Dijon mustard
1 egg yolk
freshly ground black pepper

2 x 12oz (350g) salmon filets, skinned and bones removed
17oz package all-butter puff pastry

a little all-purpose flour, to dust
1 egg beaten with 1 tbsp milk

For the dressing

2 large firm but ripe tomatoes
salt
2 scallions, finely chopped
2 tsp sugar
2 tbsp white wine vinegar
¼ cup olive oil
½ tsp Dijon mustard
1 tbsp freshly chopped parsley

Serves 12

For the salsa verde

½ cup flat-leaf parsley
¼ cup fresh basil leaves
¼ cup fresh mint leaves
2 garlic cloves, halved
6 anchovy filets
¼ cup Dijon mustard
1 egg
freshly ground black pepper

2 x 1lb 10oz (750g) salmon filets, skinned and bones removed
17oz package all-butter puff pastry

a little all-purpose flour, to dust
1 egg beaten with 1 tbsp milk

For the dressing

4 large firm but ripe tomatoes
salt
3 scallions, finely chopped
1 tbsp sugar
¼ cup white wine vinegar
½ cup olive oil
1 tsp Dijon mustard
2 tbsp freshly chopped parsley

1 To make the salsa verde, put the herbs into a processor and blend until smooth. Add the garlic, anchovies, mustard, egg yolk (egg for 12), and some freshly ground black pepper (but no salt) and blend again until smooth.

2 Arrange one filet on a cutting board and spread the salsa verde over the top in an even layer. Sit the other filet on top so it looks like a whole fish.

3 Roll out the pastry so it is long enough and wide enough to enclose the filets completely (freeze the rest for later) and place on a piece of lightly floured baking parchment. Sit the filets in the center and brush the pastry with the beaten egg (reserving some for later). Fold the ends of the pastry over the filet and bring the sides up to meet at the top. Pinch the edges together with your fingers. Chill for a minimum of 30 minutes.

4 Preheat the oven to 425°F (220°C) and put a baking sheet in to get hot. Brush the en croûte with beaten egg, then coarsely grate the frozen pastry and scatter on top.

5 Transfer the en croûte (still on the baking parchment) to the hot baking sheet and bake for 25–30 minutes (35–40 minutes for 12) or until the pastry is golden and cooked at the top and bottom. Allow to rest at room temperature for about 15 minutes.

6 Meanwhile, make the dressing. Plunge the tomatoes into boiling salted water for 1 minute, then remove with a slotted spoon, plunge into cold water, and drain. Remove the skins, then seed, cut into dice (see page 166), and put in a bowl. Add the remaining ingredients, season with salt and freshly ground black pepper, and stir to combine.

7 Carve the en croûte into thick slices and serve the dressing alongside in a bowl.

PREPARE AHEAD AND FREEZE
The en croûte can be made up to 12 hours ahead. The dressing can be made up to 2 days ahead. Freeze the uncooked en croûte for up to 2 months.

We find this the best way to poach salmon and over the years we have perfected the method so it's foolproof. We do it in a fish poacher, which are available in kitchen supply stores.

GREAT FOR A CROWD

Classic poached salmon

Serves 12

6–6½lb (2.7–3kg) salmon
  (head on), gutted
small handful of salt
12 black peppercorns
cucumber, very thinly sliced,
  to garnish
24 cooked shrimp, peeled but
  heads left on, to garnish
parsley or dill, to garnish

For the sauce

2 tbsp fresh dill
2 tbsp fresh chives
2 tbsp fresh mint
2 tbsp fresh flat-leaf parsley
6oz crème fraîche
6oz Greek yogurt
1¼ cups mayonnaise
1 tbsp sugar
juice of 1 lemon

Serves 20

11–12lb (5–5.5kg) salmon
  (head on), gutted
small handful of salt
20 black peppercorns
cucumber, very thinly sliced,
  to garnish
40 cooked shrimp, peeled but
  heads left on, to garnish
parsley or dill, to garnish

For the sauce

¼ cup fresh dill
¼ cup fresh chives
¼ cup fresh mint
¼ cup fresh flat-leaf parsley
12oz crème fraîche
12oz Greek yogurt
2 cups mayonnaise
2 tbsp sugar
juice of 2 lemons

1 Put the salmon in the fish poacher and pour in enough cold water from the tap to cover it completely. Remove the fish.

2 Add the salt and peppercorns to the water, then bring to a full rolling boil. Carefully lower the salmon into the water, bring back to a boil, and boil for 1 minute per pound (2 minutes per kilo) and no more. Do not cover with a lid.

3 Remove from the heat and cover with a tight-fitting lid. Set in a cool place (not the fridge) and leave undisturbed for about 8 hours—the salmon will continue to cook as it cools.

4 Transfer the salmon to a chopping board or work surface and carefully peel off the skin while it is still lukewarm. Using two large spatulas and taking care not to damage the flesh, turn the fish over and peel the skin from the other side, leaving a little over the end of the tail and the head. Cut off the fins with scissors and cut a neat "V" in the tail.

5 To make the sauce, put the herbs into a processor and whiz until chopped. Add the rest of the ingredients and season well with salt and freshly ground black pepper. Spoon into a serving dish (not silver as the sauce will discolor), cover, and chill until required.

6 To serve, arrange the salmon on a platter and overlap cucumber slices along the spine. Take pairs of the shrimp and interlock the tails, then arrange them around the fish. Finish with the sprigs of parsley or dill. Serve cold with the lemon and herb sauce.

Great for a crowd... Buy extra salmon and poach separately. Don't be tempted to buy one really huge salmon—you may have trouble fitting it in the fish poacher.

BIG FISH

If you are cooking a very large salmon and it is too big for the fish poacher, cut off the head before poaching. The timing will be the same.

PREPARE AHEAD

The salmon can be poached up to 1 day ahead, then skinned and wrapped tightly in plastic wrap to keep it moist. The herb sauce is better made in advance and it can be made up to 3 days ahead. Not suitable for freezing.

Served with rice, this Hungarian classic is perfect bowl food. We like it made with pork shoulder, but you could also use pork filet if you prefer. Reduce the cooking time by half for filet.

Paprika pork goulash

Serves 6

2 tbsp olive oil

2lb (900g) boneless pork shoulder, cut into 1½in (4cm) pieces

2 medium onions, sliced

2 garlic cloves, crushed

2 tbsp paprika

3 tbsp tomato purée

1¼ cups chicken stock or beef stock

salt and freshly ground black pepper

2 red peppers, peeled, seeded, and thinly sliced

1 tbsp balsamic vinegar

1 tsp brown sugar

2–3 tbsp sour cream or crème fraîche (depending on taste)

2 tbsp freshly chopped flat-leaf parsley

Serves 12

¼ cup olive oil

4lb (1.8kg) boneless pork shoulder, cut into 1½in (4cm) pieces

3 large onions, sliced

4 garlic cloves, crushed

3 heaped tbsp paprika

¾ cup tomato purée

2 cups chicken stock or beef stock

salt and freshly ground black pepper

4 red peppers, peeled, seeded, and thinly sliced

2 tbsp balsamic vinegar

2 tsp brown sugar

¾ cup sour cream or crème fraîche

¼ cup freshly chopped flat-leaf parsley

1 Preheat the oven to 325°F (160°C). Meanwhile, heat the oil in a deep frying pan or casserole. Add the pork and brown quickly on all sides. You may need to do this in batches. Remove with a slotted spoon and set aside.

2 Add the onions to the pan and fry for 3 minutes or until starting to soften. Stir in the garlic and paprika and fry for 1 minute. Add the tomato purée and stock and return the meat to the pan. Bring to a boil, season with salt and freshly ground black pepper, cover with a lid, and transfer to the oven for 1¼–1½ hours (2 hours for 12) or until the pork is tender.

3 Add the peppers, vinegar, and sugar, bring to a boil, then check the seasoning. Stir in the sour cream or crème fraîche to taste and serve garnished with the parsley.

PREPARE AHEAD AND FREEZE

You can make the goulash up to 1 day ahead. The flavor will improve, in fact. Freeze without the cream for up to 2 months.

PREPARING RED PEPPERS

STEP 1 Blacken the skin of the pepper under the grill, then pop it into a plastic bag and seal.

STEP 2 When cold, peel off the charred skin with your fingers, then pull out the core and seeds.

Hot or cold, ham is irresistible and perfect for any buffet table. We like to serve it with Cumberland sauce (see facing page). It feeds twice the number when cold because it's easier to slice thinly.

Watercroft glazed ham

Serves 6–12

3lb (1.35kg) boneless, uncured ham
½ onion, cut in half
1 small celery stalk, cut into three
1 small bay leaf

¼ cup light or dark brown sugar
2 tbsp red currant jelly
2 tsp wholegrain mustard

Serves 12–20

6½lb (3kg) boneless, uncured ham
1 onion, quartered
1 celery stalk, cut into four
1 bay leaf

½ cup light or dark brown sugar
¼ cup red currant jelly
1 tbsp wholegrain mustard

1 Weigh the ham and calculate the cooking time based on 20 minutes per 1lb (450g). A 3lb (1.35kg) ham will take 1 hour. A 6½lb (3kg) joint will take 2 hours 10 minutes.

2 Place it skin side down in a large deep saucepan. Add the vegetables, bay leaf, and sugar, then cover with cold water and a lid.

3 Bring to a boil (this takes longer than you may imagine) and, once boiling, start the timing. Simmer very gently until cooked. Check from time to time and top up with boiling water, if needed, to ensure the ham is covered.

4 Once the ham is cooked through, carefully lift it out of the pan and, using a small sharp knife, remove the skin, leaving a very thin layer of fat on the joint. Preheat the oven to 400°F (200°C).

5 Meanwhile, put the red currant jelly and mustard into a bowl and stir until combined. Spread the mixture over the layer of fat, then score it in a lattice pattern with a knife.

6 Line a large roasting pan with foil and sit the ham in the center with the glaze at the top. Bring the foil up so the flesh is completely covered and only the glaze is exposed—this prevents the ham drying out.

7 Bake for 15–20 minutes or until the glaze has melted and started to caramelize. If serving hot, rest for a good 10 minutes before carving. If serving cold, set aside until needed.

Great for a crowd... Cook one large ham—it looks more impressive than two smaller ones. In an emergency, you could even buy a cooked ham. Add your own glaze, and brown as in the recipe.

BUYING HAM
When you're buying the ham, ask the butcher if it needs soaking to remove any excess saltiness. If you get it from a supermarket, it is usually presoaked, but always check the label.

PREPARE AHEAD
The ham can be prepared up to 5 days ahead. To serve warm, it can be boiled up to 5 days ahead and then glazed on the day. Not suitable for freezing.

This is a wonderfully rich vibrantly colored sauce. We suggest serving it with our baked ham (see facing page), but it is also very good with cold meats, turkey at Christmas, and game pie.

Cumberland sauce

Serves 6

1 orange
12oz jar red currant jelly
2½fl oz (75ml) red wine
1 tsp Dijon mustard
a dash of Worcestershire sauce

salt and freshly ground
    black pepper
juice of ½ lemon

Serves 12

2 oranges
2 x 12oz jars red currant jelly
5fl oz (150ml) red wine
2 tsp Dijon mustard
a dash of Worcestershire sauce

salt and freshly ground
    black pepper
juice of 1 lemon

1 Using a potato peeler, remove very thin strips of peel from the orange. Scrape off any white pith from the underside. Cut into needle-thin strips and transfer to a pan. Cover with water, bring to a boil, and simmer over low heat for 3–4 minutes or until soft. Drain, refresh in cold water, then dry well with paper towels and set aside.

2 Put the red currant jelly and wine into a saucepan. Squeeze the orange and add the juice to the pan with the mustard and Worcestershire sauce. Whisk over high heat until the jelly has melted, then boil rapidly for 4–5 minutes or until reduced by half.

3 Season with salt and freshly ground black pepper, add lemon juice to taste, then spoon into a serving dish and sprinkle with the orange strips. Serve warm or cold.

PREPARE AHEAD
The sauce can be made up to 1 week ahead.
To serve warm, reheat gently in a pan. Not
suitable for freezing.

Coronation chicken is a delicious twist on traditional chicken salad. It's also delicious made with cooked turkey—ideal for the day after Thanksgiving. Serve with baby new potatoes and dressed salad.

GREAT FOR A CROWD

21st-century coronation chicken

Serves 6

2 tbsp apricot jam

1 tbsp curry powder

1 cup mayonnaise

¾ cup low-fat sour cream

1 tbsp tomato purée

finely grated zest and juice of 1 lemon

1lb (450g) cooked chicken, cut into bite-sized pieces

2 scallions, finely chopped

salt and freshly ground black pepper

6oz (175g) black and green seedless grapes, cut in half lengthwise

arugula, to garnish

Serves 12

¼ cup apricot jam

2 tbsp curry powder

2 cups mayonnaise

1¼ cups low-fat sour cream

2 tbsp tomato purée

finely grated zest and juice of 2 lemons

2lb (900g) cooked chicken, cut into bite-sized pieces

4 scallions, finely chopped

salt and freshly ground black pepper

11oz (300g) black and green seedless grapes, cut in half lengthwise

arugula, to garnish

1 Put the jam and curry powder in a small saucepan and heat gently, stirring until the jam has melted. Set aside to cool a little.

2 Meanwhile, put the mayonnaise, sour cream, and tomato purée in a mixing bowl with the lemon zest and lemon juice and mix together until combined.

3 Stir in the jam mixture, then add the chicken and scallions. Season with salt and freshly ground black pepper, add half the grapes, and stir until combined.

4 Spoon on to a serving platter and garnish with the remaining grapes and the arugula.

Great for a crowd... Make the sauce up to three days ahead so the flavors have time to infuse.

PREPARE AHEAD

The dish can be made up to 1 day ahead.
The sauce can be made up to 3 days ahead.
Not suitable for freezing.

BACK IN THE DAY

The original recipe for Coronation chicken—created for the Queen's coronation in 1953—was made with red wine and apricots and took ages to prepare. This is considerably simpler, but every bit as good.

This is a wonderful dish to serve on a cold winter day. The savory beef is complemented by the light and fluffy dumplings. Served with creamy mashed potatoes.

Beef casserole with thyme and mustard dumplings

Serves 6

2lb (900g) beef stew chunks
5fl oz (150ml) red wine
2 tbsp sunflower oil
2 tbsp butter
2 large leeks, sliced
4 celery stalks, sliced
1 apple, peeled, cored, and
    chopped into small cubes
1 tbsp brown sugar
½ cup all-purpose flour
2 cups beef stock
1 tbsp Worcestershire sauce
2 tsp Dijon mustard
1 tbsp balsamic vinegar
salt and freshly ground
    black pepper

For the dumplings

2¼ cups biscuit mix
¾ cup milk
2 tbsp wholegrain mustard
1 tsp freshly chopped
    thyme leaves, plus extra
    to garnish

Serves 12

4lb (1.8kg) beef stew chunks
10fl oz (300ml) red wine
¼ cup sunflower oil
¼ cup butter
4 large leeks, sliced
8 celery stalks, sliced
2 apples, peeled, cored, and
    chopped into small cubes
2 tbsp brown sugar
1 cup all-purpose flour
3 cups beef stock
2 tbsp Worcestershire sauce
1 heaped tbsp Dijon mustard
2 tbsp balsamic vinegar
salt and freshly ground
    black pepper

For the dumplings

4½ cups biscuit mix
1½ cups milk
¼ cup wholegrain mustard
2 tsp freshly chopped
    thyme leaves, plus extra
    to garnish

1 Put the beef and wine into a bowl and leave to marinate for a few hours or overnight.

2 Preheat the oven to 325°F (160°C). Meanwhile, heat the oil in a large frying pan or casserole. Drain the meat from the marinade (reserving the marinade) and brown quickly over high heat. Remove with a slotted spoon and set aside. You may need to do this in batches.

3 Melt the butter in the frying pan, add the leeks, celery, and apple, and fry for 2 minutes. Add the brown sugar and fry for 2 minutes more or until the leeks are starting to soften.

4 Add the flour, then blend in the reserved marinade and stock. Return the meat to the pan and add the Worcestershire sauce, mustard, balsamic vinegar, and some salt and freshly ground black pepper.

5 Bring to a boil, cover with a lid, then transfer to the oven for 1–1½ hours (1½–2 hours for 12) or until the meat is tender.

6 Remove from the oven and increase the temperature to 400°F (200°C).

7 To make the dumplings, mix all the ingredients together in a large mixing bowl until combined. Add a tablespoon or two of water, if necessary, to make a sticky but manageable dough. Shape into 12 small balls (24 for 12).

8 Put the dumplings on top of the casserole and bake without a lid near the top of the oven for 15 minutes or until the dumplings have risen and are golden brown on top. Garnish with chopped thyme.

PREPARE AHEAD AND FREEZE
The casserole can be made up to the end of step 5 up to 2 days ahead. The dumplings are best freshly made. Freeze without the dumplings for up to 2 months.

STRIPPING THYME LEAVES

Hold each sprig in one hand, then run the forefinger and thumb of your other hand along the stalk.

"This is the perfect casserole for a winter buffet or bowl party. Start it the day before so that the beef has chance to absorb all the flavors of the wine."

Game casserole with thyme and mustard dumplings (see overleaf) ●●●>

The hotness of chili con carne is a personal choice. Taste it at the end and, if you like yours hot, add more chili powder, then bring to a boil to cook it through. The chutney adds a touch of sweetness.

Chili con carne

Serves 6

1 tbsp olive oil
2lb (900g) raw ground beef
2 medium onions, coarsely chopped
2 garlic cloves, crushed
2 red chiles, halved, seeded, and finely chopped
2 tbsp paprika
2 tsp cumin powder
½–1 tsp hot chili powder (depending on taste)

7fl oz (200ml) red wine
2 x 14oz cans chopped tomatoes
2 tbsp tomato purée
salt and freshly ground black pepper
2 x 14oz cans kidney beans in water, drained and rinsed
1–2 tbsp mango chutney (depending on taste)

Serves 12

2 tbsp olive oil
4lb (1.8kg) raw ground beef
3 large onions, coarsely chopped
4 garlic cloves, crushed
4 red chiles, halved, seeded, and finely chopped
¼ cup paprika
1 heaped tbsp cumin powder
1–2 tsp hot chili powder (depending on taste)

14fl oz (400ml) red wine
4 x 14oz cans chopped tomatoes
¼ cup tomato purée
salt and freshly ground black pepper
4 x 14oz cans kidney beans in water, drained and rinsed
2–3 tbsp mango chutney (depending on taste)

1 Preheat the oven to 350°F (180°C). Meanwhile, heat the oil in a deep, non-stick frying pan or casserole, add the beef, and fry over high heat for 5 minutes or until brown all over. You may need to do this in batches.

2 Add the onions, garlic, and chiles and fry with the beef for a few minutes.

3 Sprinkle in the paprika, cumin, and chili powder and fry for a few minutes more. Blend in the wine, tomatoes, and tomato purée and stir as you bring to a boil. Season with salt and freshly ground black pepper, cover with a lid, and transfer to the oven for about an hour.

4 Add the kidney beans and chutney, return to the oven, and continue to cook for a further 30 minutes (1 hour for 12) or until the meat is completely tender. Serve immediately.

Great for a crowd... This is perfect for making in one large batch if you have a saucepan big enough. Remember to stir often. If the mixture gets too thick, add a little stock. Freezes well.

SERVING SUGGESTIONS

Serve with long-grain rice, grated Cheddar cheese, and a dollop of sour cream. Teenagers love it with tortilla chips or served in taco shells.

PREPARE AHEAD AND FREEZE
The chili can be made up to 2 days ahead. Freeze for up to 2 months.

This traditional stew has lots of flavor and is a favorite of Lucy's family, especially at holiday times when everyone is gathered together. Serve with creamy mashed potatoes and green vegetables.

Good old-fashioned beef stew

Serves 6

2 tbsp sunflower oil

2lb (900g) stewing beef, cut into bite-sized pieces

12 small shallots, peeled

2 medium carrots, diced

¼ cup all-purpose flour

10fl oz (300ml) red wine

1¾ cup beef stock

1 tbsp red currant jelly

1 tbsp Worcestershire sauce

5 thyme sprigs

salt and freshly ground black pepper

9oz (250g) button mushrooms

Serves 12

2 tbsp sunflower oil

4lb (1.8kg) stewing beef, cut into bite-sized pieces

24 small shallots, peeled

4 medium carrots, diced

¾ cup all-purpose flour

20oz (600ml) red wine

3 cups beef stock

2 tbsp red currant jelly

2 tbsp Worcestershire sauce

small bunch of thyme sprigs

salt and freshly ground black pepper

1lb 2oz (500g) button mushrooms

1 Preheat the oven to 325°F (160°C). Meanwhile, heat the oil in a large frying pan or casserole and quickly brown the beef all over. Remove with a slotted spoon and set aside. You may need to do this in batches.

2 Add the shallots and carrots to the pan and brown over high heat. Add the flour and stir to coat the vegetables, then blend in the wine and stock. Add the red currant jelly, Worcestershire sauce, thyme, and some salt and freshly ground black pepper. Add the mushrooms and return the beef to the pan.

3 Bring to a boil, cover with a lid, and cook in the oven for 2–2½ hours (2½–3 hours for 12) or until the beef is tender. Serve piping hot.

PREPARE AHEAD AND FREEZE

The stew can be made up to 1 day ahead.
Freeze for up to 2 months.

A wonderful untemperamental casserole—warming and spicy. Serve with Cheese-topped dauphinois potatoes (page 125) and peas.

Hot mustard spiced beef

Serves 6

1 tbsp sunflower oil

2lb (900g) chuck steak, cut into ¾in (2cm) cubes

2 large onions, chopped

3½oz (100g) button mushrooms, cut into quarters

1 tbsp Dijon mustard

2 tsp medium curry powder

1 tbsp muscovado sugar

2 tbsp Worcestershire sauce

3 tbsp all-purpose flour

2 cups beef stock or 2 beef stock cubes dissolved in 2 cups water

salt and freshly ground black pepper

1lb (450g) peeled baby carrots

freshly chopped parsley, to garnish (optional)

Serves 12

2 tbsp sunflower oil

4lb (1.8kg) chuck steak, cut into ¾in (2cm) cubes

4 large onions, chopped

8oz (225g) button mushrooms, cut into quarters

2 tbsp Dijon mustard

4 tsp medium curry powder

2 tbsp muscovado sugar

¼ cup Worcestershire sauce

½ cup all-purpose flour

1 quart beef stock or 4 beef stock cubes dissolved in 1 quart water

salt and freshly ground black pepper

2lb (900g) peeled baby carrots

freshly chopped parsley, to garnish (optional)

1 Preheat the oven to 325°F (160°C). Meanwhile, heat the oil in a large non-stick frying pan or casserole, add the cubes of meat, and fry quickly until golden brown all over. Remove with a slotted spoon and drain on paper towels. You may need to do this in batches.

2 Add the onions and mushrooms to the pan and fry over high heat, stirring occasionally, for 3 minutes or until starting to soften.

3 Put the mustard, curry powder, sugar, Worcestershire sauce, and flour into a bowl and add ½ cup of the stock (1 cup for 12). Whisk by hand until smooth.

4 Add the remaining stock to the pan and bring to a boil. Spoon about half the hot stock into the mustard mixture and whisk by hand to give a smooth paste. Pour the mixture back into the pan, whisking over high heat until thickened.

5 Season with salt and freshly ground black pepper, then return the meat to the pan. Bring to a boil, cover with a lid, and transfer to the oven for 2–2½ hours (2½–3 hours for 12) or until the meat is tender.

6 While the meat is cooking, cook the carrots in boiling salted water for a few minutes or until just tender. Drain and refresh in cold water.

7 To serve, bring the casserole to a boil on the stovetop. Add the carrots, check the seasoning, and boil until the carrots are hot. Sprinkle with parsley, if using, and serve.

Great for a crowd... Make in batches and freeze ahead of time.

PREPARE AHEAD AND FREEZE
The dish can be made up to the end of step 5 up to 2 days ahead. Freeze without the carrots for up to 2 months.

There's nothing nicer on a buffet table than slices of pink beef filet.
Serve with new potatoes and the salad on page 224.

Cold filet of beef with mustard sauce

Serves 6

2¾lb (1.25kg) center-cut
  filet of beef
salt and freshly ground
  black pepper
1 tbsp olive oil
a small pat of butter

For the mustard sauce
6oz crème fraîche
2 tbsp Dijon mustard
1 tsp white wine vinegar
1 tsp black mustard seeds
1 tsp sugar

Serves 12

4lb (1.8kg) whole center-cut
  filet of beef
salt and freshly ground
  black pepper
2 tbsp olive oil
a pat of butter

For the mustard sauce
16oz crème fraîche
¼ cup Dijon mustard
2 tsp white wine vinegar
2 tsp black mustard seeds
2 tsp sugar

1 Preheat the oven to 425°F (220°C). Meanwhile, season the beef with salt and freshly ground black pepper, then rub the oil over the meat.

2 Heat a wide-based frying pan over high heat until very hot and brown the beef quickly on all sides.

3 Transfer to a small roasting pan, spread with the butter, and roast for 18–20 minutes (25 minutes for 12) or until medium rare. Set aside until cold.

4 To make the sauce, put all the ingredients into a bowl, season with salt and freshly ground black pepper, and stir to combine.

5 Thinly carve the beef and serve cold with the sauce.

Great for a crowd... Brown the filets individually and roast two at a time.

PREPARE AHEAD
The filet can be roasted up to 2 days ahead.
The sauce can be made up to 3 days ahead.
Not suitable for freezing.

CARVING THE BEEF
If carved too early and arranged on a platter, the meat will turn gray fairly quickly as it is exposed to the air. To prevent this, carve the cold beef up to 6 hours ahead, then reassemble into its original shape and wrap tightly in plastic film. Chill until needed and arrange on the plate just before serving.

Whether it's on a buffet table or at a supper party, vegetarians will love this. Serve with dressed salad leaves.

Mushrooms and spinach en croûte

Serves 6

1 tbsp olive oil
½ large onion, chopped
1 garlic clove, crushed
5½oz (150g) cremini
 mushrooms, sliced
8oz (225g) baby spinach
4½oz (125g) ricotta
2½oz (75g) Gruyère cheese,
 grated

1 egg yolk
dash of Tabasco
salt and freshly ground
 black pepper
a little all-purpose flour, to dust
1 sheet of frozen puff pastry,
 thawed
1 egg yolk beaten with
 1 tbsp milk

Serves 12

1 tbsp olive oil
1 large onion, chopped
2 garlic cloves, crushed
9oz (250g) cremini
 mushrooms, sliced
1lb (450g) baby spinach
7oz (200g) ricotta
6oz (175g) Gruyère cheese,
 grated

1 egg
dash of Tabasco
salt and freshly ground
 black pepper
a little all-purpose flour, to dust
2 sheets of frozen puff pastry,
 thawed
1 whole egg beaten with
 1 tbsp milk

1 Preheat the oven to 425°F (220°C) and put a baking sheet in the oven to get hot. Meanwhile, heat the oil in a non-stick frying pan, add the onion, and fry for 2 minutes. Lower the heat, cover with a lid, and cook for 15 minutes or until soft.

2 Add the garlic, mushrooms, and spinach and cook over high heat for 3 minutes or until the spinach has wilted and the mushrooms have softened. Set aside to cool.

3 Meanwhile, put the ricotta, Gruyère, egg yolk (whole egg for 12), and Tabasco into a bowl, season with salt and freshly ground black pepper, and mix until combined. Stir into the cold spinach mixture.

4 Lay the sheet of pastry on a lightly floured work surface and roll it out into a 11 x 13in (28 x 33cm) rectangle (13 x 15in/33 x 38cm rectangle for 12).

5 Pile the spinach mixture into the middle, leaving a 1½in (4cm) gap around the edge. Brush the pastry with the egg mixture, then fold the ends over the filling and bring the sides up so they meet at the top. Crimp the ends together to seal, then brush the pastry with egg.

6 Transfer to the hot baking sheet and bake for 30 minutes (45 minutes for 12) or until golden all over. Leave to rest at room temperature for 5 minutes, then slice and serve hot.

Great for a crowd... Make more en croûtes and bake two to a baking sheet. Never make an en croûte larger than for 12, as the pastry may split.

PUFF PASTRY
Be sure to buy all-butter puff pastry, as it has a much better flavor than other kinds and is a little softer to handle.

PREPARE AHEAD
The en croûte can be made up to the end of step 5 up to 8 hours ahead. Not suitable for freezing.

This is great for vegetarians and meat-eaters alike—the mushrooms are delicious and the cornichons (baby gherkins) give a lovely texture and sweetness. Serve with rice.

Mushroom stroganoff

Serves 6

1½ tbsp butter
1 large onion, thinly sliced
2 garlic cloves, crushed
1 tbsp paprika
1 tbsp all-purpose flour
3½fl oz (100ml) Marsala
7oz crème fraîche
1lb 7oz (650g) mixed mushrooms, such as oyster, cremini, and portabella, sliced

salt and freshly ground black pepper
juice of ½ lemon
1 tsp tomato purée
1 tsp sugar
1¾oz (50g) cornichons, chopped

Serves 12

3 tbsp butter
2 large onions, thinly sliced
4 garlic cloves, crushed
2 tbsp paprika
2 tbsp all-purpose flour
7fl oz (200ml) Marsala
14oz crème fraîche
2½lb (1.1kg) mixed mushrooms, such as oyster, cremini, and portabella, sliced

salt and freshly ground black pepper
juice of 1 lemon
2 tsp tomato purée
2 tsp sugar
3½oz (100g) cornichons, chopped

1 Melt the butter in a deep frying pan, add the onion, and fry for 1 minute. Lower the heat, cover with a lid, and simmer for 15 minutes or until soft.

2 Stir in the garlic, then sprinkle in the paprika and flour and mix well. Add the Marsala and crème fraîche and stir until thickened slightly.

3 Add the mushrooms, season with salt and freshly ground black pepper, and simmer over low heat for 4 minutes (5–10 minutes for 12) or until the mushrooms are just cooked.

4 Stir in the lemon juice, tomato purée, and sugar and check the seasoning. Scatter over the cornichons and serve hot.

VARIATION
If you don't have any Marsala, you can use another fortified wine such as medium sherry or Port.

PREPARE AHEAD
This is best made and served immediately.
Not suitable for freezing.

We always try to keep the number of ingredients to a minimum, but by nature a curry has many—it's the blend of spices that give it flavor. Sorry! Serve with naan breads and Pilaf rice (pages 206–207).

Vegetable korma

Serves 6

3½oz (100g) green beans, sliced into three

salt and freshly ground black pepper

2 tbsp olive oil

1 large onion, roughly chopped

¾in (2cm) piece fresh ginger root, peeled and grated

1 tsp cardamom seeds, crushed

1½ tbsp ground cumin

1½ tbsp ground coriander

1½ tbsp garam masala

1lb (450g) potatoes, chopped into ⅜in (1½cm) cubes

12oz (350g) carrots, chopped into ⅜in (1½cm) cubes

12oz (350g) cauliflower, cut into even-sized florets

14oz can coconut milk

15fl oz (450ml) vegetable stock

3½oz (100g) ground almonds

juice of 1 lemon

2 tbsp mango chutney

Serves 12

6oz (175g) green beans, sliced into three

salt and freshly ground black pepper

3 tbsp olive oil

2 large onions, roughly chopped

2in (5cm) piece fresh ginger root, peeled and grated

2 tsp cardamom seeds, crushed

3 tbsp ground cumin

3 tbsp ground coriander

3 tbsp garam masala

2lb (900g) potatoes, chopped into ⅜in (1½cm) cubes

1lb 9oz (700g) carrots, chopped into ⅜in (1½cm) cubes

1lb 9oz (700g) cauliflower, cut into even-sized florets

2 x 14oz cans coconut milk

3 cups vegetable stock

8oz (225g) ground almonds

juice of 2 lemons

¼ cup mango chutney

1 Cook the beans in boiling salted water for 4 minutes or until just cooked. Drain, refresh in cold water, and set aside.

2 Heat the oil in a deep frying pan or casserole, add the onion, and fry over high heat for 2 minutes.

3 Add the ginger and spices, stir to coat the onions, and fry for 1 minute. Add all the vegetables except the beans, then stir in the coconut milk and stock. Season well with salt and freshly ground black pepper and bring to a boil.

4 Cover with a lid and simmer over low heat for 30–40 minutes (45 minutes for 12) or until the vegetables are tender.

5 Stir in the ground almonds (they will thicken the sauce), then add the reserved beans, the lemon juice, and chutney. Check the seasoning and serve.

Great for a crowd... This is perfect for making in one large batch if you have a saucepan big enough. Measure the spices accurately so you get the balance of flavors right. And remember to stir often.

PREPARE AHEAD

The korma can be made up to the end of step 4 up to 12 hours ahead. Not suitable for freezing.

Jumbo shrimp are expensive, but this is a great dish for a special occasion. Serve with Pilaf rice (page 207) or, as part of a buffet, with Vegetable korma (page 199) and Aromatic beef curry (page 203).

Jumbo shrimp balti

Serves 6

3 tbsp sunflower oil

2 large onions, finely chopped

2 red peppers, halved, seeded, and roughly chopped

2½in (6cm) piece fresh ginger root, peeled and finely grated

3 red chiles, halved, seeded, and roughly chopped

1 tsp turmeric

2 tsp ground coriander

2 tsp garam masala

1 tsp black mustard seeds

2 x 14oz cans chopped tomatoes

1¼ cups water

¼ cup tomato purée

4 tsp lime pickle

juice of 1 lime

2 tbsp honey

salt and freshly ground black pepper

2¼lb (1kg) raw peeled jumbo shrimp

1 heaped tbsp freshly chopped cilantro, to garnish

Serve 12

5 tbsp sunflower oil

4 large onions, finely chopped

4 red peppers, halved, seeded, and roughly chopped

7in (18cm) piece fresh ginger root, peeled and finely grated

6 red chiles, halved, seeded, and roughly chopped

2 tsp turmeric

4 tsp ground coriander

4 tsp garam masala

2 tsp black mustard seeds

4 x 14oz cans chopped tomatoes

2 cups water

½ cup tomato purée

2 heaped tbsp lime pickle

juice of 2 limes

¼ cup honey

salt and freshly ground black pepper

4½lb (2kg) raw peeled jumbo shrimp

2 heaped tbsp freshly chopped cilantro, to garnish

1 Heat the oil in a large frying pan or saucepan, add the onions, peppers, ginger, and chiles and fry over high heat for 2 minutes or until starting to soften.

2 Cover with a lid, then reduce the heat and cook for 10 minutes or until the onions and peppers are nearly soft. Add the spices and stir over high heat to coat the vegetables.

3 Add the tomatoes, water, tomato purée, lime pickle, lime juice, and honey. Bring to a boil and simmer for 10 minutes (15 minutes for 12). Season with salt and freshly ground black pepper, add the shrimp, and cook for 5 minutes (5–10 minutes for 12) or until they turn pink and are cooked through. Garnish with the cilantro and serve immediately.

Great for a crowd… This is perfect for making in one large batch if you have a saucepan big enough. Measure the spices accurately so you get the balance of flavors right. And remember to stir often. Freezes well.

PREPARE AHEAD AND FREEZE

The sauce can be made up to 1 day ahead. Reheat to serve, adding the shrimp at the end. Freeze the sauce without the shrimp for up to 1 month.

VARIATION

Lime pickle can often be found in the international aisle of the supermarket. If you cannot find it, substitute hot mango chutney instead.

Bright and full of flavor, this is one of the most popular curries we make. Serve with naan breads and Pilaf rice (pages 206–207).

Chicken tikka masala

Serves 6

12 skinless boneless chicken
    thighs, each cut into 6 pieces
1 tbsp medium curry powder
1 tsp paprika
1 tbsp olive oil
3 onions, roughly chopped
2 garlic cloves, crushed
2½in (6cm) piece fresh ginger
    root, peeled and finely grated
2 tbsp garam masala
½ tsp turmeric

1 cup water
16oz tomato purée
2 tbsp tomato paste
1 tbsp sugar
salt and freshly ground
    black pepper
juice of ½ lime
¾ cup heavy cream
1 heaped tbsp freshly chopped
    cilantro, to garnish

Serves 12

24 skinless boneless chicken
    thighs, each cut into 6 pieces
2 tbsp medium curry powder
2 tsp paprika
2 tbsp olive oil
5 onions, roughly chopped
4 garlic cloves, crushed
3in (7.5cm) piece fresh ginger
    root, peeled and finely grated
¼ cup garam masala
1 tsp turmeric

1¾ cups water
2 x 16oz can tomato purée
¼ cup tomato paste
2 tbsp sugar
salt and freshly ground
    black pepper
juice of 1 lime
1¼ cups heavy cream
2 tbsp freshly chopped
    cilantro, to garnish

1 Put the chicken pieces into a bowl, sprinkle over the curry powder and paprika, cover, and chill for 15 minutes.

2 Heat the oil in a deep frying pan or casserole, add the chicken, and quickly brown all over. Remove with a slotted spoon and set aside. You may need to do this in batches.

3 Add the onions, garlic, and ginger and fry until starting to soften. Add the garam masala and turmeric and fry for 1 minute. Blend in the water, tomato purée and paste, and sugar, return the chicken to the pan, and season with salt and freshly ground black pepper.

4 Bring to a boil, cover with a lid, and simmer, stirring occasionally, for 30–40 minutes (1 hour for 12) or until the chicken is tender.

5 Add the lime juice, check the seasoning, bring to a boil again, then add the cream. Serve garnished with the cilantro.

Great for a crowd... This is perfect for making in one large batch if you have a saucepan big enough. Measure the spices accurately so you get the balance of flavors right. And remember to stir often. Freezes well.

PREPARE AHEAD AND FREEZE
The curry can be made up to the end of step 4 up to 2 days ahead. Freeze without the lime juice and cream for up to 2 months.

A warming curry with lots of spice. Serve with poppadoms, naan breads, and Pilaf rice (pages 206–207).

Aromatic beef curry with ginger and tomatoes

Serves 6

1 heaped tsp each ground cumin, ground coriander, and garam masala

½ tsp turmeric

10 cardamom pods, crushed, pods discarded, and seeds finely crushed

2 tbsp olive oil

2lb (900g) stewing beef, chopped into 1in (2.5cm) pieces

1 large onion, roughly chopped

1 red chile, halved, seeded, and chopped

4 garlic cloves, crushed

¾in (2cm) piece fresh ginger root, peeled and grated

14oz can chopped tomatoes

1¼ cups beef stock

1 cinnamon stick

¼ cup tomato purée

3 tbsp mango chutney

salt and freshly ground pepper

7oz (200g) okra or green beans, sliced into ¾in (2cm) pieces

Serves 12

2 heaped tsp each ground cumin, ground coriander, and garam masala

1 tsp turmeric

20 cardamom pods, crushed, pods discarded, and seeds finely crushed

¼ cup olive oil

4lb (1.8kg) stewing beef, chopped into 1in (2.5cm) pieces

2 large onions, roughly chopped

2 red chiles, halved, seeded, and chopped

8 garlic cloves, crushed

2in (5cm) piece fresh ginger root, peeled and grated

2 x 14oz cans chopped tomatoes

2 cups beef stock

2 cinnamon sticks

½ cup tomato purée

6 tbsp mango chutney

salt and freshly ground pepper

1lb (450g) okra or green beans, sliced into ¾in (2cm) pieces

1 Preheat the oven to 325°F (160°C). Heat a large frying pan or casserole over high heat, add all the spices, and fry for 1 minute or until just toasted, then spoon into a small bowl.

2 Add the oil to the pan and quickly brown the beef until golden all over. Remove with a slotted spoon and set aside. You may need to do this in batches. Add the onion to the pan with the toasted spices, the chile, garlic, and ginger and fry for 3–4 minutes.

3 Add the chopped tomatoes, stock, cinnamon, tomato purée, and chutney. Return the beef to the pan, season with salt and freshly ground pepper, cover with a lid, and transfer to the oven for 2–2¼ hours (2½ hours for 12) or until the beef is tender.

4 Cook the okra or green beans in boiling salted water for 3 minutes, drain, and stir into the pan. Fish out the cinnamon and discard and serve immediately.

Great for a crowd... Make in batches. Don't try to brown too much beef in one go or it will go gray instead of golden brown. Freezes well.

TOASTING SPICES

Heat a frying pan until hot, add the spices, and fry, stirring constantly, until lightly colored and toasted.

PREPARE AHEAD AND FREEZE

The curry can be made up to 2 days ahead. Freeze without the okra or green beans for up to 2 months.

Aromatic beef curry with ginger and tomatoes (see overleaf) ●●●>

True naan breads are a little tricky to make, so these are a bit of a cheat. But a really delicious one! Serve them with any of the curries on pages 199–203.

Garlic and cilantro naan breads

Serves 6

3 large or 6 small plain
  naan breads
1½ tbsp butter,
  at room temperature
2 garlic cloves, crushed
3 tbsp freshly chopped cilantro
salt and freshly ground
  black pepper

Serves 12

6 large or 12 small plain
  naan breads
3 tbsp butter,
  at room temperature
4 garlic cloves, crushed
6 tbsp freshly chopped cilantro
salt and freshly ground
  black pepper

1 Preheat the oven to 400°F (200°C). Arrange the naan breads on a baking sheet without overlapping them.

2 Put the butter, garlic, and cilantro into a bowl and mix until combined. Season with salt and freshly ground black pepper and mix again.

3 Spread evenly over the naan breads so the whole of each bread is covered.

4 Bake for 5–8 minutes (8 minutes for 12) or until the butter has melted and the bread is crisp.

PREPARE AHEAD AND FREEZE
The naan breads can be prepared up to the end of step 3 up to 12 hours ahead. Freeze for up to 3 months.

Pilaf (sometimes called pilaff or pilau) rice is a dish that originates from the near East. It's the perfect accompaniment to any of the curries on pages 199–203.

Pilaf rice

Serves 6

8oz (225g) basmati rice
salt and freshly ground
  black pepper
3 tbsp butter
1 onion, roughly chopped
4 garlic cloves, crushed
1 red chile, halved, seeded,
  and finely chopped

8oz (225g) cremini
  mushrooms, sliced
1 tsp paprika
juice of 1 lemon
1¾oz (50g) golden raisins
scant 1oz (25g) sliced almonds
3½oz (100g) cooked baby peas

Serves 12

1lb (450g) basmati rice
salt and freshly ground
  black pepper
5 tbsp butter
2 onions, roughly chopped
6 garlic cloves, crushed
2 red chiles, halved, seeded,
  and finely chopped

12oz (350g) cremini
  mushrooms, sliced
2 tsp paprika
juice of 2 small lemons
3½oz (100g) golden raisins
1¾oz (50g) sliced almonds
8oz (225g) cooked baby peas

1 Cook the rice in boiling salted water according to the package instructions. Drain, refresh in cold water, and set aside.

2 Meanwhile, melt the butter in a large saucepan, add the onion, garlic, and chile and fry for 2 minutes. Lower the heat, cover with a lid, and simmer for 20 minutes or until the onion is soft.

3 Add the mushrooms, turn up the heat, and fry for 3 minutes or until soft. Sprinkle in the paprika, lemon juice, golden raisins, almonds, and baby peas and fry for a few minutes, stirring. Add the rice and stir until it is piping hot. Season with salt and freshly ground black pepper and serve.

PREPARE AHEAD
The pilaf can be cooked up to 12 hours ahead. To reheat, transfer to a buttered, wide-based ovenproof dish, cover with buttered foil, and place in an oven preheated to 400°F (200°C) for 15 minutes (25 minutes for 12) or until piping hot. Not suitable for freezing.

Summer
in the backyard

The warm-weather recipes in this chapter have all been chosen with sunny days and balmy evenings in mind. And if you're a city dweller, many of them are just as good at a picnic in the park.

Summer in the backyard

Food needs to be gutsy to taste good outdoors. Kebabs and terrines, burgers and frittatas all fit the bill. When you're eating outside, it's often nice to dispense with cutlery, so the food should be easy to eat. No one's going to bother with a knife and fork in any case when they're tucking into finger food like chicken drumsticks.

Many of us prefer cold food or warm food when the weather hots up, so we've also included a selection of salads substantial enough to be served as a main course, along with a goat cheese and onion marmalade galette that's as delicious warm as it is hot.

Food for every occasion

During the summer months we entertain in lots of different ways.

● Perhaps the most laid-back is laying food out buffet-style, either outside in the backyard or in the kitchen if it backs on to the lawn. See overleaf for our guide to setting a buffet table outside.

● Barbecues are always great fun, and you can't help but whet people's appetites with burgers and sausages sizzling on the grill. The cooking often becomes part of the entertainment, too, and can be shared—men, in particular, often like to show off their barbecuing skills.

● Placed in a shady spot, our tables and chairs are often the scene for a meal that lasts well into the afternoon or evening. If it's not quite warm enough to eat outside, we'll have lunch in the sun room—but with the doors open, so we're reminded that summer's on its way.

● And a picnic in the country or in a town park never ceases to hold its appeal.

"You can't help but whet people's appetites with burgers and sausages sizzling on the grill. The cooking often becomes part of the entertainment at a barbecue, too."

Picnics

If you're venturing further afield than your own backyard, there's no need to resort to sandwiches. Take the right food along and a picnic becomes an open-air feast.

● Keep the food simple and don't give too much choice—if it's been sitting outside in the sunshine for hours, it can't be used afterward.

● Pick dishes that are easy to eat with your hands or just a plate and fork.

● Choose dishes you can transport in insulated bags. If you've run out of ice blocks, freeze water in plastic bottles—they'll do the job just as well.

● If you're taking a dish such as a frittata, quiche, or galette, cut it into wedges or slices, then reassemble the pieces to transport it. Wrap it in foil then a dish towel to keep it warm. If the weather looks as if it might rain, however, wrap food in individual foil parcels.

● Keep food covered until you serve it or it will discolor, dry out, and attract flies.

● Dress salads when you get there. If you do it beforehand, the leaves will go soggy and limp. Coleslaw is a good choice because it can be taken along ready to serve.

● Take napkins and garbage bags for trash.

Barbecuing

● Depending on the type of fuel you're using, light the barbecue at least an hour before you want to start cooking. If you're using a gas barbecue, follow the instructions carefully.

● Before you start, put a table next to the barbecue and gather together everything you'll need so you don't have to keep running into the house for utensils or whatever.

● If you're cooking lots of food, give chicken and sausages a headstart by part-cooking them in the oven until nearly done but not brown.

● Don't overbrown the outside of food before the middle is cooked.

● Have a clean plate or platter to put cooked meat on. And don't confuse it with the plate the raw meat was on or there could be a risk of food poisoning.

How to set the table for a buffet in the backyard

Arrange the food from right to left (as here) or left to right, whichever works best. To make it easier for guests to help themselves, place food in the order they'll put it on their plates, so main dishes first. If more than 30 people are coming and your yard is large, set two tables with the same food on each.

Chopping board
Place whole pieces of meat on a chopping board with a carving knife and fork. Carve a few slices and lay them on the board, then leave guests to cut themselves more.

Bread basket
Cut the bread into evenly sized pieces and place it next to the butter.

Napkins and cutlery
To make them easier for people to carry, wrap the knives and forks in napkins.

Salad bowls
Put bowls of salad at the end and supply serving implements for each one.

Salt and pepper
Place the salt and pepper after the food, so guests can season it as they wish.

Side dishes
Place the side dishes with serving spoons after the main dishes.

Finish ‹·········

‹·········

"With so much food on display, keep bugs at bay with a citronella candle. And never leave food unattended if your dog or cat is on the loose."

Sauces
Place sauces next to the main dish they accompany.

Butter plate
Put cubes of cold butter on a plate with a butter knife.

Plates
Guests will need these first, so place them in a pile at the start.

Serving platters
Arrange the main dish(es) next to the plates and provide appropriate serving implements for each one.

Small burgers are the perfect finger food and, with only half a bun, these are even easier to eat (and less stodgy). They are great for children's parties. Serve with a large bowl of fries and mayonnaise.

Manhattan mini burgers

Serves 6

1¾oz (50g) fresh white
   breadcrumbs
1lb 2oz (500g) raw lean
   ground beef
½ onion, finely diced
4 small pickles, finely chopped
2 tsp Dijon mustard
2 tbsp Worcestershire sauce
1 egg yolk
salt and freshly ground
   black pepper
sunflower oil, to fry

To serve

6 slider buns
tomato ketchup
yellow mustard
pickle slices

Serves 12

3½oz (100g) fresh white
   breadcrumbs
2¼lb (1kg) raw lean ground beef
1 onion, finely diced
8 small pickles, finely chopped
1 heaped tbsp Dijon mustard
¼ cup Worcestershire sauce
1 large egg
salt and freshly ground
   black pepper
sunflower oil, to fry

To serve

12 slider buns
tomato ketchup
yellow mustard
pickle slices

1 Put the first seven ingredients into a large bowl and mix well with your hands. Season well with salt and freshly ground black pepper and shape into 12 round burgers (24 burgers for 12). Chill in the fridge for 30 minutes.

2 Heat a little sunflower oil in a frying pan, add the burgers, and fry for 3 minutes on each side or until golden brown on the outside and cooked through in the middle. You may need to do this in batches. Alternatively, cook them on the grill.

3 Spread the cut side of the buns with ketchup, place a burger on top, then squirt with a little mustard and top with a slice of pickle. Arrange on a large platter and serve.

PREPARE AHEAD AND FREEZE
The burgers can be made up to the end of step 1 up to 1 day ahead. Freeze the raw burgers for up to 2 months.

Drumsticks are always a favorite at a barbecue—with adults and children alike. Marinating aside, they are also quick to make. Serve hot or cold with corn on the cob and potato salad.

Sticky chicken drumsticks

Serves 6

6 tbsp tomato ketchup
2 tbsp Worcestershire sauce
2 tbsp grainy mustard
2 tbsp honey

salt and freshly ground
    black pepper
6 chicken drumsticks (skin on)

Serves 12

¾ cup tomato ketchup
¼ cup Worcestershire sauce
¼ cup grainy mustard
¼ cup honey

salt and freshly ground
    black pepper
12 chicken drumsticks (skin on)

1 Put the first four ingredients into a bowl, mix together well, then season with salt and freshly ground black pepper.

2 Add the chicken and marinate for a minimum of 2 hours or overnight.

3 Preheat the oven to 425°F (220°C). Season the drumsticks with salt and freshly ground black pepper and cook for 30–40 minutes (45 minutes for 12) or until golden brown and sticky. Turn halfway through. Alternatively, cook on the grill.

PREPARE AHEAD AND FREEZE
The drumsticks can be marinated overnight.
Freeze in the marinade for up to 2 months.

These lemony chicken burgers are so easy to make and are perfect for a barbecue. Make them larger if you prefer, but cook them for longer.

Mini chicken burgers

Serves 6

2 slices white bread
1lb 2oz (500g) skinless boneless chicken breasts or thighs, roughly chopped
zest and juice of 1 small lemon
1¾oz (50g) freshly grated Parmesan cheese
small bunch of chives, snipped
1 egg yolk
salt and freshly ground black pepper
a little olive oil, to fry

To serve

6 slider buns
grainy mustard
lettuce leaves
mayonnaise
2 tomatoes, sliced

Serves 12

4 slices white bread
2¼lb (1kg) skinless boneless chicken breasts or thighs, roughly chopped
zest and juice of 2 small lemons
3½oz (100g) freshly grated Parmesan cheese
large bunch of chives, snipped
1 large egg
salt and freshly ground black pepper
a little olive oil, to fry

To serve

12 slider buns
grainy mustard
lettuce leaves
mayonnaise
4 tomatoes, sliced

1 Put the bread into a food processor and pulse to fine breadcrumbs. Transfer to a large mixing bowl. Put the chicken into the processor and pulse till coarsely ground. You may need to do this in batches. Add to the bowl with the breadcrumbs.

2 Add the lemon zest, lemon juice, cheese, chives, and egg yolk (whole egg for 12) and mix together with your hands. Season with salt and freshly ground black pepper, then shape the mixture into 12 small burgers (24 for 12) and chill in the fridge for 30 minutes.

3 Heat a little oil in a frying pan and fry the burgers for 3–3½ minutes on each side or until lightly golden and cooked through. You may need to do this in batches. Alternatively, cook on a barbecue.

4 Use the top and bottom of the buns. Spread each with a little mustard, then add a lettuce leaf. Place a burger on top, add a blob of mayonnaise, and garnish with a slice of tomato. Arrange the burgers on a platter and serve.

PREPARE AHEAD AND FREEZE
The burgers can be prepared up to the end of step 2 up to 1 day ahead. Freeze for up to 3 months.

In this chunky-textured terrine with an herby crust the chicken is kept in pieces. It is perfect for a picnic, lunch, or buffet.

French country terrine

Serves 6

Special equipment *1lb (450g) loaf pan*

1 tbsp olive oil

1 small onion, very finely chopped

1 garlic clove, crushed

6oz (175g) good pork sausagemeat

1¾oz (50g) lamb's liver

1½ tbsp brandy

8oz (225g) boneless skinless chicken breast, cut into thin even strips

1 heaped tbsp freshly chopped mixed herbs, such as parsley, thyme, and chives

salt and freshly ground black pepper

freshly chopped parsley and chives, to garnish

Serves 12

Special equipment *2lb (900g) loaf pan*

1 tbsp olive oil

1 medium onion, very finely chopped

2 garlic cloves, crushed

12oz (350g) good pork sausagemeat

3½oz (100g) lamb's liver

3 tbsp brandy

1lb (450g) boneless skinless chicken breast, cut into thin even strips

2 heaped tbsp freshly chopped mixed herbs, such as parsley, thyme, and chives

salt and freshly ground black pepper

freshly chopped parsley and chives, to garnish

1 Preheat the oven to 350°F (180°C). Meanwhile, heat the oil in a frying pan over high heat, add the onion and garlic, and fry for 1 minute. Lower the heat, cover with a lid, and cook for 15 minutes or until the onion is soft. Set aside to cool slightly.

2 Put the sausagemeat, liver, and brandy into a processor and pulse until smooth. Spoon into a bowl. Add the cooled onion and garlic and stir well. Add the chicken and herbs and season with salt and freshly ground black pepper. Mix together with your hands.

3 Spoon into the loaf pan, making sure the chicken strips are lying horizontally. If you're making the small terrine, the mixture will only come two-thirds up the side of the pan. Level the top with the back of a spoon, cover with foil, and seal tightly around the edges.

4 Sit the loaf pan in a small roasting pan and pour enough boiling water into the roasting pan to come halfway up the sides of the pan. Bake for 45 minutes–1 hour (1½ hours for 12) or until shrinking away from the sides of the pan and firm to the touch. Set aside to cool.

5 Sit weights or cans of soup on top of the foil to weigh the terrine down, then transfer to the fridge for a minimum of 4 hours.

6 To serve, turn the terrine out on to a plate and press the chopped parsley and chives on top. Cut into slices and serve.

SERVE WITH

The terrine goes really well with the Cumberland sauce on page 185, but it is equally delicious with good chutney. Serve some crusty bread alongside.

PREPARE AHEAD

The terrine can be made and garnished with herbs up to 2 days ahead. Wrap in foil. Not suitable for freezing.

A meal in itself. We serve it cold with crusty bread, but you can keep the bacon, croûtons, and chicken warm and add just before serving.

Chicken and bacon Caesar salad

Serves 6

7oz smoked slab bacon, cut into ¼in pieces

4 thick slices white bread, crusts removed

3 tbsp olive oil

3 boneless skinless chicken breasts

2 romaine lettuces, cut into 2in (5cm) slices

1¾oz (50g) coarsely grated Parmesan cheese

salt and freshly ground black pepper

For the dressing

¼ garlic clove, crushed

2 tbsp white wine vinegar

½ tsp Dijon mustard

2 tbsp olive oil

6 tbsp mayonnaise

3 tbsp water

scant 1oz (25g) finely grated Parmesan cheese

1 tsp sugar

Serves 12

14oz smoked slab bacon, cut into ¼in pieces

8 thick slices white bread, crusts removed

6 tbsp olive oil

6 boneless skinless chicken breasts

4 romaine lettuces, cut into 2in (5cm) slices

3½oz (100g) coarsely grated Parmesan cheese

salt and freshly ground black pepper

For the dressing

½ garlic clove, crushed

¼ cup white wine vinegar

1 tsp Dijon mustard

¼ cup olive oil

¾ cup mayonnaise

¼ cup water

1¾oz (50g) finely grated Parmesan cheese

2 tsp sugar

1 Preheat the oven to 425°F (220°C). Meanwhile, scatter the bacon pieces over the base of a roasting pan. Cut each slice of bread into 20 even-sized cubes and scatter next to the bacon. Drizzle over two-thirds of the oil and cook in the oven for 15–20 minutes (20 minutes for 12) or until golden and crisp. Shake the pan occasionally.

2 Lay the chicken breasts between two sheets of plastic wrap and bash with a rolling pin until half as thick. Heat the remaining oil in a frying pan, add the chicken, and fry for 3 minutes on each side or until golden all over and cooked through. You may need to do this in batches. Allow to cool slightly, then cut into thin slices.

3 Put the lettuce and Parmesan into a large salad bowl and season with salt and freshly ground black pepper. Add the bacon and croûtons and toss together.

4 To make the dressing, put the garlic, vinegar, mustard, and oil into a bowl and whisk by hand until smooth. Add all the other ingredients and whisk again. Season with salt and freshly ground black pepper. Pour the dressing over the salad and toss to combine. Arrange the chicken on top and serve at once.

PREPARE AHEAD

The lettuce and Parmesan can be placed in a bowl up to 6 hours ahead. The dressing can be made up to 3 days ahead. Not suitable for freezing.

Chicken and bacon Caesar salad (see overleaf) •••▶

This is a wonderfully fresh and light salad, perfect for a picnic or for eating al fresco. You can replace the chicken with turkey if you prefer. Serve with salad leaves and your favorite bread.

Mediterranean lemon and herb chicken salad

Serves 6

For the dressing

2 tbsp Dijon mustard

2 tbsp pesto

juice of 1 lemon

¼ cup olive oil

1 tbsp sugar

salt and freshly ground
   black pepper

1lb 10oz (750g) cooked
   boneless skinless chicken,
   cut into thin strips

5½oz (150g) pitted green
   olives, halved

10oz jar roasted red peppers,
   drained and thinly sliced

2 tbsp freshly chopped basil

2 tbsp freshly chopped
   flat-leaf parsley

7oz (200g) feta cheese, broken
   into small pieces

Serves 12

For the dressing

¼ cup Dijon mustard

¼ cup pesto

juice of 2 lemons

½ cup olive oil

2 tbsp sugar

salt and freshly ground
   black pepper

3lb 3oz (1.5kg) cooked
   boneless skinless chicken,
   cut into thin strips

11oz (300g) pitted green
   olives, halved

2 x 10oz jars roasted red peppers,
   drained and thinly sliced

¼ cup freshly chopped basil

¼ cup freshly chopped
   flat-leaf parsley

14oz (400g) feta cheese,
   broken into small pieces

1 Put all the ingredients for the dressing into a large bowl and whisk by hand until well combined.

2 Add the chicken and toss well. Add the olives, half the peppers, the basil, parsley, and two-thirds of the feta. Season with salt and freshly ground black pepper and toss to combine.

3 Arrange on a platter and scatter the remaining peppers and feta attractively along the center. Chill in the fridge before serving.

PREPARE AHEAD
The salad can be made up to 8 hours ahead.
Not suitable for freezing.

A frittata is a kind of Italian omelette and this one—cooked in the oven rather than in a frying pan—is ideal for picnics. Cut into wedges and serve warm or cold with dressed salad and bread.

Summer frittata

Serves 6

Special equipment *8in (20cm) round springform pan, greased and lined with parchment*

12oz (350g) potatoes, cut into 1¼in (3cm) cubes
1 small onion, roughly chopped
salt and freshly ground
  black pepper

8 large eggs
1 tsp freshly chopped
  thyme leaves
3½oz (100g) goat cheese, cut into small cubes
2½oz (75g) Black Forest ham, cut into thin strips

Serves 12

Special equipment *2 x 8in (20cm) round springform pan, greased and lined with parchment*

1lb 9oz (700g) potatoes, cut into 1¼in (3cm) cubes
2 small onions, roughly chopped
salt and freshly ground
  black pepper

16 large eggs
2 tsp freshly chopped
  thyme leaves
2 x 3½oz (100g) goat cheese, cut into small cubes
5½oz (150g) Black Forest ham, cut into thin strips

1 Preheat the oven to 400°F (200°C). Cook the potatoes and onion in boiling salted water for 5–8 minutes or until tender. Drain and refresh in cold water.

2 Crack the eggs into a large mixing bowl, add the thyme, and season with salt and freshly ground black pepper. Whisk by hand until combined. Add the potatoes and onion and stir in the cheese.

3 Pour into the pan(s) and scatter over the strips of ham.

4 Bake for 12–15 minutes (15–20 minutes for 12) or until slightly risen and just firm. To make slicing easier, leave to cool slightly before serving.

VARIATION
Black Forest ham is one of the most reasonably priced cured hams. If you can't get hold of it, use Serrano ham or Parma ham.

PREPARE AHEAD
The frittata can be made up to 8 hours ahead.
Not suitable for freezing.

Buy the freshest peppers and eggplants you can find, with smooth skins, not wrinkly. Toast the pine nuts in a dry frying pan until golden. Watch them carefully, as they burn quickly. Serve with crusty bread.

Red pepper and eggplant salad with basil dressing

Serves 6

2 red peppers, cut in half and seeded

2 large eggplants, sliced in half lengthwise and cut into ¼in (5mm) slices

2 tbsp olive oil

salt and freshly ground black pepper

3½oz (100g) baby spinach

For the dressing

2 tbsp olive oil

2 tbsp balsamic vinegar

1½ tbsp fresh pesto

1¾oz (50g) pine nuts, toasted

Serves 12

4 red peppers, cut in half and seeded

4 large eggplants, sliced in half lengthwise and cut into ¼in (5mm) slices

¼ cup olive oil

salt and freshly ground black pepper

7oz (200g) baby spinach

For the dressing

¼ cup olive oil

¼ cup balsamic vinegar

3 tbsp fresh pesto

2½oz (75g) pine nuts, toasted

1 Preheat the oven to 425°F (220°C). Arrange the pepper halves cut side down in a single layer on one end of a baking sheet, then lay the eggplant slices in a single layer at the other. (For 12, lay the peppers on one sheet and the eggplants on another sheet.) Drizzle over the oil and season with salt and freshly ground black pepper.

2 Roast for 25–30 minutes or until the peppers are charred and the eggplant is tender and golden. Put the hot peppers into a plastic bag, seal tightly, and set aside until cold. This allows them to sweat, which makes it easier to remove the skins.

3 Peel the skin from the peppers and discard. Cut the flesh into thin slices and transfer to a serving bowl. Add the eggplant and spinach and season with salt and freshly ground black pepper.

4 To make the dressing, put the oil, vinegar, and pesto into a jam jar, seal with a lid, and shake vigorously.

5 To serve, pour the dressing over the salad, toss well, then scatter with the pine nuts. For the flavors to infuse, it is best to do this about an hour before serving.

PREPARE AHEAD
The salad can be made up to the end of step 2 up to 12 hours ahead. The dressing can be made up to 4 days ahead. Not suitable for freezing.

Packed with lentils, herbs, and vegetables, this side salad makes a fantastic accompaniment to grilled meats and fish.

Globe artichoke and Puy lentil salad

Serves 6

7oz (200g) dried Puy lentils
2 large celery stalks, finely diced
½ small red onion, finely diced
3½oz chargrilled artichokes
    in oil, drained and sliced into
    large pieces
2 tbsp freshly chopped
    flat-leaf parsley
2 tbsp freshly chopped mint
8oz (225g) cherry tomatoes,
    quartered

For the dressing

2 tbsp white wine vinegar
¼ cup olive oil
1 garlic clove, crushed
2 tbsp tomato paste
1 tbsp balsamic vinegar
salt and freshly ground
    black pepper

Serves 12

11oz (400g) dried Puy lentils
4 large celery stalks, finely diced
1 small red onion, finely diced
7oz chargrilled artichokes
    in oil, drained and sliced into
    large pieces
small bunch of flat-leaf
    parsley, chopped
small bunch of mint, chopped
1lb 2oz (500g) cherry tomatoes,
    quartered

For the dressing

¼ cup white wine vinegar
½ cup olive oil
2 garlic cloves, crushed
¼ cup tomato paste
2 tbsp balsamic vinegar
salt and freshly ground
    black pepper

1 Cook the lentils in boiling water for 15–20 minutes or until tender. Don't add salt or they might not soften. Drain and refresh in cold water.

2 Put the celery, onion, artichokes, herbs, and tomatoes into a large mixing bowl and stir in the lentils.

3 Mix the ingredients for the dressing in a small bowl and pour over the salad.

4 Season well with salt and freshly ground black pepper and chill in the fridge for 1 hour before serving.

PREPARE AHEAD
The salad can be made up to the end of step 2 up to 12 hours ahead. Add the dressing up to 3 hours ahead. Not suitable for freezing.

This is a great main course for a picnic, but it's also good as a side dish—in which case it will feed more. Serve with French bread.

Tuna salade niçoise

Serves 6

3½oz (100g) green beans, trimmed

salt and freshly ground black pepper

6 eggs

3 small Baby Gem lettuces

6 tomatoes, quartered

8oz (225g) baby new potatoes, cooked and halved lengthwise

2 x 7oz cans tuna in oil, drained

12 canned anchovy fillets, drained

3½oz (100g) pitted black olives, halved lengthwise

1 red onion, finely sliced

For the dressing

¼ cup good olive oil

2 tbsp grainy mustard

2 tbsp white wine vinegar

2 tsp sugar

juice of 1 lemon

Serves 12

7oz (200g) green beans, trimmed

salt and freshly ground black pepper

12 eggs

6 small Baby Gem lettuces

12 tomatoes, quartered

1lb (450g) baby new potatoes, cooked and halved lengthwise

2 x 14oz cans tuna in oil, drained

24 canned anchovy fillets, drained

8oz (225g) pitted black olives, halved lengthwise

2 red onions, finely sliced

For the dressing

½ cup good olive oil

¼ cup grainy mustard

¼ cup white wine vinegar

4 tsp sugar

juice of 2 lemons

1 Cook the beans in boiling salted water for 4 minutes or until just tender. Drain, refresh in cold water, and set aside.

2 Put the eggs into a saucepan, cover with water, and bring to a boil. Boil for 5 minutes, then drain and cover again with cold water. Peel, slice into quarters, and set aside.

3 Cut each lettuce into six wedges. Place in a serving bowl with the beans, tomatoes, potatoes, tuna, anchovies, olives, and onion and mix together. Season with salt and freshly ground black pepper.

4 Mix the ingredients for the dressing in a bowl, pour over the salad, and toss gently.

5 Scatter over the eggs and serve.

PREPARE AHEAD

The salad can be prepared up to the end of step 3 up to 6 hours ahead. Dress just before serving. Not suitable for freezing.

The sweet marinade for these kebabs helps the vegetables and cheese turn golden. Serve with salad and baked potatoes.

Chargrilled vegetable and halloumi skewers

Serves 6

Special equipment *6 metal or wooden skewers (soak wooden skewers in water for 12 hours beforehand to prevent them burning)*

2 medium red onions
salt
1 yellow pepper, halved, seeded, and cut into 12 large pieces
1 red pepper, halved, seeded, and cut into 12 large pieces

9oz (250g) halloumi cheese, cut into 18 cubes
12 small cherry tomatoes
2 tbsp olive oil, for frying

For the marinade

2 tbsp soy sauce
1 tbsp honey
1 red chile, halved, seeded, and finely chopped
1 large garlic clove, crushed

Serves 12

Special equipment *12 metal or wooden skewers (soak wooden skewers in water for 12 hours beforehand to prevent them burning)*

4 medium red onions
salt
2 yellow peppers, halved, seeded, and cut into 12 large pieces each
2 red peppers, halved, seeded, and cut into 24 large pieces

1lb (450g) halloumi cheese, cut into 36 cubes
24 small cherry tomatoes
¼ cup olive oil, for frying

For the marinade

¼ cup soy sauce
2 tbsp honey
2 red chiles, halved, seeded, and finely chopped
2 large garlic cloves, crushed

1 Slice each onion into six wedges, leaving the root end intact on each wedge so that the layers stay together during cooking. Bring a pan of salted water to a boil, add the onion wedges, the pieces of yellow pepper and the pieces of red pepper, and bring back to a boil. Boil for 5 minutes, then drain, refresh in cold water, and drain again.

2 In the order of your choice, thread two onion wedges, two pieces of yellow pepper, two pieces of red pepper, and three cubes of cheese on to each skewer. Place in a shallow dish.

3 Put all the ingredients for the marinade into a small bowl and mix well. Pour over the kebabs and leave to marinate for at least 1 hour and up to 8 hours.

4 Heat the oil in a large frying pan or griddle pan, add the kebabs, and fry for 2–3 minutes on each side or until chargrilled and brown and the cheese is just soft. You may need to do this in batches. Alternatively, cook under the broiler or on a grill. Serve hot on the skewers.

PREPARE AHEAD
The kebabs can be made up to the end of step 2 up to 1 day ahead. They can be marinated for up to 8 hours. Not suitable for freezing.

This unusual salad goes well with grilled meat or fish. To allow the flavors to infuse, make it up to six hours ahead.

Spicy roast squash and feta salad

Serves 6

1 large butternut squash
1 red onion, thinly sliced
2 tbsp olive oil
salt and freshly ground
    black pepper
1 tsp ground cumin
3½oz (100g) feta cheese,
    crumbled
2 tbsp freshly chopped parsley

For the dressing

1 tbsp white wine vinegar
2 tbsp olive oil
1 tsp honey
½ garlic clove, crushed

Serves 12

2 large butternut squash
2 red onions, thinly sliced
¼ cup olive oil
salt and freshly ground
    black pepper
1 tbsp ground cumin
7oz (200g) feta cheese,
    crumbled
¼ cup freshly chopped parsley

For the dressing

2 tbsp white wine vinegar
¼ cup olive oil
2 tsp honey
1 garlic clove, crushed

1 Preheat the oven to 425°F (220°C). Cut the squash in half lengthwise, scoop out the seeds and discard, then peel and cut the flesh into thin half-moon slices.

2 Scatter the squash and onion over the base of a roasting pan. Drizzle with the oil, season with salt and freshly ground black pepper, and toss to combine.

3 Roast for 25–30 minutes (30–35 minutes for 12) or until pale golden and just tender. Transfer to a mixing bowl with a slotted spoon, scatter over the cumin, and toss together. Set aside to cool.

4 When completely cool, stir in the feta and parsley. Put the ingredients for the dressing into a clean jam jar, tighten the lid, and shake well.

5 Pour the dressing over the salad and mix together. Transfer to a salad bowl and chill for up to six hours before serving.

PREPARE AHEAD
The salad can be made up to 6 hours ahead.
Not suitable for freezing.

PREPARING SQUASH

STEP 1 Cut the squash in half lengthwise, then scoop out the seeds and fibers with a spoon.

STEP 2 Cut into sections and use a peeler to remove the skin. You may need a knife for larger squash.

A fantastic vegetarian lunch. Make two separate galettes for 12. Allow to cool slightly before slicing and serving warm with salad.

Goat cheese, thyme, and onion marmalade galette

Serves 6

2 red peppers, halved and seeded

1 tbsp olive oil

salt and freshly ground black pepper

1 sheet frozen puff pastry, thawed

a little flour, to dust

10oz soft goat cheese

1 tbsp fresh thyme leaves, plus a few sprigs to garnish

1 egg, beaten

For the onion marmalade

2 tbsp olive oil

3 large onions, sliced

1 tbsp sugar

1 tbsp balsamic vinegar

Serves 12

4 red peppers, halved and seeded

2 tbsp olive oil

salt and freshly ground black pepper

2 sheets frozen puff pastry, thawed

a little flour, to dust

20oz soft goat cheese

2 tbsp fresh thyme leaves, plus a few sprigs to garnish

1 egg, beaten

For the onion marmalade

3 tbsp olive oil

6 large onions, sliced

2 tbsp sugar

2 tbsp balsamic vinegar

1 Preheat the oven to 400°F (200°C). Arrange the peppers cut side down on a baking sheet, drizzle over the oil, and season with salt and freshly ground black pepper. Roast for 25–30 minutes or until blackened. Transfer to a plastic bag, seal, and set aside.

2 Meanwhile, make the onion marmalade. Heat the oil in a non-stick frying pan over high heat, add the onions, and fry for 3 minutes or until starting to soften. Sprinkle in the sugar and vinegar and season with salt and freshly ground black pepper. Cover with a lid, lower the heat, and cook for 20 minutes or until the onions are soft. Set aside to cool.

3 Pop a baking sheet in the oven to get hot (two sheets for 12). Lightly flour a piece of baking parchment (two pieces for 12) and roll the pastry out into a 9 x 13in (23 x 33cm) rectangle (two rectangles for 12). Prick the base with a fork, leaving a border of 2in (5cm). Spread the cheese inside the border, scatter over the thyme, and spoon the onion marmalade on top. Peel the peppers, cut into strips, and scatter over the top. Brush the border with beaten egg.

4 Transfer the baking parchment and galette(s) to the baking sheet and bake for 20–25 minutes (30–35 minutes for 12) or until the pastry is golden. Garnish with thyme sprigs.

CHEAT

If you don't have the time to roast the peppers and make the onion marmalade, use store-bought, but buy the best you can.

PREPARE AHEAD

The galette can be made up to the end of step 3 up to 8 hours ahead. Not suitable for freezing.

Coleslaw should be light and fresh rather than rich and sloppy. This recipe comes from our lovely friend Joanna.

Sweet chili coleslaw

Serves 6

11oz (300g) white cabbage
1 small white onion
2 celery stalks
2 carrots, coarsely grated
salt and freshly ground
    black pepper

3 tbsp cider vinegar
2 tsp Dijon mustard
½ cup light or regular
    mayonnaise
5 tbsp sweet chili dipping sauce

Serves 12

1lb 5oz (600g) white cabbage
1 large white onion
4 celery stalks
4 carrots, coarsely grated
salt and freshly ground
    black pepper

6 tbsp cider vinegar
1 heaped tbsp Dijon mustard
1 cup light or regular mayonnaise
5fl oz (150ml) sweet chili
    dipping sauce

1 Slice the cabbage, onion, and celery in a food processor, using the slicing blade. If you have a mandolin, use the thin blade. Alternatively, slice them very finely by hand.

2 Transfer to a bowl, add the carrots, and season with salt and freshly ground black pepper.

3 Put the vinegar, mustard, mayonnaise, and dipping sauce into a jam jar. Seal with a lid and shake vigorously to combine.

4 Pour over the dressing and toss well. Transfer to the fridge for a minimum of 3 hours. Serve chilled or at room temperature.

SWEET CHILI DIPPING SAUCE
Look for this in the Asian section of the supermarket. It gives coleslaw a sweet kick and stops the sauce being too thick.

PREPARE AHEAD
The dressing can be made and kept in the jar for up to 4 days. The coleslaw can be made up to 1 day ahead. The flavors improve, in fact. Not suitable for freezing.

Some classic recipes are unbeatable, but our quiche lorraine—with added parsley—has the edge, we think. Serve warm with salad.

Quiche lorraine

Serves 6

Special equipment 8in (20cm) round 2in (5cm) deep removeable bottom tart pan or quiche dish

1½ cup all-purpose flour, plus a little extra to dust
6 tbsp cold butter, cubed
1 egg

For the filling
a pat of butter
1 large onion, roughly chopped

8oz (225g) unsmoked bacon, snipped into small pieces
1 heaped tbsp freshly chopped flat-leaf parsley
2½oz (75g) mature Cheddar cheese, grated
3 eggs
6oz crème fraîche
¾ cup heavy cream
salt and freshly ground black pepper

Serves 12

Special equipment 11in (28cm) round 2in (5cm) deep removeable bottom tart pan or quiche dish

Heaping 1¾ cup all-purpose flour, plus a little extra to dust
1 stick cold butter, cubed
1 egg
1–2 tbsp water

For the filling
a pat of butter
2 large onions, roughly chopped

12oz (350g) unsmoked bacon, snipped into small pieces
2 heaped tbsp freshly chopped flat-leaf parsley
6oz (175g) mature Cheddar cheese, grated
6 eggs
1¼ cup crème fraîche
1¼ cup heavy cream
salt and freshly ground black pepper

1 Put the flour and butter into a processor and pulse until the mixture resembles breadcrumbs. Add the egg (and the water if you're making the larger one) and pulse again until you have a smooth dough. Dust a work surface with flour and knead the dough lightly. Roll the dough out and use to line the flan pan (see page 243). Pierce the base all over with a fork and chill for 15 minutes.

2 Preheat the oven to 400°F (200°C). Put a baking sheet in to get hot. Line the crust with baking parchment, fill with dried beans, and bake for 15–20 minutes (see page 275). Remove the beans and paper, lower the temperature to 325°F (160°C), and return the crust to the oven to dry out for 5–10 minutes. Set aside to cool. Turn the oven up to 375°F (190°C).

3 To make the filling, melt the butter in a frying pan, add the onion and bacon, and fry over high heat for 2 minutes or until starting to crisp. Cover with a lid, lower the heat, and cook slowly for 15–20 minutes or until the onion is tender and the bacon cooked. Spoon into the crust and spread out evenly. Scatter with half the parsley and half the cheese.

4 Put the eggs, crème fraîche, and heavy cream into a mixing bowl and whisk by hand until combined. Add the remaining parsley and season with salt and freshly ground black pepper. Pour into the crust and sprinkle over the remaining cheese.

5 Bake in the oven for 25 minutes (30–35 minutes for 12) or until golden brown and the egg mixture is just set.

PREPARE AHEAD AND FREEZE
The quiche lorraine can be made up to 2 days ahead. Freeze for up to 2 months.

From left Hazelnut meringue roulade with raspberries (page 272), Individual tiramisus (page 256), Exotic fruit salad (page 265).

Our favorite desserts

The grand finale to any feast is the dessert. In this chapter, you'll find desserts of all kinds—wicked and indulgent, delicate and fruity, warm and comforting.

Our favorite desserts

We're huge fans of dessert. We love the classics like soufflés and crème brûlées, puddings and pavlovas, tarts and tiramisus, as well as our own variations on family favorites such as apple crumble and lemon meringue pie. In fact, the only thing we dislike about dessert is having to choose which ones to cook!

In general, for 8–12 people we'll serve one dessert that's rich and indulgent and another that's light and fruity—a fresh fruit salad or a fruit compote perhaps. These are always popular and if there's any left over it's delicious for breakfast the following day. Go to town with the decoration—fresh mint leaves, lime wedges, or a sprinkling of pomegranate seeds all look fantastic.

Serving dessert

● Plates must be hot if you're serving a warm dessert.

● So you know there'll be enough to go around, cut large desserts such as cheesecakes, pies, tarts, and roulades into wedges or slices. Place them on a flat platter or cake stand—the pieces can be difficult to remove from a bowl—and reassemble them so they look whole.

● If you're offering a selection of desserts on one plate, keep the portions small and arrange them in an attractive way.

● Take containers of ice cream out of the freezer and leave at room temperature for an hour or until beginning to thaw at the edges. Scoop balls of the ice cream on to a cold tray, cover with plastic wrap, and return to the freezer until required. Serve piled into a mound.

Cutlery
Provide both dessert forks and dessert spoons so that guests can help themselves to the ones they need.

Finish

Pitcher of cream or custard
If you're worried about drips, sit the pitcher on a plate. Put crème fraîche, ice cream, or whipped cream, into a small bowl.

How to set a buffet table of desserts

Desserts should be presented in the same way as main courses—from right to left (as here) or from left to right, depending on the layout of your room—and in the order guests will put them on their plates, so the desserts themselves should come before any cream or custard.

Doing it like this makes it quicker and easier for people to serve themselves. For a buffet of a dozen guests or more, we offer two desserts, plus a fruit salad. If you've invited over 30 people and have enough room, set two buffet tables with the same desserts on each.

Large desserts
Cut cheesecakes and tarts into slices or wedges and place on a flat platter or cake stand with a spatula to serve them with. Present other desserts in the dish you've made them in.

Table decoration
Place the table decoration in a prominent position, but well out of guests' way.

Start

Fruit salad
A glass bowl will show off the jewel-bright colors of a fruit salad to their best advantage. Provide a serving spoon.

Individual desserts
Serve individual desserts in tumblers, wine glasses, Martini glasses, shot glasses, or ramekins. Place them on a tray to make them easier to take to the table.

Bowls and plates
Provide dessert bowls and dessert plates. Which people take will depend on the dessert they choose—although most guests will likely eat more than one!

This is also very good made with thinly sliced unpeeled eating apples instead of apricots. Use about three per galette. Serve the tart warm with ice cream.

Apricot and almond galette

Makes 1 (serves 6)

a little all-purpose flour, to dust
½ of 1 sheet frozen puff pastry, thawed
a little milk
14oz can apricots in natural juices, drained
5½oz (150g) marzipan, coarsely grated
1 tbsp apricot jam
1 tsp water

Makes 2 (serves 12)

a little all-purpose flour, to dust
1 sheet frozen puff pastry, thawed
a little milk
2 x 14oz cans apricots in natural juices, drained
9oz (250g) marzipan, coarsely grated
2 tbsp apricot jam
2 tsp water

1 Preheat the oven to 425°F (220°C). Put a baking sheet in to get hot. Lightly flour a piece of parchment and roll the pastry out into a 5 x 12in (12.5 x 30cm) rectangle. For 12, roll it out into a 10 x 12in (25 x 30cm) rectangle, cut it in half lengthwise to make two strips, then arrange them neatly side by side.

2 With a knife, score a ½in (1cm) border around the rectangle(s), taking care not to cut all the way through—this allows the strip to rise up around the apricots and stops any liquid or fruit leaking out. Brush the border(s) with a little milk.

3 Slice each apricot into four slices and arrange them in rows inside the border(s). Sprinkle over the marzipan.

4 Slide the paper on to the hot baking sheet and bake for 20 minutes (20–25 minutes for two galettes) or until golden brown. Check halfway through cooking and, if they are getting too brown, cover loosely with foil.

5 Heat the apricot jam in a pan with the water, whisking until smooth. Brush the apricots with a thin layer to glaze them. Serve warm.

PREPARE AHEAD AND FREEZE
The galette(s) can be made up to 2 days ahead.
Freeze for up to 1 month.

COLD IS BEST
Take the pastry and marzipan straight from the fridge—they are easier to handle when cold. If you're not using all the pastry immediately, freeze any left over until needed.

These individual crumbles are scrumptious and so easy to make. Serve with cream, crème fraîche, or warm custard.

Mini apple, apricot, and hazelnut crumbles

Serves 6

Special equipment *6 x size 5fl oz (150ml) ramekins*

2lb (900g) Granny Smith apples, peeled and cut into ½in (1cm) cubes
6oz (175g) ready-to-eat dried apricots, snipped
into small pieces
½ cup apple juice
scant ½ cup demerara sugar
¾ cup all-purpose flour
3 tbsp cold butter, cubed
1oz (30g) hazelnuts, chopped

Serves 12

Special equipment *12 x size 5fl oz (150ml) ramekins*

4lb (1.8kg) Granny Smith apples, peeled and cut into ½in (1cm) cubes
12oz (350g) ready-to-eat dried apricots, snipped
into small pieces
1 cup apple juice
¾ cup demerara sugar
1½ cup all-purpose flour
6 tbsp cold butter, cubed
1¾oz (50g) hazelnuts, chopped

1 Preheat the oven to 400°F (200°C). Put the apples, apricots, apple juice, and all but 1 heaped tablespoon (3 level tablespoons for 12) of the demerara sugar into a saucepan. Bring to a boil, cover with a lid, and simmer for 5–7 minutes or until the apples are just soft. Remove from the heat and divide among the ramekins.

2 Put the flour and butter into a mixing bowl and rub together. Add the remaining sugar and the hazelnuts and mix together.

3 Sprinkle the crumble topping over the apples in the ramekins, then place on a baking sheet and bake for 15 minutes or until the crumble is light golden brown and the fruit is bubbling around the edges.

PREPARE AHEAD AND FREEZE
The crumbles can be made up to 2 days ahead.
Freeze for up to 1 month.

MAKING CRUMBLE TOPPING

Using the tips of your fingers, rub the cold butter into the flour until the mixture resembles breadcrumbs.

VARIATION
You could equally make one large crumble. Use a 1 quart (1.2 liter) ovenproof dish for six or a 2 quart (2.4 liter) dish for 12. Bake for 30 minutes (45 minutes for 12).

What makes this crumble so unusual is the layer of creamy custard in the middle. Serve it as it is or with a little more cream.

Apricot custard crumble pie

Makes a 11in (28cm) pie (serves 8–10)

Special equipment 11in (28cm) round tart pan

1½ cup all-purpose flour, plus a little extra to dust
6 tbsp butter
2 tbsp superfine sugar
1 egg

For the filling

5fl oz (150ml) sour cream
3 egg yolks
Heaping ¾ cup superfine sugar
scant ¼ cup all-purpose flour
2 x 14oz cans apricot halves in natural juices, drained and each apricot cut into three

For the crumble topping

3 tbsp butter
scant ½ cup all-purpose flour
Heaping ¾ cup superfine sugar

1 Preheat the oven to 425°F (220°C). Put a baking sheet in to get hot. Meanwhile, make the pastry. Put the flour and butter into a processor and pulse until the mixture resembles breadcrumbs. Add the sugar and egg and pulse again to form a ball.

2 Place the base of the tart pan on a work surface. Lightly dust the base of the tart pan and the work surface with flour, then roll the pastry out and line the tart pan.

3 To make the filling, put the sour cream, egg yolks, sugar, and flour into a mixing bowl and whisk by hand until smooth.

4 Arrange the apricots over the base of the pastry and pour the custard filling over the top. Sit the pie on the hot baking sheet and bake for 20 minutes or until the filling is just beginning to set.

5 Meanwhile, make the crumble topping. Put the butter, flour, and sugar into a mixing bowl and rub with your fingertips until the mixture resembles coarse breadcrumbs.

6 Sprinkle the crumble topping over the just-set custard. Return to the oven and bake for a further 15 minutes or until golden and the custard is completely set. If the crumble topping starts to get too brown, cover with foil. Serve warm or cold.

PREPARE AHEAD
The pie can be made the day before and gently reheated. Not suitable for freezing.

LINING A TART PAN

STEP 1 Place the pastry ball in the middle of the base of the pan and roll into a circle 2in (5cm) bigger. Carefully fold in the edge.

STEP 2 Return the base of the pan to the surround, then unfold the edge and neaten. Pierce the disk of pastry all over with a fork.

Crisp, buttery pastry packed with fruit—this apple pie is perfect for a special Sunday lunch. Serve warm with cream or ice cream.

Melt-in-the-mouth apple pie

Makes a 9½in (24cm) pie (serves 8)

Special equipment one 9in deep-dish pie pan

Heaping 1¾ cup all-purpose flour, plus a little extra to dust

1¼ sticks cold butter, cubed

2 tbsp superfine sugar, plus a little extra to decorate

1 egg, beaten

1–2 tbsp water

For the filling

3lb (1.35kg) Granny Smith apples, peeled, cored, and thinly sliced

¾ cup superfine sugar

½ tsp ground cinnamon

1 egg, beaten, to glaze

1 Preheat the oven to 400°F (200°C). Meanwhile, put the flour, butter, and sugar into a processor and pulse until the mixture resembles breadcrumbs. Add the egg and water and pulse again until it forms a ball. The dough will weigh about 1lb (450g). Divide it into a 9oz (250g) piece and a 7oz (200g) piece.

2 Lightly flour a work surface and roll the larger piece out very thinly, then use to line the inside of the dish, leaving a little hanging over at the sides.

3 To make the filling, put the apples, sugar, and cinnamon into a bowl, mix well, then spoon into the base of the dish. The apples will be higher than the pastry, but they will sink down as they cook.

4 Lightly flour the work surface and roll the remaining pastry out slightly larger than the surface of the dish. Brush the top of the pastry rim in the dish with water, then sit the pastry circle on top and gently push down to seal the edges. Using a small sharp knife, trim off any excess pastry and crimp the edges together with your fingertips. Use any leftover pastry for decoration (see right). Brush the pie with the beaten egg.

5 Bake for 45–50 minutes or until golden brown and crisp. Allow to cool slightly, then sprinkle with a little extra caster sugar and serve.

PREPARE AHEAD AND FREEZE
The pie can be made up to the end of step 4 up to 1 day ahead. Freeze for up to 2 months.

PASTRY DECORATIONS
Roll any leftover pastry out thinly, then place on a piece of baking parchment and pop in the freezer for 15 minutes or until frozen. When crisp, use a knife to cut into the shapes or letters you want.

These individual soufflés look impressive and, despite their rather complicated-sounding name, are extremely simple to make.

Twice-baked lemon soufflés

Serves 6

Special equipment 6 x size 5fl oz (150ml) ramekins, greased and base-lined with a disk of baking parchment

3 eggs, separated
¾ cup superfine sugar
2 tbsp corn starch
finely grated zest of
  2 large lemons

juice of 1 large lemon
9oz (250g) low-fat cream cheese
1 large tbsp lemon curd

For the lemon sauce

1¼ cup heavy cream
1 tbsp lemon curd
finely grated zest and juice
  of 1 lemon

Serves 12

Special equipment 12 x size 5fl oz (150ml) ramekins, greased and base-lined with a disk of baking parchmen

6 eggs, separated
1½ cup superfine sugar
¼ cup corn starch
finely grated zest of
  4 large lemons

juice of 2 large lemons
1lb 2oz (500g) low-fat
  cream cheese
2 large tbsp lemon curd

For the lemon sauce

2 cups heavy cream
2 tbsp lemon curd
finely grated zest and juice
  of 2 lemons

1 Preheat the oven to 375°F (190°C). Put the egg yolks and half the sugar into a mixing bowl and whisk with an electric whisk until pale, thick, and frothy.

2 Mix the corn starch, lemon zest, and lemon juice in a bowl until smooth. Fold in the egg-yolk mixture, then beat in the cream cheese and lemon curd with a spatula.

3 Whisk the egg whites with an electric whisk until they resemble clouds. Whisking constantly, add the remaining sugar a teaspoon at a time until the whites are stiff and shiny.

4 Carefully fold the egg-white mixture into the mixing bowl, then spoon into the ramekins. Run a knife around the edge of each one to ensure they rise evenly. Sit the ramekins snugly in a roasting pan, then pour enough boiling water to come halfway up the sides of the pan.

5 Bake for 15–20 minutes or until the soufflés have risen well and are just cooked. Set aside to cool completely.

6 Turn the soufflés out of the ramekins, remove the paper bases, and arrange snugly in one layer in an ovenproof dish.

7 To make the sauce, put all the ingredients into a mixing bowl and whisk until smooth. Pour the sauce around the soufflés in the dish, then bake in an oven preheated to 400°F (200°C) for 10 minutes (20–25 minutes for 12). Serve at once.

PREPARE AHEAD

The soufflés can be made up to the end of step 6 and the sauce poured around them up to 8 hours ahead. Not suitable for freezing.

This is a truly wonderful LMP. It takes a bit of time to make but, for a really special occasion, it's worth it. Serve warm or cold, but not hot, as the pie will be too soft to cut.

Lemon meringue pie

Makes a 11in (28cm) pie (serves 8–10)

Special equipment 11in (28cm) fluted removeable-bottom tart pan

Heaping 1¾ cups flour, plus a little extra to dust
1¼ sticks cold butter, cubed
½ cup confectioners' sugar
1 large egg, beaten
1 tbsp water

For the lemon filling

finely grated zest and juice of 6 lemons
½ cup corn starch
2 cups water
1¼ cups superfine sugar
6 egg yolks

For the topping

4 egg whites
1 cup superfine sugar
2 level tsp corn starch

1 Put the flour and butter into a processor and pulse until the mixture resembles breadcrumbs. Add the confectioners' sugar, egg, and water and pulse until it forms a ball. Transfer to a lightly floured work surface and roll the dough out thinly until slightly larger than the pan, then use to line the pan. Cover with plastic wrap and chill for about an hour.

2 Preheat the oven to 400°F (200°C). Line the crust with baking parchment, fill with dried beans, and bake for 15 minutes (see page 275). Remove the beans and parchment and return to the oven for 5 minutes to dry out, then remove from the oven and set aside. Reduce the oven temperature to 350°F (180°C).

3 To make the filling, mix the lemon zest, lemon juice, and corn starch to a smooth paste in a small bowl. Bring the water to a boil in a pan, add the lemon mixture, and stir over the heat until thickened, then boil for 1 minute. Mix the sugar and yolks in a bowl and carefully add to the pan. Stir over medium heat until you have a thick custard. Set aside to cool slightly, then pour into the crust.

4 To make the topping, whisk the egg whites with an electric whisk until they look like clouds. Gradually add the superfine sugar, whisking on maximum speed until the whites are stiff and glossy. Add the corn starch and whisk to combine.

5 Spoon the meringue on top of the lemon filling, spreading to cover it completely and swirling the top. Bake for 30 minutes or until the filling is completely set and the meringue is lightly golden and crisp.

JUICING LEMONS

To get the most juice from lemons, cut them in half and put them in the microwave. Heat until hot (3 minutes should be about right for six lemons), then squeeze. Not only will you get more juice from them, they'll be easier to squeeze, too.

PREPARE AHEAD

The crust can be made up to 2 days ahead. The pie can be made completely up to 1 day ahead. Not suitable for freezing.

This is similar to sticky toffee pudding and it's truly scrumptious. If you're serving 12, bake the pudding in two pans.

Toffee pudding with warm toffee sauce

Serves 6

***Special equipment** 9 x 13in (23 x 33cm) baking dish, greased, lined with baking parchment, and greased*

7 tbsp butter, at
    room temperature
¾ cup light brown sugar
2 eggs
1¾ cups self-rising flour
2 tbsp molasses
5fl oz (150ml) milk
1¾oz (50g) walnuts, chopped

For the toffee sauce

scant ¾ cup light brown sugar
½ cup honey
3 tbsp butter
6oz can evaporated milk

Serves 12

***Special equipment** Two 9 x 13in (23 x 33cm) baking dishes, greased, lined with baking parchment, and greased*

14 tbsp butter, at
    room temperature
1½ cup light brown sugar
4 eggs
1lb (450g) self-rising flour
¼ cup molasses
10fl oz (300ml) milk
3½oz (100g) walnuts, chopped

For the toffee sauce

1½ cup light brown sugar
1 cup honey
6 tbsp butter
2 x 6oz cans evaporated milk

1 Preheat the oven to 350°F (180°C). Put the butter, sugar, eggs, flour, and molasses into a bowl and whisk with an electric whisk until combined. Slowly add the milk, whisking until smooth. Pour into the lined pan and sprinkle with the walnuts.

2 Bake for 30–35 minutes (40 minutes for two puddings) or until well risen, just firm in the middle, and lightly golden brown. Keep warm.

3 To make the sauce, put the sugar, honey, and butter into a saucepan and stir over low heat until the sugar has dissolved, the butter has melted, and all the ingredients are combined. Simmer for 5 minutes, then remove from the heat and stir in the evaporated milk.

4 Cut the pudding into squares and serve warm with the warm toffee sauce.

PREPARE AHEAD AND FREEZE
The pudding can be made up to 1 day ahead. Freeze for up to 2 months. The sauce can be made up to 5 days ahead. Not suitable for freezing.

Becca is a great friend of ours. She has her own catering company and has given us great advice on cooking for numbers.

Becca's white chocolate and orange mousses

Serves 6

Special equipment 6 x 2¾in (7cm) round metal cooking rings

2½oz (75g) graham crackers, crushed
3 tbsp butter, melted
1 tbsp demerara sugar

For the mousse

3½oz (100g) cream cheese
½ cup heavy cream
5½oz (150g) Belgium or Continental 100 percent white chocolate
1 tbsp Cointreau
1 large orange

Serves 12

Special equipment 12 x 2¾in (7cm) round metal cooking rings

6oz (175g) graham crackers, crushed
5 tbsp butter, melted
1½ tbsp demerara sugar

For the mousse

9oz (250g) cream cheese
1¼ cup heavy cream
11oz (300g) Belgium or Continental 100 percent white chocolate
3 tbsp Cointreau
2 large oranges

1 Put the graham crackers into a mixing bowl, add the butter and sugar, and mix to combine.

2 Line a baking sheet with plastic wrap and sit the rings on top. Spoon the biscuit mixture evenly into the rings and level the tops with the back of a teaspoon. Transfer to the fridge to chill while you make the mousse.

3 Put the cream cheese and cream into a mixing bowl and whisk with an electric whisk until thick and holding its shape.

4 Gently melt the chocolate in a bowl set over a pan of just-simmering water until smooth.

5 Add the chocolate to the cream mixture and stir in the Cointreau. Finely grate the zest of the orange(s) and add to the mousse.

6 Spoon the mousse into the rings and level the tops. Chill for a minimum of 4 hours to firm up. Meanwhile, peel the orange(s) with a small knife. Cut the segments free and place in a bowl. Squeeze over the juice from the peel.

7 Remove the rings and serve the mousses with the orange segments arranged on top.

VARIATION

If you don't have cooking rings, you can make one large mousse. Follow the recipe for 12 and spoon the mousse into a 8in (20cm) round springform pan. Cut into 12 wedges and decorate with the orange segments.

PREPARE AHEAD
You can make the mousses up to 12 hours ahead. Not suitable for freezing.

This is so impressive—two small desserts, a little of each on one plate, served with some glazed summer berries. Your friends will think they are in a three-star restaurant.

A rather special dessert collection

Serves 12

Glazed summer berries

9oz (250g) small strawberries, hulled and halved
9oz (250g) raspberries
3½oz (100g) blueberries
3 tsp confectioners' sugar

1 Place the berries in a large mixing bowl and toss together gently.

2 Sift the confectioners' sugar over the top and gently combine. Cover and chill in the fridge for up to 4 hours. The sugar will dissolve in the strawberry juices to form a shimmering glaze.

Crème brûlée

Special equipment 7in (18cm) square cake pan, greased

2 cups heavy cream
4 egg yolks
2 tbsp superfine sugar
½ tsp vanilla extract
scant ½ cup demerara sugar

1 Preheat the oven to 275°F (140°C). Heat the heavy cream gently in a saucepan until hot. Put the egg yolks, sugar, and vanilla extract into a bowl and whisk until combined. Pour the mixture into the hot cream and whisk until smooth. Transfer to a measuring cup, then strain into the cake pan.

2 Sit the cake pan in a roasting pan, pour enough boiling water into the roasting pan to come halfway up the sides of the cake pan, then transfer to the oven and bake for 30–35 minutes or until the cream mixture has just set. Set aside to cool.

3 Once cold, sprinkle the demerara sugar on top and slide under a hot broiler until the sugar dissolves and becomes caramel-colored. Set aside to firm up in the fridge for at least 1 hour and up to 5 hours.

4 When ready to serve, cut into even-sized squares with a sharp thin knife.

If you're serving fewer than 12 people, make just one of these special desserts—it will serve six. Cut the crème brûlée into six servings rather than 12. And make the chocolate pots in six 5fl oz (150ml) ramekins or wine glasses. Serve with or without the glazed summer berries.

Chocolate pots

Special equipment *12 shot glasses, about 2½fl oz (75ml) in capacity*

11oz (300g) dark or
  semi-sweet chocolate
1¼ cups heavy cream
7fl oz (200ml) crème fraîche

TO SERVE
The desserts look particularly attractive on long white plates. Arrange a chocolate pot at one end, place a pile of the berries in the center, and a square of crème brûlée at the other end.

1 Reserve two squares of chocolate for decoration, then put the rest in a bowl set over a pan of simmering water. Add 7fl oz (200ml) of the heavy cream and stir until the chocolate has melted. Set aside to cool slightly.

2 Stir in the crème fraîche, then pour into the shot glasses. Leave to set in the fridge for at least 2 hours.

3 Once set, pour the remaining heavy cream over the top. Coarsely grate the reserved chocolate and sprinkle on top.

PREPARE AHEAD
The custard for the crème brûlée can be made up to 2 days ahead. Add the topping up to 5 hours before serving. The chocolate pots can be made up to 2 days ahead. The berries can be prepared up to 4 hours ahead. Not suitable for freezing.

A rather special dessert collection (see overleaf) ●●>

The combination of rhubarb and lemon is delicious. This dessert looks particularly pretty made with young pink rhubarb, which may be available in stores toward the end of the winter.

Rhubarb and lemon pots

Serves 6

1lb 10oz (750g) rhubarb, sliced into 1¾in (4cm) pieces
finely grated zest of ½ orange, plus 2 tbsp orange juice
2 tbsp superfine sugar

For the lemon topping

1¼ cups heavy cream
3 tbsp superfine sugar
finely grated zest and juice of 1½ lemons
six mint leaves, to decorate

Serves 12

3lb 3oz (1.5kg) rhubarb, sliced into 1¾in (4cm) pieces
finely grated zest of 1 orange, plus ¼ cup orange juice
3 tbsp superfine sugar

For the lemon topping

2 cups heavy cream
6 tbsp superfine sugar
finely grated zest and juice of 3 lemons
12 mint leaves, to decorate

1 Put the rhubarb, orange zest, orange juice, and sugar into a saucepan. Stir over high heat for 2 minutes, cover with a lid, lower the heat, and simmer for 10 minutes (15 minutes for 12) or until the rhubarb is just tender. Set aside to cool.

2 To make the topping, put the cream, sugar, and lemon zest into a pan. Heat gently over low heat until the sugar dissolves and the mixture reaches simmering point. Remove from the heat, stir in the lemon juice, and set aside to cool slightly.

3 Spoon the rhubarb and a little of the liquid into the base of some pretty glasses or tumblers. Pour the lemon topping on top, then transfer to the fridge for a minimum of 4 hours to set.

4 Serve chilled, decorated with mint leaves.

PREPARE AHEAD
The pots can be made up to 12 hours ahead.
Not suitable for freezing.

We all love tiramisu. This version is served individually, with the added decadence of a splash of Baileys Irish Cream. Serve the tiramisus in tumblers or wine, martini, or champagne glasses.

Individual tiramisus

Serves 6

1½ tsp instant coffee granules
½ cup boiling water
3 tbsp Baileys Irish Cream
2 eggs
½ cup superfine sugar
1¼ cups heavy cream
8oz mascarpone

12 soft ladyfingers
2½oz (75g) dark chocolate, coarsely grated

Serves 12

1 tbsp instant coffee granules
1¼ cup boiling water
6 tbsp Baileys Irish Cream
4 eggs
¾ cup superfine sugar
2 cups heavy cream
1lb mascarpone

24 soft ladyfingers
5½oz (150g) plain chocolate, coarsely grated

1 Put the coffee granules and boiling water into a measuring glass and stir to dissolve. Allow to cool slightly, then stir in the Baileys.

2 Break the eggs into a mixing bowl, add the sugar, and whisk with an electric whisk until pale, thick, and frothy and the whisk leaves a trail on the surface when lifted.

3 Whip the cream till just lightly whipped and holding its shape.

4 Put the mascarpone into a bowl, stir in 2 tablespoons of the whipped cream, and mix with a spatula. Gently fold in the rest of the whipped cream, followed by the egg mixture, taking care not to knock out any of the air.

5 Cut the ladyfingers in half horizontally and then in half crosswise. Push a piece into the base of each tumbler or glass, drizzle over half the coffee mixture, then spoon over half the cream mixture. Repeat to give another layer of ladyfingers, coffee, and cream. Finish with a sprinkling of the grated chocolate.

6 Cover and chill in the fridge for a minimum of 4 hours.

VARIATION
If you don't have any Baileys Irish Cream, you can replace it with the same quantity of brandy.

PREPARE AHEAD AND FREEZE
The tiramisus can be made up to 12 hours ahead.
Freeze for up to 1 month.

A rich, indulgent cheesecake that requires no gelatine—ideal for vegetarians. Serve on its own or with fresh summer fruits such as raspberries and strawberries.

Chocolate truffle cheesecake

Serves 12

Special equipment 7½in (19cm) square pan or an 7in (18cm) round springform pan, lined with plastic wrap

7oz (200g) dark chocolate
2 eggs, separated
3 tbsp superfine sugar

6oz (175g) cream cheese
½ tsp vanilla extract
5fl oz (150ml) heavy cream, lightly whipped
175g (6oz) chocolate wafers, crushed
5 tbsp butter, melted

1 Break the chocolate into small pieces into a bowl. Sit the bowl over a pan of hot water on low heat and stir until melted. Take care not to allow the chocolate to get too hot or it will lose its shine and become too thick.

2 Put the egg yolks and sugar into a large bowl and whisk with an electric whisk until light and thick and a trail is left when the whisks are lifted from the bowl.

3 Mix the cream cheese and vanilla extract in a bowl, then stir in the melted chocolate. Fold in the whisked egg yolks and sugar, taking care not to knock out any air. Fold in the whipped cream.

4 Whisk the egg whites with an electric hand whisk until like clouds. Stir a spoonful of egg whites into the chocolate mixture with a spatula, then cut and fold the rest in until smooth.

5 Spoon into the prepared pan and level the top. Transfer to the fridge for 1 hour or until just set.

6 Mix the wafer crumbs and butter together until combined. Carefully press on top of the cheesecake in an even layer. Return to the fridge for a minimum of 6 hours.

7 To serve, turn the cheesecake upside-down on to a board or plate and cut into 12 fingers or wedges.

PREPARE AHEAD AND FREEZE
The cheesecake can be made up to the end of step 6 up to 2 days ahead. Freeze for up to 3 months.

FOLDING IN EGG WHITES

STEP 1 Cut down through the spoonful of egg white and bring some chocolate mixture up over it.

STEP 2 Continue the cut, lift, and sweep and, when no whites are visible, add the rest and repeat.

This was the favorite dessert at a charity buffet for 40 that Mary was a guest at—it went like lightning. The other good news is that once you've collected the ingredients together, it takes 10 minutes.

Heavenly lemon cheesecake on a ginger crust

Makes a 20cm (8in) cheesecake (serves 8)

Special equipment *8in (20cm) round removeable-bottom tart pan, greased and lined with baking parchment*

3½oz (100g) ginger cookies, crushed
3 tbsp butter, melted
8oz mascarpone
11oz jar lemon curd
juice of 1 small lemon
fresh raspberries and blueberries, to decorate
confectioners' sugar, to dust

1 Mix the cookies with the butter in a bowl, then press into the base of the pan (but not up the sides).

2 Put the mascarpone, lemon curd, and lemon juice in a bowl and beat with a spatula until smooth.

3 Spoon on to the cookie base and level the top. Chill in the fridge for at least 4 hours and up to 24 hours to firm up.

4 To serve, remove the cheesecake from the pan, peel off the baking parchment, and arrange on a platter. Decorate with the fruit and dust with confectioners' sugar.

Great for a crowd... You can make up to three cheesecakes at a time (but do not to overbeat the mixture at step 2). If you're making more cheesecakes than that, prepare them in separate batches.

PREPARE AHEAD
The cheesecake can be made up to the end of step 3 up to 1 day ahead. Not suitable for freezing.

This unusual chilled cheesecake has a delicious raspberry-ripple filling. If we don't have any Framboise raspberry liqueur to hand, we make a cherry-ripple cheesecake, using kirsch instead.

Chilled marbled raspberry cheesecake

Makes a 9in (23cm) cheesecake (serves 8)

Special equipment 9in (23cm) round springform pan, greased and lined with parchment

1 cup graham cracker crumbs
3 tbsp butter, melted
2 tbsp demerara sugar

For the raspberry filling
1lb 2oz (500g) fresh raspberries
2 tsp powdered gelatine
2 tbsp water
2 tbsp Framboise liqueur

For the creamy filling
3 tsp powdered gelatine
3 tbsp water
9oz (250g) cream cheese,
   at room temperature
2 eggs, separated
7oz (200g) low-fat sour cream
scant ½ cup superfine sugar

1 Mix the crumbs, butter, and sugar together in a bowl and press into the base of the pan. Transfer to the fridge to chill.

2 Meanwhile, make the raspberry filling. Blend the raspberries in a processor until smooth, then push through a sieve into a bowl. Put the gelatine into another bowl and add the water. Allow to soak until the gelatine becomes spongy, then stand the bowl in a saucepan of hot water until it dissolves. Once dissolved, add the Framboise, then pour into the raspberry purée. Stir and set aside.

3 To make the creamy filling, prepare the gelatine and water as above. Put the cream cheese, egg yolks, and sour cream into a bowl and beat with an electric mixer combine.

4 Spoon 2 tablespoons of the creamy mixture into the liquid gelatine and mix, then pour the whole lot into the creamy mixture and stir until smooth.

5 Whisk the egg whites with an electric hand whisk until stiff, then add the sugar a teaspoon at a time, whisking constantly until shiny and stiff. Fold the egg whites into the creamy mixture until smooth.

6 Carefully fold the raspberry filling into the creamy mixture to give a ripple effect.

7 Spoon into the pan and chill in the fridge for a minimum of 6 hours or until firm.

8 To serve, remove from the pan, discard the disk of paper, and cut into slices.

PREPARE AHEAD AND FREEZE
The cheesecake can be made up to the end of step 7 up to 2 days ahead. Freeze for up to 3 months.

One of the great things about this ice cream (apart from its flavor) is that you don't need an ice-cream maker. It's made with raw meringue, which means it doesn't need whisking as it freezes.

Rum and raisin ice cream

Serves 10–12

Special equipment *1½ quart (1.5 liter) freezerproof container*

6oz (175g) black raisins
5 tbsp dark rum
4 eggs, separated
scant ½ cup sugar
1¼ cups heavy cream

1 Put the raisins into a bowl and add the rum. Leave to soak—ideally overnight.

2 Put the egg yolks into a small bowl and whisk with a fork until blended.

3 Whisk the egg whites with an electric whisk until stiff. Whisking on maximum speed, add the sugar a teaspoon at a time until the whites are stiff and glossy.

4 Whip the cream until soft peaks form, then fold into the egg-white mixture until smooth. Stir in the egg yolks and soaked raisins. If there is any rum left in the bowl, add this too.

5 Transfer to the freezerproof container and freeze for a minimum of 24 hours.

6 Remove from the freezer 10 minutes before serving to make scooping easier.

PREPARE AHEAD AND FREEZE
Freeze for up to 2 months.

SERVING TIP
To make serving speedier, once the ice cream is frozen, scoop out the number of balls of ice cream you need and arrange on a tray (make sure it fits in the freezer first). Cover with plastic wrap and slide the tray into the freezer. Then all you need to do is arrange the balls in the bowls when you are ready to serve.

A fruit-based dessert is so welcome after a rich main course and these poached pears make a great change from fruit salad. The sauce for them is vivid and vibrant in color.

Poached pears with blackberry sauce

Serves 6

1¼ cups granulated sugar
1 quart water
a few strips of lemon zest
6 pears, peeled, but stem left on

For the blackberry sauce

1lb (450g) blackberries
¼ cup granulated sugar

Serves 12

2½ cups granulated sugar
2 quarts water
a few strips of lemon zest
12 pears, peeled, but stem left on

For the blackberry sauce

2lb (900g) blackberries
½ cup granulated sugar

1 Put the sugar, water, and lemon peel into a saucepan just large enough to take the pears upright in a single layer.

2 Heat gently, stirring until the sugar has dissolved, then boil rapidly for 2 minutes.

3 Place the pears in the hot syrup, cover with a wet sheet of parchment paper (this ensures the top of the pears do not dry out), and bring to a boil. Cover with a lid and simmer gently for 30–45 minutes (50 minutes for 12) or until the pears are just tender. Set aside to cool.

4 Put the blackberries and sugar into a pan and cook for 5 minutes or until the juices start to run. Push through a sieve into a bowl to get a thickish purée.

5 When the pears are cold, remove from the syrup and pat dry with paper towels.

6 Serve one pear per person or cut each one in half lengthwise through the stem, remove the core, and serve two halves. Drizzle over the sauce.

PREPARE AHEAD AND FREEZE
The pears can be poached up to 12 hours ahead and kept in the syrup until ready to serve. The sauce can be made up to 3 days ahead. Freeze the sauce for up to 2 months.

VARIATION
Black currants work just as well as blackberries. Whichever fruit you use, make the pudding extra special by adding 1 tablespoon of crème de cassis to the purée.

One of the quickest, most delicious desserts you'll ever make! Serve with shortbread cookies to make it extra special.

Magenta fruit compote with white chocolate sauce

Serves 6

2 tbsp superfine sugar
2 tbsp crème de cassis or
   blackcurrant liqueur
¼ cup water
8oz (225g) blueberries
8oz (225g) raspberries

8oz (225g) strawberries,
   quartered
5oz (150g) Belgian 100 percent
   white chocolate
1¼ cup heavy cream

Serves 12

¼ cup superfine sugar
¼ cup crème de cassis or
   blackcurrant liqueur
½ cup water
1lb 2oz (500g) blueberries
1lb 2oz (500g) raspberries

1lb 2oz (500g) strawberries,
   quartered
11oz (300g) Belgian 100 percent
   white chocolate
2 cups heavy cream

1 Put the sugar, crème de cassis, and water into a shallow saucepan. Gently heat, then add the blueberries and simmer for a few minutes or until just starting to soften. Remove from the heat and add the raspberries and strawberries. Mix together and leave in the pan to cool completely.

2 Put the chocolate and cream into a bowl set over a pan of just-simmering water and stir until runny. Take care not to overheat the chocolate or it will lose its shine and sieze. Leave to cool and thicken slightly.

3 Divide the fruit among wine or cocktail glasses. Pour the white chocolate sauce over the top, then place in the fridge for 2 hours to set slightly.

PREPARE AHEAD
The fruit can be prepared up to 2 days ahead and the desserts assembled up to 12 hours ahead. Not suitable for freezing.

This is a lovely refreshing fruit salad and any left over is a real treat for breakfast the next day. Serve on its own or with cream.

Exotic fruit salad

Serves 6

½ large cantaloupe melon

1 large mango, stone removed and flesh cut into cubes (see page 273)

3 passion fruit

3 oranges

1 grapefruit

8oz (225g) black seedless grapes

¼ cup Cointreau or Grand Marnier (optional)

Serves 12

1 large cantaloupe melon, cut in half

2 large mangoes, stones removed and flesh cut into cubes (see page 273)

6 passion fruit

6 oranges

2 grapefruits

1lb 2oz (500g) black seedless grapes

½ cup Cointreau or Grand Marnier (optional)

1 Scoop the seeds from the melon and discard. Using a sharp knife, cut into wedges and remove the skin. Slice the flesh into 1in (2.5cm) chunks and put into a serving bowl with the mango cubes.

2 Slice the passion fruit in half and scoop the seeds into the bowl.

3 Remove the skin from the oranges and grapefruit(s) and cut the flesh into segments, making sure you catch the juices. Add to the bowl.

4 Slice the grapes in half and add to the bowl.

5 Add the Cointreau or Grand Marnier, if using, and mix lightly together, then chill in the fridge until you are ready to serve.

PREPARE AHEAD

The salad can be made up to 12 hours ahead. Not suitable for freezing.

OTHER FRUITS TO USE

Raspberries and strawberries are good in a fruit salad, but add them at the last minute or they will bleed into the other fruits and turn mushy. Bananas go soft after a while, too. Avoid apples, pears, and peaches, as they discolor.

SEGMENTING ORANGES

STEP 1 Cut a piece from the top and base, then slice down around the flesh, removing skin and pith.

STEP 2 Slide the knife down one side of a segment, then cut down the other side and pull it free.

A classic dessert that's brilliant for serving numbers. For a recipe for six, turn to page 250. This is delicious served with soft summer fruits such as raspberries or a fruit coulis.

Party crème brûlée

Serves 12–16

Special equipment 2 quart shallow wide-based ovenproof dish, greased

½ cup superfine sugar
12 egg yolks
3 tsp vanilla extract
1 quart heavy cream
1¼ cups half-and-half
1 cup demerara sugar
3½oz (100g) raspberries, to decorate
mint leaves, to decorate

1 Preheat the oven to 325°F (160°C). Meanwhile, put the sugar, egg yolks, and vanilla extract into a large mixing bowl and whisk together by hand.

2 Put the heavy cream and half-and-half into a saucepan and heat until just below boiling point (just hot enough to put your finger in).

3 Pour the hot cream into the egg yolk mixture, whisking quickly until combined.

4 Pour the custard through a sieve into the prepared ovenproof dish.

5 Put the dish into a large roasting pan and pour enough boiling water into the pan so that it comes halfway up the sides of the dish.

6 Carefully slide into the oven and cook for 35–45 minutes or until set but with a slight wobble in the middle. Check after 30 minutes to see how it's doing.

7 Remove from the oven and leave to cool in the roasting pan, then place in the fridge and chill until stone cold.

8 Sprinkle over the demerara sugar, then put under a hot broiler, watching it very carefully, for 20–25 minutes or until melted and golden brown. You could also use a blowtorch to do this. To give the topping time to soften slightly, chill in the fridge for at least 5 hours and up to 10 hours, but no more or it will liquify.

9 To serve, cut into portions with a sharp thin knife and decorate with raspberries and mint leaves.

Great for a crowd... Make in batches and store in the fridge for 5–10 hours.

VARIATION

You could also serve the crème brûlée in individual portions—there will be enough for 12 size 5fl oz (150ml) ramekins. The baking time will be shorter, though—around 20 minutes—but keep an eye on them when they're in the oven.

PREPARE AHEAD

The custard can be made up to the end of step 7 up to 2 days ahead. Not suitable for freezing.

Pear and ginger is one of our all-time favorite combinations. This pavlova is sprinkled with pomegranate seeds just before serving—they look so pretty and glisten like little gems.

Pear and ginger pavlova

Serves 6

3 egg whites
6oz (175g) superfine sugar
1 level tsp corn starch
1 tsp white wine vinegar

¼ cup superfine sugar
1¼ cups heavy cream, whipped
6 bulbs stem ginger (from a jar), drained and coarsely chopped
1 small pomegranate

For the topping

5 fairly ripe pears, peeled, cored, and chopped into chunky slices
juice of ½ lemon

Serves 12

6 egg whites
1½ cups superfine sugar
2 level tsp corn starch
2 tsp white wine vinegar

juice of 1 lemon
½ cup superfine sugar
2 cups heavy cream, whipped
12 bulbs stem ginger (from a jar), drained and coarsely chopped
2 small pomegranates

For the topping

10 fairly ripe pears, peeled, cored, and chopped into chunky slices

1 Preheat the oven to 325°F (160°C). Whisk the egg whites with an electric whisk until they look like clouds. Gradually add the sugar a little at a time, whisking on maximum speed until the whites are stiff and glossy. Mix the corn starch and vinegar in a cup until smooth, then stir into the pavlova mixture.

2 Line a baking sheet with baking parchment and draw a 8 x 12in (20 x 30cm) rectangle on it (two rectangles side by side for 12). Spread the pavlova mixture out into the rectangle(s) with a knife, then create a well in the middle by building up the sides.

3 Slide the baking sheet into the oven, immediately reduce the temperature to 300°F (150°C), and bake for 1 hour. Turn the oven off and leave the pavlova in the oven for a further hour to dry out.

4 To make the topping, put the pears, lemon juice, and sugar into a small pan and barely cover with water. Simmer gently over low heat for 10 minutes or until the pears are just tender. Leave in the liquid until needed, then drain, reserve a few for decoration, and stir the rest into the whipped cream with the ginger.

5 Arrange the pavlova on a serving plate, spoon the cream into the well, and decorate with the reserved pears. Cut the pomegranate(s) in half, pick out the seeds, and sprinkle over the top. Serve at room temperature.

PREPARE AHEAD AND FREEZE
The pavlova can be made up to the end of step 3 up to 1 month ahead. Wrap in plastic wrap and then foil and keep in a cool place. The pears can be poached up to 8 hours ahead. The pavlova can be assembled up to 4 hours ahead. Freeze the pavlova without the topping for up to 6 months.

You don't get successful pavlovas if you use more than six egg whites at one time, which is why we make them in two batches for this party pyramid. It is the most spectacular dessert you'll ever make.

Party pavlova pyramid

Serves 35–40

2 x 6 egg whites
1½ cups superfine sugar
2 x 1 tsp white wine vinegar
2 x 1 tsp corn starch

For the filling
6 cups heavy cream
18oz Greek yogurt
2lb (900g) strawberries, hulled

1lb 10oz (750g) raspberries
1lb (450g) blueberries
a few mint leaves, to decorate, optional

1 Preheat the oven to 325°F (160°C). Make a first batch of pavlova by putting six egg whites into a mixing bowl and whisking with an electric whisk until they look like clouds. Gradually add the sugar a little at a time, whisking on maximum speed until they are stiff and glossy. Mix the vinegar and corn starch in a cup until smooth, then stir into the bowl.

2 Line a baking sheet with baking parchment and spread the pavlova mixture out—it should be about 12in (30cm) in diameter and about 2in (5cm) thick. This will be the base for the pyramid.

3 Slide into the oven, then immediately reduce the temperature to 300°F (150°C) and bake for 1 hour. Turn the oven off and leave the pavlova in the oven for an hour or overnight to dry out.

4 Prepare a second batch of pavlova mixture in the same way. Use to make one pavlova measuring 10in (25cm) in diameter, another measuring 8in (20cm) in diameter, and a third that is 5in (12cm) in diameter. The smallest one can be fairly thin and should fit on a baking sheet with the 8in (20cm) pavlova.

5 Cook in the same way: put the 10in (25cm) pavlova in the oven and bake for 15 minutes, then pop the two smaller pavlovas in as well and bake for a further 45 minutes. Switch off the oven and leave to dry out for an hour or overnight.

6 To assemble, whip the cream until just stiff and mix with the yogurt. Place the largest pavlova on a foil-covered board or tray (it needs to be sturdy), then cover with whipped cream and half the fruit. Make sure the fruit can be seen around the edge, so the pyramid will look attractive.

7 Place the next-largest pavlova on top and cover with cream and fruit. Continue in the same way with the other pavlovas. Finish with the last of the cream and a pretty arrangement of fruit and mint leaves on top, if using. To serve, cut in wedges, starting from the top.

Great for a crowd... To make a larger pyramid, make another meringue layer as opposed to making larger meringues.

PREPARE AHEAD AND FREEZE
The pavlovas can be made up to 1 month ahead and stored (see page 268). Freeze for up to 6 months. The pyramid can be assembled up to 4 hours ahead. This is best done in situ, so you don't need to move it.

Party pavlova pyramid (see overleaf) •••>

Meringue roulade is such a classic dessert. As a twist, we've added chopped roasted hazelnuts to give a lovely nutty flavor that goes sublimely well with raspberries and cream.

Hazelnut meringue roulade with raspberries

Makes a 13in (33cm) roulade (serves 8–10)

Special equipment 9 x 13in (23 x 33cm) jelly roll pan, greased and lined with baking parchment

4 egg whites
1 cup superfine sugar

1¾oz (50g) roasted hazelnuts, chopped
1¼ cups heavy cream, whipped
7oz (200g) fresh raspberries

1 Preheat the oven to 400°F (200°C). Meanwhile, put the egg whites into a large clean bowl and whisk with an electric whisk on full speed until very stiff. With the whisk still on full speed, gradually add the sugar a teaspoon at a time, whisking well between each addition. The meringue is ready when it is glossy and very, very stiff.

2 Spread the mixture into the prepared pan and sprinkle with the hazelnuts. Bake for 8 minutes or until very golden.

3 Remove the meringue from the oven and turn hazelnut side down on to a sheet of non-stick baking parchment. Remove the paper from the base of the meringue and allow to cool for 10 minutes.

4 Spread the whipped cream over the meringue and scatter over the raspberries. Using the parchment to help you, roll the meringue up fairly tightly from one of the long ends to form a roulade. Wrap in non-stick baking parchment and chill well before serving.

5 To serve, unwrap and cut into slices.

Great for a crowd... Prepare individual roulades rather than multiplying the quantities and making one big one. Bake one at a time. The roulades freeze well, remember.

PREPARE AHEAD AND FREEZE
The roulade can be made up to 12 hours ahead.
Freeze without the raspberries for up to 2 months.
Serve with the raspberries on the side.

Eton mess is a favorite pudding of meringues, cream, and fruit. We love the combination of lime and mango in our version. Don't crush the meringues too much—the pieces should be the size of grapes.

Mango Eton mess

Serves 6

1 large ripe mango
1¼ cups heavy cream
scant ¼ cup confectioners' sugar

finely grated zest and juice
   of 1 lime
3½oz (100g) crisp meringue
   cookies, crushed

Serves 12

2 large ripe mangoes
2½ cups heavy cream
½ cup confectioners' sugar

finely grated zest and juice
   of 2 limes
7oz (200g) crisp meringue
   cookies, crushed

1 Cut the mango(es) in half, then remove the flesh (see right). Put half the cubes into a processor and whiz to a smooth purée. Put the other half to one side.

2 Whip the cream until it just holds its shape. Carefully fold in the mango purée, the reserved mango cubes, icing sugar, lime zest, lime juice, and meringues.

3 Spoon into pretty wine glasses or tumblers or into one large glass bowl and serve chilled.

PREPARE AHEAD
The cream can be whipped and folded with all the ingredients except the meringues up to 12 hours ahead. Fold in the meringues a maximum of 6 hours ahead. Not suitable for freezing.

PREPARING A MANGO

STEP 1 Sit the mango on its side, then slice it in half at either side of the large flat stone in the center.

STEP 2 Cut the flesh into cubes, but don't cut through the skin. Press the skin so the cubes burst upward.

These creamy desserts are one of those foolproof desserts you'll go back to time and again and all your friends will ask for the recipe.

Lemon and lime puddings

Serves 6

2 cups heavy cream
scant ¾ cup superfine sugar
finely grated zest and juice
   of 2 lemons

finely grated zest and juice
   of 2 limes
lime zest, sprigs of mint, or
   borage flowers, to decorate

Serves 12

1 quart heavy cream
1½ cups superfine sugar
finely grated zest and juice
   of 4 lemons

finely grated zest and juice
   of 4 limes
lime zest, sprigs of mint, or
   borage flowers, to decorate

1 Put the cream, sugar, lemon zest, and lime zest into a wide-based saucepan.

2 Heat gently over low heat, stirring until the sugar has dissolved and the cream is just under scalding point (just hot enough to touch).

3 Remove from the heat and stir in the lemon juice and lime juice.

4 Pour into small coffee cups or shot glasses and leave to set in the fridge for at least 6 hours.

5 Serve chilled, decorated with lime zest, sprigs of mint, or borage flowers.

PREPARE AHEAD
The puddings can be made up to the end of step
4 up to 2 days ahead. Not suitable for freezing.

This looks stunning and makes the most of all the lovely summer fruits. It's a top favorite of Lucy's.

Summer berry tart

Makes a 11in (28cm) tart (serves 8–10)

Special equipment 11in (28cm) removeable-bottom fluted tart pan

1¾ cup all-purpose flour, plus a little extra to dust
7 tbsp cold butter, cubed
2 tbsp confectioners' sugar
1 egg
2 tbsp water

For the crème pâtissière
3 eggs
½ cup superfine sugar
1 tsp vanilla extract
¼ cup all-purpose flour
1¾ cups milk

For the topping
14oz (400g) strawberries, hulled and quartered
8oz (225g) raspberries
225g (8oz) blueberries
6–8 tbsp red currant jelly
1 tbsp water

1 Preheat the oven to 400°F (200°C). Put the flour, butter, and confectioners' sugar into a processer and pulse until the mixture resembles breadcrumbs. Add the egg and water and pulse again until it forms a smooth dough. Lightly dust a work surface with flour and knead the dough for a few minutes or until it forms a smooth ball. Roll it out and use to line the tart pan (see page 243). Chill while you make the crème pâtissière.

2 Put the eggs, sugar, vanilla extract, and flour into a mixing bowl and mix with a wooden spoon until smooth. Add 2 tablespoons of the milk and stir again. Heat the remaining milk until just below boiling, then pour into the mixing bowl and whisk until smooth. Return to the pan and gently heat, whisking until thick and nearly simmering, but don't let it boil. Set aside to cool.

3 Bake the crust blind for 20 minutes, then remove the beans and paper (see right). Lower the oven temperature to 325°F (160°C) and return the tart crust to the oven for 10 minutes to dry out. Set aside to cool.

4 Pour the crème pâtissière into the tart crust and arrange the fruit in circles on top—strawberries on the outside, then a circle of raspberries, and the blueberries in the center.

5 Heat the red currant jelly and water together in a pan over gentle heat, whisking until smooth. Brush this glaze over the fruit, then place the tart in the fridge and serve chilled.

PREPARE AHEAD
The crust can be baked up to 2 days ahead. The crème pâtissière can be made up to 1 day ahead. The tart can be assembled up to 8 hours ahead. Not suitable for freezing.

BAKING BLIND

STEP 1 Cut a baking parchment circle just larger than the pan. Fold into a triangle and snip the edge.

STEP 2 Line the crust with the baking parchment, pushing it into the rim. Fill with dried beans.

STEP 3 After 20 minutes' baking, the crust is partly cooked and won't go soggy when the filling is added.

Snacks for a crowd

Plates of neatly cut sandwiches, tiers of homemade cookies and cakes—it's everyone's idea of a traditional English tea. In this chapter you'll find all the recipes you need to make it.

Snacks for a crowd

Birthdays, christenings, and funerals, friends dropping by at the weekend, a visit from granny—it's at times like these that a reviving cup of tea or coffee and a selection of sweet and savory treats go down well. As it is likely to be a special occasion, it seems only fitting to pull out all the stops and go with tradition. And if you don't have a reason for inviting people around for a get-together, invent one! We often do—as a way of catching up with family, friends, and neighbors.

Small is best

For an informal get-together, forget those huge slices of cake and oversized cookies you so often see in bakeries and fast-food outlets. Keep the food small, so it's easier for guests to eat, particularly if they'll be standing up.

● When making sandwiches, remove the crusts, then cut across into neat squares, triangles, or fingers.

● Cut large cakes into manageable wedges and traybakes into smallish squares or slices.

● Offer a selection of individual items such as cupcakes and muffins, cookies and scones—these are simple to eat as you stand and chat.

"If you don't have a reason for inviting people around for a get-together, invent one! We often do—as a way of catching up with family, friends, and neighbors."

For freshness

● Bake scones on the day. If you do have to prepare them in advance, freeze them and then gently reheat in a low oven once defrosted. At a buffet, serve them with bowls of jam and cream (there's no need for butter) for guests to help themselves. Otherwise top them before you serve them.

● Although you can frost cakes ahead, the frosting will be at its shiniest if you do it on the day itself. Serve forks with frosted cakes as they can be messy to eat with your hands.

● Depending on the filling you're using, most sandwiches can be prepared up to a day ahead. Kept correctly, they will taste as fresh as the moment you made them. Other sandwiches, such as cucumber and tomato, are best made no more than 10 hours ahead. For more on this, turn to page 283.

Make it an occasion

● Use cups and saucers, never mugs (unless you're outside—at a sporting event, say—or having something from the back of the car).

● Provide napkins—this occassion is as much of a meal as any other.

● Arrange cakes, scones, and cookies on tiered cake stands. They look so pretty presented like that. You'll find lots of designs in stores and they won't cost the earth if you buy them from charity shops.

● To give cakes a final flourish, decorate them with a sprinkling of confectioners' sugar. You can do it before or after you've arranged them on the plates or stands—it doesn't much matter. Fresh flowers and crystallized fresh flowers look great as decorations, too.

Quantities

● When serving cakes, serve one round of sandwiches (two slices of bread) per person.

● Most people will drink a couple of cups of tea. For 20 cups, you'll need about 15 teabags (although it depends of course on how strong you make it) and 1¼ pints (600ml) milk.

WHICH TEAS TO SERVE *We always make a pot of black tea and one of Earl Grey. We also provide a pot of boiling water, a selection of fancy herbal teas, and a jar of instant coffee. Sprigs of fresh mint or lemon balm make a refreshing cup in summer.*

How to set a table for a snack buffet

Place the table against a wall, with just enough room behind it for someone to stand and pour guests a cup of tea or coffee. Alternatively, you can let people serve themselves. Depending on the layout of your room, display the food from right to left (as here) or from left to right, and in the order guests will eat it, so sandwiches should come before cakes, traybakes, and scones. This will make it quicker. If you've invited over 30 people and have enough room, set two buffet tables with the same food on each.

Individual cakes
Arrange individual cakes such as muffins and cupcakes on a tiered cake stand.

Large traybakes or cakes
Cut large cakes or traybakes into small wedges or slices and arrange on a flat platter.

Scones or cookies
Arrange scones or cookies on a serving platter.

Jam
Serve the jam for scones in a bowl with a spoon.

Napkins
Place a pile of napkins at the end of the table.

Cream
Serve the cream for scones in a bowl with a teaspoon.

Plates
Stand a pile of small plates next to the sandwiches.

Finish <·········

<·········

Pots of tea
Stand the teapots on a tray to catch any drips. If you're serving more than one kind of tea, label them so guests know what's what.

Table decoration
Place the table decoration in a prominent position, but well out of guests' way.

Sugar
Put the sugar in a bowl with a teaspoon.

Cups
The first thing your guests will want is a cup of tea or coffee, so place cups and saucers at the start.

Sandwiches
Arrange the sandwiches on serving platters or plates and present them before the cookies and cakes.

Lemon
Put lemon slices in a bowl with a small fork.

Milk
Use a large pitcher so you don't have to keep refilling it.

Teaspoons
Place teaspoons handle up in a glass or mug. Provide cake forks as well for iced cakes.

⟨ • • • • • • • •

⟨ • • • • • • • • Start

As a snack, sandwiches should be small rather than filling. Some fillings can be added up to 10 hours ahead. Others can be added up to one day ahead with no compromise on freshness or taste.

Sandwiches

Makes 24 (serves 6)

soft butter
12 slices bread from a thin-cut or
    medium-cut white or brown loaf
the filling(s) of your choice (see below)
salt and freshly ground black pepper

Fillings you can add 1 day ahead

Rare roast beef with horseradish sauce
    and arugula
Egg salad with lots of watercress
Smoked salmon and cream cheese
Hummus, olive, and grated carrot
Ham and English mustard
Cream cheese, mango chutney,
    and watercress
Gravadlax and mustard mayonnaise
    (see page 81)
Mature Cheddar, pickle, and watercress
Goat cheese, arugula, and sun-dried
    tomatoes
Thin strips of pan-fried steak and mustard
Crispy bacon with egg salad

Fillings to add on the day

Shrimp with lemon mayonnaise
Feta cheese, sun-dried tomatoes,
    and cucumber
Cucumber and black pepper
Sardine, mayonnaise, and lemon
Fresh salmon and cucumber
Avocado and bacon
Crab and avocado with lime mayonnaise
Pastrami and sweet dill pickle with cream
    cheese and horseradish sauce
Tomato, basil, and mozzarella
Smoked mackerel, tomato, and aïoli

1 Butter the bread on one side, top half the slices with the filling(s) of your choice, and sandwich together. Leave the crusts on.

2 Arrange the sandwiches in piles of four on a large tray (check first that it will fit in your fridge). Cover with a layer of damp paper towels, then cover tightly with plastic wrap, and place the tray in the fridge.

3 Two hours before serving, slice off the crusts and cut the sandwiches into fingers or quarters—either triangles or squares. Cover with plastic wrap and keep at room temperature until ready to serve. They will taste as fresh as the moment you made them.

CUCUMBER AND TOMATOES
Fillings containing cucumber or tomato should only ever be added on the day. To stop the bread going soggy, you also need to remove the seeds. Slice the cucumber in half lengthwise and scoop out the seeds with a teaspoon. To seed tomatoes, see page 166.

Cut into squares, traybakes are great at large gatherings. This unusual recipe has a wonderful zesty taste.

Lime marmalade traybake

Cuts into 12 squares

Special equipment *9 x 12in (23 x 30cm) sheet pan, lined with foil and greased*

2 sticks butter, at room temperature
1 cup superfine sugar
2½ cups self-rising flour
4 eggs
2 tsp baking powder
finely grated zest of 1 lime, plus
  2 tbsp lime juice
2 tbsp lime marmalade

For the icing
2¾ cups confectioners' sugar
3½oz (100g) cream cheese
3 tbsp butter, at room temperature
2 tbsp lime marmalade
juice and finely grated zest of 1 small lime

1 Preheat the oven to 350°F (180°C). Put all the ingredients for the cake into a mixing bowl and beat by hand or with an electric whisk until combined and smooth.

2 Spoon into the sheet pan and level the top.

3 Bake for 30–35 minutes or until risen and golden. Set aside to cool completely.

4 To make the icing, sift the confectioners' sugar into a mixing bowl, add all the other ingredients, and beat with a wooden spoon or an electric whisk until well combined and smooth.

5 Spread the icing over the cake, making a pretty pattern on it with a palette knife. Cut into 12 squares and serve.

PREPARE AHEAD AND FREEZE
The cake can be made up to 1 day ahead and iced on the day. Freeze without the icing for up to 3 months.

A lemon traybake is always a big hit and we think this variation with orange is particularly delicious. It's also very easy to make.

Iced orange and lemon traybake

Cuts into 12 squares

Special equipment *9 x 12in (23 x 30cm) sheet pan, lined with foil and greased*

2 sticks butter, at room temperature

1 cup superfine sugar

2½ cups self-rising flour

2 tsp baking powder

4 eggs

¼ cup milk

grated zest of ½ lemon

grated zest of ½ small orange

For the icing

1¾ cups confectioners' sugar

1 tbsp lemon juice

2 tbsp orange juice

grated zest of ½ lemon

grated zest of ½ small orange

1 Preheat the oven to 350°F (180°C). Put the butter, sugar, flour, baking powder, eggs, and milk into a bowl and mix with a wooden spoon or electric hand whisk until smooth. Stir in the lemon zest and orange zest and pour into the sheet pan. Level the top.

2 Bake for 30 minutes or until shrinking away from the sides of the pan and springy to the touch. Leave to cool in the pan.

3 To make the icing, sift the confectioners' sugar into a bowl, mix in the lemon juice and orange juice, and beat until smooth. Spread evenly over the cold cake, then sprinkle with the lemon zest and orange zest and leave to set. To serve, cut into 12 squares.

PREPARE AHEAD AND FREEZE

The traybake can be made and iced up to 1 day ahead. Freeze without the icing for up to 3 months.

These are delicious with a cup of coffee. If you're preparing them ahead, stop them going soggy by storing them in an airtight container with pieces of paper towel between the layers.

Almond cookies

Makes 30–35

Special equipment 2in (5cm) fluted biscuit cutter

7 tbsp butter, at room temperature
½ cup superfine sugar
1½ cups all-purpose flour, plus a little extra to dust
2½oz (75g) ground almonds
½ tsp almond extract
1¾oz (50g) sliced almonds

1 Put the butter and sugar into a mixing bowl and whisk with an electric whisk until light and fluffy. Add the flour, ground almonds, and almond extract and whisk again until smooth.

2 Lightly dust a work surface with flour and knead the dough for a few minutes until smooth. Wrap in plastic wrap and chill for 30 minutes.

3 Preheat the oven to 325°F (180°C). Grease two baking sheets or line with baking parchment. Lightly flour the work surface again and roll the dough out until it is ¼in (5mm) thick. Using a 2in (5cm) fluted biscuit cutter, cut out 30–35 rounds.

4 Transfer to the baking sheets with a spatula. Sprinkle a few sliced almonds on top of each cookie and press them down gently so they stick to the dough.

5 Bake for 10–12 minutes (checking after 8 minutes) or until lightly golden. Leave to cool slightly, then transfer to a wire rack to cool completely.

PREPARE AHEAD AND FREEZE
The cookies can be made up to 4 days ahead.
Keep, layered with paper towels, in a cookie jar.
Freeze for up to 3 months.

Everyone loves cookies. And no one will be able to resist this deliciously gooey combination of pecan nuts and chocolate. The cookies keep well in a jar for a couple of days.

Pecan and chocolate chip cookies

Makes 24

7 tbsp butter, at room temperature
¼ cup superfine sugar
1¼ cups self-rising flour, plus
   a little extra to dust
½ tsp vanilla extract
1¾oz (50g) milk chocolate chips
1¾oz (50g) pecan nuts, chopped

1 Preheat the oven to 350°F (180°C). Put the butter and sugar into a bowl and mix together with a wooden spoon until light and fluffy. Stir in the flour, then add the vanilla extract, chocolate chips, and pecans and mix to a soft dough.

2 Knead the dough lightly on a floured work surface, then divide into 24 balls. Flatten the balls with the palm of your hand and arrange on two baking sheets lined with baking parchment. Space them out so they have room to spread.

3 Bake for 20–25 minutes or until lightly golden. Transfer to a wire rack to cool.

PREPARE AHEAD AND FREEZE
The cookies can be made up to 2 days ahead and kept in a sealed container. Freeze the raw mixture or the cooked cookies for up to 2 months.

Cupcakes are the cake of the moment, with some stores specializing in just them. These are made in muffin pans, which are fairly large, but make them in smaller pans if you wish.

Coffee and walnut cupcakes

Makes 12

Special equipment 12-hole muffin pan lined with 12 paper muffin cases

1 tbsp instant coffee granules
1 tbsp boiling water
7 tbsp butter, softened
1¼ cups self-rising flour
¾ cup superfine sugar
2 tbsp milk
2 large eggs
scant 1oz (25g) walnuts, chopped

For the coffee icing

2 tsp instant coffee granules
2 tsp boiling water
7 tbsp butter, at room temperature
1¾ cups confectioners' sugar
12 walnut halves, to decorate

SOFTENING BUTTER

To make sure the butter is soft enough to work with, cut it into small cubes and put into a bowl of lukewarm water. After 10 minutes or so, squeeze one of the cubes—it should be lovely and soft. You can then drain them and use them.

1 Preheat the oven to 350°F (180°C). Put the coffee granules and water into a mixing bowl and stir until smooth. Add the butter, flour, sugar, milk, and eggs and mix with an electric whisk until smooth. Stir in the walnuts, then spoon into the muffin cases.

2 Bake in the center of the oven for 20–25 minutes or until risen and golden brown. Transfer to a wire rack until stone cold.

3 To make the icing, put the coffee granules and boiling water into a bowl and stir until smooth. Add the butter, sift in the confectioners' sugar, and stir until smooth and free of streaks.

4 Spoon on to the cupcakes, then decorate each one with a walnut half.

PREPARE AHEAD AND FREEZE

The cupcakes can be made and iced up to 1 day ahead. Freeze without the icing for up to 1 month.

Arranged on a tiered cakestand, a dozen cupcakes (see page 288) make a spectacular centerpiece for any tea party. We like to bake them in silver or floral muffin cases. Serve one per person.

Cupcake tier

Serves 12

For the glacé icing
juice of 1 lemon
1¾ cups confectioners' sugar

For the chocolate curls
bar of white chocolate, at room
  temperature
bar of dark chocolate, at room
  temperature

DECORATING CUPCAKES
When it comes to decorating cupcakes, let your imagination run riot. But keep the tier looking elegant and classy—not chaotic. Crystallized flowers look pretty, as do silver balls or silver hearts. Or decorate the edges of the cakestand with fresh flowers. The beauty of the cupcake tier is that you can match the decorations to suit the occasion. For a child's birthday party, for instance, you could decorate one of the cupcakes with a candle. Sprinkles or tiny colored candies such as jelly beans and M&Ms also work well.

1 Make a dozen cupcakes, following the recipe on page 288. You won't need the coffee icing and walnuts.

2 To make the glacé icing, warm the lemon juice in a pan. Put the confectioners' sugar into a mixing bowl and gradually add enough lemon juice to make a smooth glossy icing. Spoon the icing on to the cupcakes and leave to set.

3 Meanwhile, shave curls from the chocolate bars with a vegetable peeler.

4 Once the icing has set, decorate the cupcakes with a mixture of white chocolate curls and dark chocolate curls.

PREPARE AHEAD AND FREEZE
The cupcakes can be iced up to 1 day ahead.
Freeze without the icing for up to 1 month.

Fairy cakes are always so popular. These are a basic vanilla sponge mix with lemon icing. Decorate them with creative flair. We like to use jelly beans and other small, brightly colored candies.

Fairy cakes

Makes 24

Special equipment 2 x 12-hole muffin pans, greased or lined with paper cases

1¼ sticks butter, softened
  (see page 288)
¾ cup superfine sugar
1¼ cups self-rising flour
1½ tsp baking powder
1½ tsp vanilla extract
3 eggs

For the icing
1¼ cups confectioners' sugar
about 3 bsp lemon juice

To decorate
candies of your choice

1 Preheat the oven to 350°F (180°C). Put all the ingredients for the cakes into a large mixing bowl and beat with an electric whisk until smooth. Spoon evenly into the pans.

2 Bake for 12–15 minutes or until risen and pale golden brown. Set aside to cool, then remove the cakes from the pans.

3 To make the icing, sift the confectioners' sugar into a bowl and add enough lemon juice to make a fairly stiff paste. Spoon a circle of the icing on the top of each cake. While the icing is still soft, decorate with the candies of your choice.

PREPARE AHEAD AND FREEZE
The cakes can be made and iced up to 1 day ahead. Freeze for up to 2 months.

VARIATIONS

Chocolate chip fairy cakes
Add scant 1oz (25g) dark chocolate chips to the basic sponge mix.

Lemon party cakes
Add the grated zest of 1 lemon to the basic sponge mix.

Orange fairy cakes
Add the grated zest of 1 orange to the basic sponge mix. For the icing, use orange juice or orange blossom water instead of lemon juice.

Rosewater fairy cakes
For the icing, use 2 tbsp rosewater and 1 tbsp water instead of the lemon juice.

This lovely cake has no flour—just cocoa powder—so it is as light as a feather. For children, replace the Cointreau with orange juice. Bake it at Easter and decorate with mini chocolate eggs.

Chocolate and orange mousse cake

Serves 8

Special equipment 9in (23cm) springform pan, greased and lined

7oz (200g) bar orange milk chocolate
3 tbsp butter
6 eggs, separated
1¼ cups superfine sugar
2–3 tbsp Cointreau
2 level tbsp cocoa powder

For the topping

3½oz (100g) orange milk chocolate, coarsely grated
1–2 tbsp Cointreau
1 cup heavy cream, lightly whipped
cocoa powder, to dust

1 Preheat the oven to 350°F (180°C). Meanwhile, break the chocolate into pieces and place in a small heatproof bowl with the butter. Sit the bowl over a pan of hot water and stir until the chocolate and butter have melted. Set aside to cool slightly.

2 Whisk the egg whites with an electric whisk until stiff. Put the egg yolks and sugar into a separate bowl and whisk until light and creamy.

3 Pour the melted chocolate into the egg-yolk mixture, add the Cointreau, and gently fold together, taking care not to knock out any of the air. Add the egg whites and gently fold to combine. Sift in the cocoa powder and fold until combined. Spoon evenly into the pan.

4 Bake for 40 minutes or until risen, shrinking away from the sides of the pan, and just firm to the touch in the center. Leave to cool, then remove from the pan.

5 For the topping, stir half the chocolate and the Cointreau into the cream. Spread over the top of the cake and sprinkle with the remaining chocolate. Sift the cocoa powder on top.

LINING THE PAN

Put baking parchment over the pan base, clip the ring in place, and trim the parchment with scissors.

PREPARE AHEAD
The cake can be made up to the end of step 4 up to 1 day ahead. Add the topping on the day of serving. Freeze without the topping for up to 2 months.

Seeded bars are extremely popular in the stores. They are also healthier than a slice of cake, so why not make your own. When we were testing these, the whole pan was eaten at once!

Figgy seeded bites

Makes 12 bars or 24 bites

Special equipment 7in (18cm) square shallow pan, lined with baking parchment and greased

5 tbsp butter
3 tbsp honey
scant ½ cup superfine sugar
6oz (175g) rolled oats
scant 1oz (25g) sunflower seeds
scant 1oz (25g) pumpkin seeds
scant 1oz (25g) desiccated coconut
3½oz (100g) dried figs, snipped
   into tiny pieces
1¾oz (50g) dried apricots, snipped
   into tiny pieces

1 Preheat the oven to 350°F (180°C). Heat the butter, honey, and sugar in a pan over gentle heat, stirring until melted and dissolved.

2 Put the remaining ingredients into a large mixing bowl, add the melted butter mixture, and stir well. Pour into the pan and level the top.

3 Bake for 30–35 minutes or until lightly golden and firm in the middle. Leave to cool slightly, then cut into 12 rectangles or 24 squares. Leave in the pan to harden, then transfer to a wire rack to cool completely.

PREPARE AHEAD
The bites can be made up to 3 days ahead and kept in a cool place. Not suitable for freezing.

These are perfect for a children's tea party. For a slightly more sophisticated touch, replace the white chocolate chips with dark chocolate chips.

White chocolate and strawberry muffins

Makes 12

Special equipment Deep 12-hole muffin pan lined with paper muffin cases

2½ cups self-rising flour
1 tsp baking powder
¾ cup superfine sugar
2 eggs
1 cup milk
7 tbsp butter, melted
2 tsp vanilla extract
3½oz (100g) white chocolate chips
12 tsp strawberry jam
confectioners' sugar, to dust

1 Preheat the oven to 400°F (200°C). Put all the ingredients except the chocolate chips and jam into a large bowl and whisk with an electric whisk until smooth. Stir in the chocolate chips.

2 Divide half the mixture evenly between the cases, spoon 1 teaspoon of jam on top of each one, then spoon the remaining mixture on top.

3 Bake for 25–30 minutes or until well risen and lightly golden brown.

4 Dust with a little confectioners' sugar and serve warm or cold.

PREPARE AHEAD AND FREEZE
The muffins can be made up to 2 days ahead.
Freeze for up to 1 month.

White chocolate and strawberry muffins (see overleaf) ●●●>

Mincemeat buns are traditional at Christmas, but there's no reason why you shouldn't make them at any time of year. Use vegetarian mincemeat if you don't eat meat.

Mincemeat buns

Makes 24

Special equipment *2 x 12-hole muffin pans, lined with paper cases*

11 tbsp butter, softened
  (see page 288)
scant ¾ cup superfine sugar
heaping 1¾ cups self-rising flour
2 eggs
2 tbsp milk
3½oz (100g) currants
3½oz (100g) mincemeat from a jar
1¾oz (50g) sliced almonds

1 Preheat the oven to 350°F (180°C). Put all the ingredients except the almonds into a bowl and beat well with a wooden spoon to combine.

2 Spoon the mixture into the paper cases, level the tops, and make sure there are no drips over the sides of the cases. Sprinkle with the almonds.

3 Bake for 15 minutes or until well risen and lightly golden.

4 Leave the buns in the pans for a few minutes, then transfer them to a cooling rack and leave to cool completely.

PREPARE AHEAD AND FREEZE
The buns can be made up to 1 day ahead and kept in the fridge. Freeze for up to 2 months.

Small loaf cakes are always lovely to make and are quicker to bake than large ones. This recipes makes two. If you don't need both immediately, you can eat one and freeze the other.

Apricot and cherry loaf cakes

Makes 2

Special equipment *2 x 1lb (450g) loaf pans, greased and the bases and sides lined with a long strip of baking parchment*

1½ cups self-rising flour

7 tbsp butter, softened (see page 288)

scant ½ cup superfine sugar

3 large eggs, beaten

5½oz (150g) ready-to-eat apricots, snipped into small pieces

1½oz (50g) raisins

1½oz (50g) glacé cherries, snipped into small pieces

1 Preheat the oven to 350°F (180°C). Put the flour, butter, sugar, and eggs into a mixing bowl and whisk with an electric whisk until combined. Stir in the dried fruit and cherries, then spoon into the pans and level the tops.

2 Bake for 45–50 minutes or until golden brown and well risen. Transfer to a wire rack to cool completely.

PREPARE AHEAD AND FREEZE

The cakes can be baked up to 2 days ahead, although they are best made and eaten on the same day. Freeze for up to 3 months.

Passing through the village of Ashburton, in Devon, Mary stopped at a tea shop and had a piece of wonderful carrot cake. The owner kindly gave Mary the recipe and it's loved by one and all.

Ashburton carrot cake

Makes a 9in (23cm) cake (serves 8)

Special equipment 2 x 9in (23cm) cake pans, greased and lined with a disk of baking parchment

heaping 1½ cups self-rising flour
1¼ cups granulated sugar
1 tsp baking powder
1½ tsp ground cinnamon
¾ cup sunflower oil
2 eggs, lightly beaten

1 tsp vanilla extract
3½oz (100g) raw carrots, grated
3½oz (100g) chopped walnuts
2oz (60g) desiccated coconut
7.5oz can pineapple slices, drained, chopped, and dried thoroughly

For the icing

7oz (200g) cream cheese
7 tbsp butter, softened (see page 288)
1½ cups confectioners' sugar
1 tsp vanilla extract

1 Preheat the oven to 350°F (180°C). Put the flour into a large mixing bowl, add the sugar, baking powder, and cinnamon and stir together.

2 Add the oil, eggs, and vanilla extract and beat well with a wooden spoon or spatula. Fold in the carrots, walnuts, coconut, and pineapple and beat until smooth.

3 Spoon evenly into the cake pans and bake for 45–50 minutes or until well risen and golden brown. To check that the cakes are cooked in the middle, insert a skewer into the center—if it comes out clean, they are done. Transfer to a wire rack and leave to cool.

4 To make the icing, put the cream cheese and butter into a bowl, sift in the confectioners' sugar, add the vanilla extract, and whisk with an electric whisk until smooth.

5 Remove the cakes from the pans and peel off the baking parchment. Turn one cake upside down on to a serving plate and spread with half the icing. Sit the other cake on top and spread the remaining icing over the top.

PREPARE AHEAD AND FREEZE
The cake can be made up to 1 day ahead, although it is best made on the day. Freeze without the icing for up to 2 months.

LINING THE PANS

STEP 1 Stand the pan on baking parchment, draw round the base with a pencil, then cut the disk out.

STEP 2 Place the disk of baking parchment in the bottom of the greased cake pan.

Scones are so quintessentially English and a traditional part of tea. For success every time, make sure the dough is good and sticky rather than dry. Serve warm with clotted cream and strawberry jam.

Buttery scones

Makes 12

Special equipment 3in (7.5cm) biscuit cutter

heaping 1¾ cups self-rising flour, plus a little extra to dust
2 tsp baking powder
3 tbsp butter, at room temperature
2 tbsp superfine sugar
1 egg
about 5fl oz (150ml) milk

1 Preheat the oven to 400°F (200°C). Put the flour, baking powder, and butter into a processor and pulse until the mixture resembles breadcrumbs. Add the sugar.

2 Break the egg into a measuring glass and beat with a fork, then pour in enough of the milk to make just over 5fl oz (150ml). Beat again to mix.

3 Switch the processor on and gradually pour in the milk and egg mixture, leaving about 1 tablespoon in the glass for glazing. Pulse until combined—the mixture should be slightly sticky. Add a little more milk if it isn't.

4 Transfer the dough to a lightly floured work surface and knead until smooth, then roll it out until it is ½in (1cm) thick. Using a 3in (7.5cm) biscuit cutter, cut out 12 scones, re-rolling the dough until it is all used up.

5 Arrange on a greased baking sheet and brush the tops with the remaining milk and egg mixture to glaze.

6 Bake for 15–20 minutes or until well risen and golden.

CUTTING THE SCONES OUT
Be careful not to twist the cutter when cutting the scones out or the scones won't rise evenly during baking.

PREPARE AHEAD AND FREEZE
The scones can be made up to 1 day ahead.
Freeze for up to 3 months.

Most brownies are dense and dark, but we use milk chocolate so ours are very light in color and texture, with gooey pieces of melted chocolate. Simply delicious.

Best-ever brownies

Makes 12

Special equipment 9 x 13in (23 x 33cm) sheet pan, lined with baking parchment and well greased

2 sticks butter, softened
12oz (350g) milk chocolate, chopped
4 eggs
1lb (450g) light muscovado sugar
5fl oz (150ml) milk
heaping 1¾ cup self-rising flour

1 Preheat the oven to 350°F (180°C). Melt the butter and 8oz (225g) of the milk chocolate in a bowl set over a pan of hot water until the mixture is smooth and glossy.

2 Break the eggs into a mixing bowl, add the sugar, milk, and the melted chocolate mixture, and beat with a wooden spoon to combine. Sift in the flour and mix until smooth.

3 Stir in the remaining chocolate, then pour into the pan and bake for 45–50 minutes or until well risen and cooked in the middle. Leave to cool, then cut into 12 squares.

PREPARE AHEAD AND FREEZE
The brownies can be made up to 2 days ahead.
Freeze for up to 3 months.

Menu planners

Winter cocktail parties

On a cold winter's day there's nothing lovelier than presenting your guests with a glass of hot mulled wine the moment they arrive. To balance your work load, serve a selection of hot eats with some cold party bites that you can prepare completely in advance. At Christmas or New Year, decorate the platters with holly and sprigs of heather tied together with swatches of tartan ribbon. As a sign that it's time for your guests to go, serve them brownies or cupcakes in pretty, individual truffle cases.

"We love the idea of giving the food for our cocktail parties a theme, as with these four party bites that all have a hint of Asia."

A hint of Asia

Allow a total of 8–10 bites per person. Serve the chicken satays first—these are the most impressive. Remember to use platters that aren't heavy to hold.

PARTY BITES

Mini chicken satays (page 36)

Pork meatballs with Asian dipping sauce (page 38)

Duck and hoisin spring rolls (page 41)

Scorching chile dip with a choice of dippers (page 49)

FOR WHEN IT'S TIME TO GO

Coffee and walnut cupcakes (page 288)

Prepare ahead

Scorching chile dip 4 days ahead.
Mini chicken satays 2 days ahead.
Pork meatballs 2 days ahead.
Coffee and walnut cupcakes 1 day ahead.
Duck and hoisin spring rolls 8 hours ahead.

New Year's Day

Allow a total of 8–10 bites per person. Bring out the sausage rolls first—these are the showstoppers. Serve mixed platters as the canapés start to disappear.

PARTY BITES

FOR WHEN IT'S TIME TO GO

Prepare ahead

Best-ever brownies 2 days ahead.

Bacon and water chestnut bites 1 day ahead.

Sausage and apple filo rolls 12 hours ahead.

Golden dough balls 12 hours ahead.

Crostini with slow-roasted tomatoes 6 hours ahead.

Summer cocktail parties

Cocktail parties are always a big hit in summer when the weather is good and your guests can spill out into the backyard or on to a patio, roof terrace, or balcony. Set the scene with pot plants or flowers in season and decorate serving platters with bunches of fresh herbs and edible blooms such as violets, pansies, and nasturtiums. When it's time for your guests to go, bring out some brownies or cupcakes in individual truffle cases.

"Buy plenty of bags of ice to keep wine, beer, and a variety of non-alcoholic drinks cool. You could even chill them in the bath tub if you have a really huge crowd coming."

Mediterranean

Cold eats are ideal in summer and are great for preparing ahead. Allow a total of 8–10 per person.

PARTY BITES

Beef remoulade rolls (page 45)

Garlicky herb dip with a choice of dippers (page 49)

Crostini with slow-roasted tomatoes and herbs (page 51)

Crostini with Parma ham and peppered cream cheese (page 52)

FOR WHEN IT'S TIME TO GO

Coffee and walnut cupcakes (page 288)

Prepare ahead

Garlicky herb dip 3 days ahead.

Coffee and walnut cupcakes 1 day ahead.

Beef remoulade rolls 8 hours ahead.

Crostini with slow-roasted tomatoes 6 hours ahead.

Crostini with Parma ham 6 hours ahead.

Sophisticated

An impressive selection of meat, fish, and vegetarian canapés. Allow 8–10 per person.

PARTY BITES

FOR WHEN IT'S TIME TO GO

Prepare ahead

Best-ever brownies 2 days ahead.
Asparagus filo rolls 12 hours ahead.
Duck and hoisin spring rolls 8 hours ahead.
Smoked salmon on rye 6 hours ahead.
Hummus and feta tartlets 4 hours ahead.

Winter lunch parties

For lunch, two courses—a main dish and dessert—are often enough. But for a special occasion, or if it's cold out there, we like to kick off with a hot starter or some piping hot soup. When serving three courses, we choose a main dish that can look after itself in the oven. A roast is ideal on Sundays and this is one of our favorite times to entertain family and friends.

Warming

A hearty meal of two upmarket pies, plus a rich and flavorsome soup to start with.

STARTER
Honey-glazed parsnip soup (page 66)

MAIN COURSE AND SIDE DISH
Loch Fyne haddock bake (page 136)

Green salad or green vegetable

DESSERT
Lemon meringue pie (page 247)

Prepare ahead
Honey-glazed parsnip soup 2 days ahead.
Lemon meringue pie 1 day ahead.
Haddock bake 8 hours ahead.

*"If you're going to Mary's for lunch on Sunday,
you can expect roast leg of lamb."*

Italian

You can't go wrong with Italian food. It's the food of love and everyone adores it.

STARTER

*Bruschette with Reblochon
and roasted vegetables (page 73)*

MAIN COURSE AND SIDE DISHES

Italian farmhouse chicken (page 161)

*Rice or mashed potatoes
Green vegetable*

DESSERT

Individual tiramisus (page 256)
and/or
Exotic fruit salad (page 265)

Prepare ahead

Italian farmhouse chicken 12 hours ahead.
Individual tiramisus 12 hours ahead.
Fruit salad 12 hours ahead.
Bruschette with Reblochon 3 hours ahead.

Sunday roast

If you're going to Mary's for lunch after church on Sunday, this is what you can expect.

STARTER

*French onion soup with mustard
Gruyère croûtons (page 64)*

MAIN COURSE AND SIDE DISHES

Slow-roast leg of lamb (page 119)

*Roast potatoes with chile
and thyme (page 126)*

Green vegetable

DESSERT

*Mini apple, apricot, and hazelnut
crumbles (page 242)*
or
Melt-in-the mouth apple pie (page 244)

Prepare ahead

French onion soup 3 days ahead.
Mini crumbles 2 days ahead.
Leg of lamb 1 day ahead.
Roast potatoes 1 day ahead.
Apple pie 1 day ahead.

Summer lunch parties

One of the most popular times of year for having a lunch party is in the summer, and it's not hard to figure out why. From May to September a fabulous range of fresh ingredients comes into season—asparagus, new potatoes, soft fruits, lamb. We can't get enough of them! If three courses seem too much, serve two—a main dish plus dessert.

Cold but sophisticated

No emerging hot and bothered from the kitchen with this menu—you'll be as cool as a cucumber.

STARTER

Crab, avocado, and smoked salmon tians (page 77)

MAIN COURSE AND SIDE DISHES

Cold filet of beef with mustard sauce (page 196)

Spicy roast squash and feta salad (page 229)

Baby new potatoes

DESSERT

A rather special dessert collection
(page 250)
or
Chilled marbled raspberry cheesecake
(page 260)

Prepare ahead

Cold filet of beef 2 days ahead.

Dessert collection 2 days ahead.

Chilled marbled raspberry cheesecake 2 days ahead.

Crab tians 6 hours ahead.

Spicy roast squash salad 6 hours ahead.

"Charity events are a huge part of our summer. It's where we got the idea for our 'Ladies that lunch' menu."

Vegetarian

We both love meat and fish, but, with recipes as special as these, how could we miss them.

STARTER
Asparagus with Parmesan and mustard sauce (page 70)

MAIN COURSE AND SIDE DISHES
Goat cheese, thyme, and onion marmalade galette (page 230)

Globe artichoke and Puy lentil salad (page 226)

Green salad

DESSERT
Magenta fruit compote with white chocolate sauce (page 264)
or
Mango Eton mess (page 273)

Ladies that lunch

Just two courses to this menu—and fairly light ones at that—for obvious reasons.

MAIN COURSE AND SIDE DISHES
Mediterranean lemon and herb chicken salad (page 222)
or
Hot baked trout with tomato and basil salsa (page 101)

Baby new potatoes and green salad

DESSERT
Pear and ginger pavlova (page 268)
or
Rhubarb and lemon pots (page 254)

Prepare ahead
Asparagus with Parmesan 1 day ahead.
Globe artichoke and lentil salad 12 hours ahead.
Fruit compote 12 hours ahead.
Goat cheese galette 8 hours ahead.
Mango Eton mess 6 hours ahead.

Prepare ahead
Rhubarb and lemon pots 12 hours ahead.
Mediterranean salad 8 hours ahead.
Hot baked trout 8 hours ahead.
Pear and ginger pavlova 4 hours ahead.

Snacks for a crowd

Elegant snacks are a special treat for guests. In the summer, tea parties in the backyard are such fun. While in winter, it's so cosy gathering in front of the fire as daylight turns to dusk. We adore a full English tea—neatly cut sandwiches followed by small cakes, large cakes, scones, jam, and cream. All washed down—of course—with pots of tea and coffee.

"Teatime can be as special as any lunch or dinner. Use it as an excuse to get out granny's china. 'Tea tastes better from a fine china cup,' as they say."

Buffet tea

An afternoon feast. Set the table along the lines we suggest on pages 280–281.

Sandwiches (page 283)

Ashburton carrot cake (page 300)

Buttery scones (page 302)

Best-ever brownies (page 303)

Prepare ahead
Best-ever brownies 2 days ahead.
Ashburton carrot cake 1 day ahead.
Buttery scones 1 day ahead.
Sandwiches 1 day–10 hours ahead, depending on the filling.

Family tea

Serve just one kind of sandwich at an informal tea party with cakes. Allow one round (two slices) per person.

Sandwiches (page 283)

Iced orange and lemon traybake
(page 285)

White chocolate and strawberry muffins (page 295)

Prepare ahead

White chocolate and strawberry muffins 2 days ahead.
Iced orange and lemon traybake 1 day ahead.
Sandwiches 1 day–10 hours ahead, depending on the filling.

Winter dinner parties

We love finding a reason to go all out in the kitchen, and dinner parties provide the perfect excuse. For us, winter is a time for casseroles and warming bakes, rich gravies and roasted meats. Set the scene with fresh flowers, candles, and music, and these meals will be special wherever you entertain your guests—in the kitchen or dining room.

Posh

Allow 1–2 blinis per person if you're serving four courses; three if you're not offering a starter.

PARTY BITES
Homemade blinis with salmon and crème fraîche (page 50)

STARTER
Roquefort and parsley mousseline creams (page 71)

MAIN COURSE AND SIDE DISHES
Mini pork en croûtes (page 120)

Heavenly potato gratin (page 123)

Green salad or green vegetable

DESSERT
Lemon and lime puddings (page 274)

Magenta fruit compote with white chocolate sauce (page 264)

Prepare ahead

Lemon and lime puddings 2 days ahead.
Heavenly potato gratin 1 day ahead.
Mini pork en croûtes 12 hours ahead.
Fruit compote 12 hours ahead.
Smoked salmon and dill blinis 6 hours ahead.
Roquefort mousseline creams 6 hours ahead.

"With the starter on the table and the candles lit, it's time to seat your guests."

Supper in the kitchen

There's no need to be lavish to turn out a special meal. Guests feel so comfortable at the kitchen table.

STARTER
Rustic mushroom liver pâté (page 82)

MAIN COURSE AND SIDE DISHES
Hot mustard spiced beef (page 195)

Cheese-topped dauphinois potatoes (page 125)

Green vegetable

DESSERT
Toffee pudding with warm toffee sauce (page 248)
or
Exotic fruit salad (page 265)

Festive

Serve both of these scrumptious desserts if you're expecting a dozen people or more.

STARTER
Celebratory fish platter (page 81)

MAIN COURSE AND SIDE DISHES
Pheasant breasts with mushrooms and Madeira (page 109)

Roast potatoes with chile and thyme (page 126)

Green salad or green vegetable

DESSERT
Chocolate truffle cheesecake (page 257)
and/or
Poached pears with blackberry sauce (page 263)

Prepare ahead

Rustic mushroom liver pâté 3 days ahead.

Hot mustard spiced beef 2 days ahead.

Toffee pudding 1 day ahead.

Fruit salad 12 hours ahead.

Cheese-topped dauphinois potatoes 8 hours ahead.

Prepare ahead

Chocolate truffle cheesecake 2 days ahead.

Pheasant breasts with mushrooms 1 day ahead.

Roast potatoes 1 day ahead.

Poached pears 12 hours ahead.

Fish platter 4 hours ahead.

Summer dinner parties

Make the most of the warm summer evenings by serving supper or dinner in the backyard. If the weather starts to get chilly, have your canapés and starter outside, then come in for the main course. Or you could do what we do—brave it and give everyone a wrap or blanket! Here's a choice of summer menus—formal or casual—to serve inside or out.

Posh

Allow three crostini per person if you're not offering a first course; one or two if you are.

PARTY BITES

Crostini with slow-roasted tomatoes and herbs (page 51)

STARTER

Roasted figs with Parma ham and goat cheese (page 68)

MAIN COURSE AND SIDE DISHES

Duck breasts with a piquant lime and ginger sauce (page 111)

Cheese-topped dauphinois potatoes (page 125)

Green vegetable

DESSERT

Becca's white chocolate and orange mousses (page 249)
and/or
Exotic fruit salad (page 265)

Prepare ahead

Duck breasts 1 day ahead.
Roasted figs 12 hours ahead.
White chocolate and orange mousses 12 hours ahead.
Fruit salad 12 hours ahead.
Cheese-topped dauphinois potatoes 8 hours ahead.
Crostini with slow-roasted tomatoes 6 hours ahead.

"Or you could do what we do—brave the evening chill and give everyone a wrap or blanket!"

Fresh and light

A showcase for the new potatoes, carrots, and soft fruits that are at their best in the summer months.

STARTER

Smoked mackerel and watercress pâté (page 79)

MAIN COURSE AND SIDE DISHES

Sardinian chicken (page 160)

Baby new potatoes and carrots

DESSERT

Magenta fruit compote with white chocolate sauce (page 264)
and/or
Heavenly lemon cheesecake on a ginger crust (page 259)

Vegetarian

Our meat-free take on two classics from Italy with a choice of fruity desserts.

STARTER

Bruschette with Reblochon and roasted vegetables (page 73)

MAIN COURSE AND SIDE DISH

Butternut squash lasagna (page 147)

Green salad

DESSERT

Hazelnut meringue roulade with raspberries (page 272)
and/or
Exotic fruit salad (page 265)

Prepare ahead

Smoked mackerel pâté 2 days ahead.
Sardinian chicken 2 days ahead.
Lemon cheesecake 1 day ahead.
Fruit compote 12 hours ahead.

Prepare ahead

Butternut squash lasagna 2 days ahead.
Hazelnut meringue roulade 12 hours ahead.
Fruit salad 12 hours ahead.
Bruschette with Reblochon 3 hours ahead.

Buffets

The goal when planning a buffet is to provide a variety of dishes that will delight your guests, but that won't require much last-minute assembly from you. These two menus are just right! To speed up serving at larger gatherings, ask some friends to help. Position them out of the way at the back of the table and tell them how much food to serve per person so you don't run out. They'll find it easier to serve the correct amount from two dishes for 12 rather than one dish for 24. For our guide to setting a buffet table, turn to pages 178–179.

"Help-yourself and hassle-free, buffets are the ultimate way of feeding a crowd—all through the year, indoor or out."

Christmas time

Unapologetically lavish. Tis the season to be jolly!

PARTY BITES
Bacon and water chestnut bites with mango chutney (page 42)
and/or
Smoked salmon on rye with cucumber pickle (page 46)

MAIN COURSES AND SIDE DISHES
Classic poached salmon (page 182)
and/or
Watercroft glazed ham with Cumberland sauce (page 184–185)
Baby new potatoes and/or Green salad

DESSERT
Party pavlova pyramid (page 269)
or
Pear and ginger pavlova (page 268)
Exotic fruit salad (page 265)

Prepare ahead
Party pavlova pyramid 1 month ahead.
Pear and ginger pavlova 1 month ahead.
Cumberland sauce 1 week ahead.
Glazed ham 5 days ahead.
Bacon bites 1 day ahead.
Classic poached salmon 1 day ahead.
Fruit salad 12 hours ahead.
Smoked salmon bites 6 hours ahead.

Mary's summer feast

There's a special something for everyone here.

PARTY BITES
*Golden dough balls with cheese
and chutney (page 35)*
and/or
*Smoked salmon on rye with
cucumber pickle (page 46)*

MAIN COURSES AND SIDE DISHES
Thai beef with lime and chili (page 114)

Thai green rice (page 116)
and/or
21st-century coronation chicken (page 187)

*Roasted Mediteranean vegetables
(page 127)*

Baby new potatoes and/or Green salad

DESSERT
*Heavenly lemon cheesecake on
a ginger crust (page 259)*

Exotic fruit salad (page 265)

Prepare ahead
Coronation chicken 1 day ahead.
Mediterranean vegetables 1 day ahead.
Cheesecake 1 day ahead.
Dough balls 12 hours ahead.
Thai beef and **Thai rice** 12 hours ahead.
Fruit salad 12 hours ahead.
Smoked salmon bites 6 hours ahead.

Bowl parties

With little choice and no fuss, bowl parties make entertaining easy. So don't worry if your bowls don't all match—these are such relaxed occasions. Use whatever bowls you have to hand—pasta bowls, cereal bowls, soup bowls, the kind you find in fancy restaurants, the kind folk drink their coffee from in the morning in France. If you don't have enough, ask your friends to bring some along.

"Just about any dish your guests can eat with a fork from a bowl while they stand and chat is perfect bowl food."

Winter curry party

Serve two of the curries for the main course. Make both for the number of people coming—it's better to have too much food than too little.

STARTER
Garlicky herb dip with dippers (page 49)

MAIN COURSES AND SIDE DISHES
Chicken tikka masala (page 202)
and/or
Aromatic beef curry with ginger and tomatoes (page 203)
and/or
Vegetable korma (page 199)

Garlic and cilantro naan breads (page 206)

Pilaf rice (page 207)

DESSERT
Rum and raisin ice cream (page 261)
and/or
Exotic fruit salad (page 265)

Prepare ahead
Rum and raisin ice cream 2 months.
Garlicky dip 3 days ahead.
Chicken tikka masala 2 days ahead.
Aromatic beef curry 2 days ahead.
Vegetable korma 12 hours ahead.
Naan breads and **Pilaf rice** 12 hours ahead.
Fruit salad 12 hours ahead.

Lucy's budget bowl party

We think the starter and main course are pretty hot, but if your guests eat jalapeño peppers for breakfast, put out the Tabasco for them to help themselves.

STARTER
Scorching chile dip with dippers (page 49)

MAIN COURSE AND SIDE DISHES
Chili con carne (page 192)

Rice or baked potatoes
Green salad

DESSERT
Party crème brûlée (page 266)
and/or
Exotic fruit salad (page 265)

Prepare ahead
Scorching chile dip 4 days ahead.
Chili con carne 2 days ahead.
Party crème brûlée 2 days ahead.
Fruit salad 12 hours ahead.

Potluck parties

If you're preparing a dish to take to a potluck gathering, be careful not to let it slop all over the car seats as you transport it. For a shepherd's pie or lasagna, wrap the ovenproof dish in foil and place it in a cardboard box or basket in the trunk of the car or inside on the floor. Insulated bags are great for keeping coronation chicken cool, but they'll also keep goulash hot (without the ice blocks, naturally). Alternatively, you could put the food in plastic containers or plastic bags and transfer it to the cooking pot or serving platter when you get there.

"Potluck parties are all about keeping it simple—you and your friends sharing the load with dishes that are easy to prepare, transport, and serve."

Winter gathering

Choose either one main and a dessert and ask everyone to prepare them or ask people to make a different dish from the menu so you have a choice.

MAIN COURSES AND SIDE DISHES
Shepherd's pie dauphinois (page 141)
and/or
Paprika pork goulash (page 183)
with
Rice or mashed potatoes
Green vegetable

DESSERT
Apricot and almond galette (page 240)
and/or
Chocolate truffle cheesecake (page 257)

Prepare ahead
Apricot and almond galette 2 days ahead.
Chocolate truffle cheesecake 2 days ahead.
Shepherd's pie 1 day ahead.
Pork goulash 1 day ahead.

Summer get-together

Serve this menu as you can the winter one—with one main course and a dessert or all the dishes, prepared by various people.

MAIN COURSES AND SIDE DISHES
Butternut squash lasagna (page 147)
and/or
21st-century coronation chicken (page 187)
with
New potatoes
Green salad

DESSERT
Hazelnut meringue roulade
with raspberries (page 272)
and/or
Summer berry tart (page 275)

Prepare ahead
Butternut squash lasagna 2 days ahead.
Coronation chicken 1 day ahead.
Hazelnut meringue roulade 12 hours ahead.
Summer berry tart 8 hours ahead.

Useful information

Eggs

We use large eggs for the recipes in this book unless we state otherwise.

Spoon measurements

All spoon measurements have been measured with standard measuring spoons and are level unless otherwise stated.

Volume equivalents

IMPERIAL	METRIC	IMPERIAL	METRIC
1fl oz	30ml	15fl oz	450ml
2fl oz	60ml	16fl oz	500ml
2½fl oz	75ml	¼ pint	600ml
3½fl oz	100ml	1½ pints	750ml
4fl oz	120ml	2 pints	900ml
5fl oz (¼ pint)	150ml	2 pints	1 liter
6fl oz	175ml	2½ pints	1.2 liters
7fl oz (⅓ pint)	200ml	3 pints	1.4 liters
8fl oz	240ml	3 pints	1.5 liters
10fl oz (½ pint)	300ml	3½ pints	1.7 liters
12fl oz	350ml	4¼ pints	2 liters
14fl oz	400ml	6¼ pints	3 liters

Weight equivalents

IMPERIAL	METRIC	IMPERIAL	METRIC
½oz	15g	5½oz	150g
¾oz	20g	6oz	175g
scant 1oz	25g	7oz	200g
1oz	45g	8oz	225g
1½oz	30g	9oz	250g
1¾oz	50g	11oz	300g
2oz	60g	1lb	450g
2½oz	75g	1lb 2oz	500g
3oz	85g	1½lb	675g
3½oz	100g	2lb	900g
4oz	115g	2¼lb	1kg
4½oz	125g	3lb 3oz	1.5kg
5oz	140g	4lb	1.8kg

Oven temperature equivalents

FAHRENHEIT	CELSIUS	DESCRIPTION
225°F	110°C	Cool
250°F	130°C	Cool
275°F	140°C	Very low
300°F	150°C	Very low
325°F	160°C	Low
350°F	180°C	Moderate
375°F	190°C	Moderately hot
400°F	200°C	Hot
425°F	220°C	Hot
450°F	230°C	Very hot
475°F	240°C	Very hot

Index

Index entries in *italics* refer to techniques and tips.

Acknowledgments

Authors' acknowledgments

Firstly, a huge thank you to the lovely Lucinda McCord, who was an essential part of the team that created the recipes with us for this book. She was also the home economist for the photography. Lucinda, thank you for your dedication, passion for your work, and friendship.

Thank you to Izzie Forrest and Rebecca Reed for their help with recipe ideas and catering tips.

Thank you, too, to Mary-Clare Jerram at Dorling Kindersley, who commissioned us to write this book and could see our vision for it. She has worked closely with us at every stage and always with a smile.

And a huge thank you to Michael Fullalove, who edited the book with such dedication and commitment, and always with humor and great understanding. It has been a joy to work with you.

Thank you to Bill Reavell for the stunning photography and the wonderful shoot.

We would also like to thank our agents, Felicity Bryan and Michele Topham, who never seem to worry about our problems, but just sort them out fast!

Finally, thank you to you our readers. You continue to support us with your emails, letters, and photos. It is always lovely to hear from you—it makes each book more and more enjoyable.

Publisher's acknowledgments

Dorling Kindersley would like to thank Barbara Shepherd at Lakeland (products available at time of going to print, www.lakeland.co.uk), Divertimenti (www.divertimenti.co.uk), Sue Rowlands and Liz Hippisley the prop stylists, Lucinda McCord and Jane Lawrie the food stylists, Liz Cook for the index, Nicky Collings for art directing the photoshoot, and Romaine Werblow for picture research.

All images © Dorling Kindersley
For further information see: www.dkimages.com